ELIZABETHAN ADVENTURER

ELIZABETHAN ADVENTURER

A LIFE OF
CAPTAIN CHRISTOPHER CARLEILL

BY

RACHEL LLOYD

'Par mer et par terre
L'art de la guerre.'

HAMISH HAMILTON
LONDON

First published in Great Britain 1974
by Hamish Hamilton Ltd
90 Great Russell Street London WC1

Copyright © 1974 by Rachel Lloyd

SBN 241 89041 1

Printed in Great Britain by
Western Printing Services Ltd, Bristol

To the memory of those who served
in 3 Commando

CONTENTS

ILLUSTRATIONS

PREFACE

THIS IS the story of a fighting Elizabethan, Captain Christopher Carleill, sailor as well as soldier. In his young days military strategy was not a science in which the English excelled; the Spaniards were far ahead, and it was during his five years of fighting for the Prince of Orange against Spain in the Low Countries that Carleill saw the Spanish army at work. The practical experience set him to the study of books on the art of war, and later his brilliant handling of the land forces in Drake's West Indies expedition revealed him as a master of military tactics. He learned how to fight at sea during his service with the Sea Beggars in Zeeland; afterwards his little fleet of ships was constantly used, from helping the Huguenots at the siege of Brouage to putting down piracy off the shores of Ireland. Round the engraving of him are the words, *Par mer et par terre l'art de la guerre*.

He was the stepson of Sir Francis Walsingham, Elizabeth's Secretary of State, who was a keen promoter, both in a public and in a private capacity, of voyages to the New World. He was also the son, grandson and nephew of three Muscovy merchants. Through his stepfather he collaborated with men whose names are famous, Richard Hakluyt, Abraham Ortelius, Sir Francis Drake, Sir Humphrey Gilbert and William Hawkins; the first three were his close friends.

Merchants were turning to colonization as a new and efficient means of harnessing the riches of the New World. This was a break-away from the traditional method of ships carrying merchandise for barter in distant lands, while factors remained in the ports to watch English interests there. Carleill had been chosen by members of the Privy Council to lead a colony into China to trade with the inhabitants; his gift for languages, his wit and diplomacy would have made him a good ambassador for his country. But the expedition, like so many others, failed to leave England. He then wrote the first treatise on colonization, expounding the advantages of this form of enterprise for merchants wishing to invest money in a voyage 'to the hithermost parts of America'. The document has its place in the history of empire.

The story of his three years in Ulster, first as a fighting captain and then as Governor of the Palace of Carrickfergus and Seneschal of Clandeboye, reveals the unique conditions of sixteenth-century Ireland. The Reformation had been slow in arriving, and during the 1580s it was not the clash between Catholic and Protestant that tore the savage land of Ulster, but ancient feuds between the chieftains and the septs, complicated by the invading Scots and the alien English. This ever-changing pattern provided ample opportunity for that great game of violence so dear to the Celtic heart. We read of the Armada wrecked on the shores of northern Ireland, of drowned and butchered Spaniards, and of the highly individual rôle adopted by Carleill in his handling of Spanish prisoners.

He escorted the Muscovy merchant fleet to Russia and brought back an ambassador from the court of Ivan the Terrible. Surprisingly, he appears at a three-day philosophical debate in a cottage near Dublin in the company of Edmund Spenser, the poet; men of the sixteenth century entered into verbal warfare as keenly as they drew their swords.

The poverty that assailed him at the end of his life was the fate shared by many of Elizabeth's servants; it was an age when men had to live by their wits, reward was not the inevitable result of service, and the goods at Elizabeth's disposal were carried off by her servants who knew how to beg. This lack of security bred strong men, and in the climate of competition the New World offered hope. We see the Elizabethan age as an age of glory, but there was the reverse side of the coin, for it was also a cruel and ruthless age and many of its best men fell by the way.

The letters written by Carleill to his stepfather, Sir Francis Walsingham, throw a new light on that enigmatic statesman who has left such scanty evidence of his private life. We do not have the replies, yet who has not listened to one end of a telephone conversation and not formed a clear impression of the unseen speaker? Walsingham had promised his first wife that her young son should 'be by him virtuously brought up'. He kept his word, but there was a great deal more to it than that. The legend of a precise, cunning and Puritanical Secretary of State, lacking many of the warmer qualities, is softened by the story of his relationship with his stepson.

I have to thank many people for the making of this book, those who have answered my many questions, and those who have offered me beds as I travelled in England, in Northern Ireland and in Holland; the Vintners' Company for permission to see their archives and their treasures, the Record Office in Belfast for its help in sending copies of documents, the Warden of King's College, Cambridge, for trying to trace Carleill in the University, the late Marquess of Salisbury for permission to read the Salisbury MSS. at Hatfield House. I am very grateful to A. W. H. Pearsall, Custodian of MSS. at the Royal Maritime Museum, for having criticized those parts of my book dealing with nautical matters. Miss Ahmet sent me much information from Edinburgh about survivors of the Armada in Scotland; Mrs. Clarke's Latin translations have been of great help. Finally my thanks to Mrs. King who has cheerfully deciphered my difficult manuscript and typed it with much skill.

I hope they will derive some pleasure from this book.

I

THE BOY

ALL WERE satisfied, some were consoled; the funeral moved slowly, slowly, through the ward of Bread Street in the City of London, and so to the Church of St. Bartholomew the Little. The body of Sir George Barne, Knight, Haberdasher and 'chief merchant of the Muscovia', muffled in a black velvet pall, was carried on the shoulders of slow-moving men, freemen of these two City companies.[1] He had been a Charter member of the Muscovy Company and one of the chief promoters of the voyage of 1553 to open up trade with Russia and the Far East; he had been Lord Mayor in 1552/3 when Mary succeeded her half-brother on the throne.[2] The Duke of Northumberland had persuaded him to attest Edward VI's will naming Lady Jane Grey as his successor.[3] But the revolution in her favour had collapsed, and Sir George Barne had conformed to the new situation. Now the Aldermen of the City of London trooped before the corpse, wearing their violet gowns as a token 'of the last love, duty and ceremony one to another', and there were sixty poor men clad in black mantles which Sir George had provided in his will. The preacher walked alone. He was followed by the pennon of the Muscovy Company, while a hooded yeoman carried the Standard emblazoned with the red cross of St. George, and on another was woven the crest and motto of Sir George Barne. There were five pennons of arms, Sir George's helmet, his crest and his coat-armour; two heralds followed, Master Clarentius and Master Lancaster. Last of all came the neat parcel carried high on the shoulders of the pallbearers, all that was left of Sir George Barne.

The chief mourners in their black gowns followed, then the Chamberlain and Town Clerk of London, and at last, clad all in black, the Lord Mayor, preceded by a black-robed swordbearer. The City Companies in their liveries and the Masters of the Hospitals with their green staves marched next. The procession, like a black and green striped snake, wound its way through the narrow City lanes.

In the gloom of St. Bartholomew's Church there blazed a huge star, the hearse, set about with four dozen torches and two great branches of white wax and a dozen little pennons and escutcheons. Here the corpse was received by the priests. The chief mourners made their offerings, and Sir George's helmet, his coat-armour and sword were presented at the altar. For a while the outward shows built a wall between the mourners and the cruel reality of death, for man in his wisdom has created ceremony to deflect pain. The arid dignity of the funeral service carried them into a rare and remote world. They were making a pause in time, erecting a barrier; this way they would begin to disentangle the dead from the arms of the living.

Henry Machyn must have been there, taking note of all the details with a professional interest, for he was a keen undertaker and had buried many of the great men of his time.

Next day the sermon was preached by Dr. Chadsay, and there was a great dinner in the Haberdashers' Hall provided by Sir George Barne in his will, and the silver gilt cup with a cover which he had left them was set on the table, and a dinner was also provided for poor men. Sir George had been generous; as well as legacies to the two Companies of which he was free, he had left two tenements to the churchwardens of St. Bartholomew the Little, the income to be used for the poor and to provide holy bread.

The chief mourners were considerable people. There was Dame Alice, Sir George's widow, a lady of strong character, whose name Alice had been given to her two granddaughters by their mothers. Her son, George Barne, was to be several times Governor of the Muscovy Company and in 1586 Lord Mayor of London. His father-in-law, Sir William Garrard,[4] was there too, the most distinguished of the mourners, who had been one of the 'principal doers' of the first voyage to Russia in 1553; he was to be four times Master of the Muscovy Company, had been Master of the Haberdashers' Company in 1557, and two years later would be Lord Mayor of London. Stow described him as 'a great sobre, wise and discreet citizen, equal with the best and inferior to none of our time'. Then there were Sir George's two daughters with their two husbands, Elizabeth, married to Sir John Rivers, a man of Kent,[5] who was to be a Consul of the Muscovy Company and Lord Mayor of London, and Anne, married to Alexander Carleill, 'that good Alexander Carleill', as Machyn was to describe him. He was Warden of the Vintners' Company and in 1561 its Master, and was also one of the Charter members of the Muscovy Company.[6] His eldest son Christopher was with him. He had two sons called Christopher,[7] a name prized in the family; the elder was to die shortly before his father's death, leaving only one Christopher, the young boy who throughout his distinguished military and naval career was to keep a contact with the Muscovy Company.

These people following Sir George Barne to his tomb were the very cream of the City of London, and some of the great merchants of their day.

In 1553 a group of enterprising merchants had bought three ships, and sent them to find the North-East Passage that would lead to fabled Cathay and all the riches of the East. Sebastian Cabot was Governor of this embryonic Company which was not in fact formally established for another two years. With the ships went a letter from Edward VI to all kings, princes, rulers and governors of the earth asking free passage for his servants and expounding the mutual aid of foreign trade.

Only one of the ships reached the White Sea, the crews of the other two having been frozen to death. Richard Chancellor travelled by land to Moscow and was received by the Tsar Ivan the Terrible, who gave him a letter for Edward VI granting English merchants 'free mart with all free liberties' in his lands.

When Chancellor returned to England he found that the young King was dead and his half-sister Mary on the throne. He spoke of the fish, train-oil and furs of the north, of the flax, hemp, wax, honey and hides of the west. The English could give the Russians broadcloth, kerseys and cotton. A new market was needed for these wares, for the export of cloth to the Low Countries had declined since 1550. In return a new trade with the East would be opened up, and gold and spices brought to Europe without Portuguese interference. Later England was to send re-exported articles to Russia, raisins, prunes, sugar, almonds, salt and pewter. In 1555 the Crown granted a charter to the new company, which became known as the Muscovy Company, giving it the monopoly of trade with Russia and all lands not yet known lying to the north, north-east or north-west of it. The original object of finding a way to the East was not however forgotten, and this was stressed in the Charter.

The Company's monopoly in Russia might be hard to defend without the Tsar's co-operation. So in 1555 Philip and Mary asked him for further grants and privileges for the Muscovy Company in return for privileges granted in England to Russian merchants. Ivan allowed the Company to land goods free of custom's duty, the merchants were provided with a house in Moscow and the right to buy one in Vologda and Kholmogory, and to build a warehouse on the river Dvina, opposite St. Nicholas. As a result of the English trade the Tsar would make contact with the West, unimpaired by the Baltic powers with whom he was constantly at war; the Tsar himself traded in wax and furs, his household enjoyed the import of sugar and he looked forward to obtaining munitions from England, and he asked for skilled workmen, doctors, apothecaries and architects. The Mephistophelian profile, sharp as a scimitar, was bent over the document as he signed it with a heavily jewelled hand; he knew the advantages he would gain by this trade.

The Muscovy Company was a joint-stock company and the members were supposed to trade as a whole and not individually. This method was not adopted by the regulated companies, whose members traded with their own capital, using their own agents and ships. The first voyage of the Muscovy Company in 1553 was financed by raising a capital of £6,000 in shares of £25 from each member, spent in buying and fitting out the three ships. The Company was to have two governors, four consuls and twenty-four assistants; Sebastian Cabot was to be Governor for life.

The Charter members were a distinguished body of men who invested in the Company but were probably not involved in its business. Among the two hundred and one members were five peers holding high office under the Crown, the two Secretaries to the Privy Council, and among the fourteen Knights, Sir William Cecil, who would one day be Elizabeth's Lord Treasurer. At least twenty-eight members were Aldermen of the City of London or were to become so, and sixteen of these were to hold the position of Lord Mayor; there was also a large number of merchants.

Thus with an enthusiasm easy for us to understand, who, too, are on the verge of discovering a new world, the enterprise was launched and brave men offered their lives.

In 1557 the first Russian Ambassador arrived in England with the Muscovy fleet returning from Russia, and was received outside Shoreditch by members of the Company and by the merchants of

London, wearing coats of velvet fringed with silk and with their gold chains round their necks. With them rode various peers 'dressed in gorgeous apparel', followed by the Lord Mayor and Aldermen in scarlet. The Ambassador was a stiff and impassive figure, clad in 'a garment of tissue broidered with pearl stones', and his men all in coarse cloth of gold. The crowds thronging the streets must have been amazed. He was to lie at Master Dymock's in Fenchurch Street, and stories flew about how when he went to bed he had put aside his cap set with pearls for a nightcap similarly encrusted, his head on its pillow like a great pin-cushion. He was to dine in state with the Lord Mayor, Aldermen and many of the merchants, and to be entertained at Drapers' Hall by the Muscovy Company. Philip and Mary would receive him in state and send him back to Russia laden with presents for the Tsar.

In these months of celebrations and diplomatic exchanges those City families, Barne, Garrard, Rivers and Carleill, all played their honourable parts.

Alexander Carleill was not only a member of the new Muscovy Company but a freeman of the Mystery of Vintners in the City of London. During the fifties he was three times its Warden; he was to die in 1561, the year he became Master.[8] The Vintners were one of the twelve Livery Companies of London, and it was as unlike the Muscovy Company as it could possibly be. For it was no new thrusting society, but a Company hallowed by age and tradition, having first been recognized by Edward III, and a Charter incorporating it into a Company having been granted it by Henry VI in 1438. In Alexander Carleill's day it had been in existence for over a hundred years, enjoying exclusive rights of loading and landing, rolling, picking and turning all wines and spirits imported into London, and within three miles of it, and exported out of it.

But for many centuries before, vintners had been active in London, landing Moselle and Bordeaux wines at Botolph's Wharf, as their Roman predecessors must have done with the wines of Gaul and Spain, before they launched the culture of the grape in Britain. In the sixteenth century there were many vineyards in southern and western England; many had been worked by the monks in the monasteries and abbeys, and at the Dissolution had passed into the hands of the great landlords. In London itself, as early as the thirteenth century, there had been vineyards in Holborn, in the parish of St. Martin Vintry, the patron saint of winegrowers. The Vintners' Company was linked with religion as were all the early guilds; after the Dissolution this tie still held, and the Company continued to spend money on the repair of City churches.

The chief street in the Vintry Ward was Three Cranes Lane, leading to the wharf where stood three strong timber cranes used to hoist the wares. Here was the Three Cranes Tavern with its painted sign which had cost a fortune to make, and here the Vintners would meet to drink wine and beer from earthenware pots with silver covers and handles and to eat soft saffron cakes speckled with raisins. Outside, the apprentices in their long navy-blue coats, white stockings and flat caps, hurried about their masters' business, while the street cries, sweet or sharp, echoed down the narrow lanes. By the Thames was the new Vintners' Hall, built in 1446 to replace the old one, and in Stodie's Lane thirteen almshouses and a fine garden for the old people; charity and the care of the poor was a large part of the guild system, and now it was continued by the Chartered Companies. In the Hall the merchants met to transact business and to give their enormous dinner on the feast of St. Martin, their patron saint. Up Broad Street went the carts laden with tuns of wine, for the other lanes were too narrow for them. Nearby was Whittington College, the new name for St. Michael Paternoster, where Alexander Carleill prayed and where one day he would be buried. Even in Roman times this must have been a busy part of the city, judging by the Roman remains that had been found there.

In Vintners' Hall was displayed its treasure, the tapestry already a hundred years old in Alexander Carleill's day, representing St. Martin of Tours mounted on an elegantly caparisoned horse, offering his coat to a beggar whom he subsequently learned, in a vision, was Christ. He was converted to Christianity by the experience, and later, became Bishop of Tours. On the right side of the tapestry was St. Dunstan saying mass and the Kyrie being sung by a choir of angels.

There had been plate enough in pre-Reformation days, gilt salts, gilt cups with chased covers, gilt spoons with grapes on their knobs, others with maidens' heads. But most of it had been sold to pay the taxes demanded by a rapacious monarch—1545 apparently having been a bad year for the Vintners. By the time that Alexander Carleill became Master there was little of the past glory left.

The Vintners owned seven swans, and the youngest Warden and a number of swan-uppers would journey up the river to set their mark on the cygnets. The swans floated on the clear water between the ferry boats and wherries that plied from one bank to the other, and when the Queen's barge came its grace rivalled that of the swans.

The Vintners had originally been divided into two classes, the Vinetarii, or importers of wine, and the Tabernii or taverners and cook-housekeepers. The Vintners were forbidden to keep taverns or to sell wine except in cities or boroughs or in certain specified towns, and the number of taverns in the town was to be limited; in London there was a limit of forty. The Vintners had protested to Queen Mary about these restrictions, and were given leave to continue their taverns and to retail wine.

In the fifth year of the reign of Philip and Mary, Alexander Carleill appears for a brief moment, for a charter was being granted to the Vintners confirming the charter of Henry VIII, and was addressed to Carleill and three others, Master and Wardens of the Company.[9] This charter, beautifully illuminated, had a drawing of St. Martin sharing his coat with a beggar, and Philip and Mary seated on their thrones with swords, sceptres and orbs in their hands.

The young Queen Elizabeth confirmed the charter in the first year of her reign, and the restrictions set on the retailing of wine by her half-brother could now be suspended at her pleasure.

Bagshot had been one of the four towns exempted from the restrictions by Edward II, and it was at Bagshot that Alexander Carleill had decided to establish his tavern, the Sign of the Saracen's Head.[10] It was a recognized stopping place on the road between London, Winchester and Salisbury, much frequented by merchants, and a good trade must have been done in wines and the provision of post-horses and beds for the night.

Young Christopher's childhood was spent among the pomps of City life, his grandfather, his father and his uncles all men whom other men revered. In his circle the making of money was eagerly discussed, and in the child's mind was linked mainly with adventure on the high seas. If he was born about 1551 he must have heard of Chancellor's first expedition to Russia, of the two ships that had carried crews that were frozen to death, of the mighty and terrible Tsar. To the small boy these stories had the magic of a fairy tale.

*

He was brought up in an age when many men were changing their religion by order of the monarch, as though it were a coat to be put on or taken off. When he was born, Edward VI was on the throne and Protestantism was the order of the day, for the young King had travelled further into the new religion than his father had done. Mary came to the throne in 1553, and Catholicism returned with her. The Spanish Philip II was not only her husband, he was King of England too. Staunch Protestants fled abroad to practise their religion in exile; the fires of Smithfield burned with an atrocious frequency, and in five years the list of the Marian martyrs grew. In 1558 came Elizabeth, and the return of the Anglican Church. The easy man, unable to see into the future, hoped that each change of religion would be replaced by the one that he secretly favoured; so outwardly he conformed.

Sir George Barne must have been one of these. After the revolution in favour of Lady Jane Grey had collapsed, he is to be found supporting Mary's marriage to Philip of Spain. Young Francis Walsingham was not so pliant, he who was later to marry the daughter of Sir George Barne, and to become the stepfather of Christopher Carleill; he went abroad for his religion's sake and clung to one faith all his life.

Five years of Mary proved enough; London received their new queen, Elizabeth, with tumultuous joy and 'there was such a shooting of guns that never was heard a-fore'. Men spoke emotionally of the old king, saying that his daughter resembled him. Thus wrote old Henry Machyn, who took a professional interest in coronations as well as in funerals.

But religious confusion grew stronger. The Marian exiles returned from Geneva, stiff with Puritanism acquired on the Continent, and began to impose their ways on a Church already weak. The Catholic priests who were faithful had disappeared into private houses or had fled abroad, and those who remained in office were not of the stuff that would resist. During the second year of Elizabeth's reign Machyn was reporting that at St. Paul's 'after the sermon they sang all, old and young, a psalm in metre, the tune of Geneva ways'.

Such a period of disputations, prophesying and quarrelling began, with breaking of images and 'popish trumpery', and defiling of roods that many men must have wished the exiles out of the country. The Queen was shocked at this challenge to her authority as Head of the Church; she would always dislike Puritanism, but as yet she was not strong enough to challenge it. London was as full of strife and revolution as any place in England.

So Christopher Carleill grew up in this seething and active town, the heart of the nation, where the Queen, riding from her Palace or taking the river in her barge, was the constant companion of her people. Alexander Carleill, in his alderman's robes, must often have bowed the knee before her. The great men about her, with their retinues, rode through the narrow streets, the ring of their horses' hoofs sending the pigeons wheeling and the apprentices to the shelter of doorways. Loyalty to the Queen came to the boy Christopher with the air he breathed. His father and his uncles threw themselves into the adventure of making money out of traffic on the high seas, for a surge of vitality had come to England with the accession of Elizabeth. This passion Christopher was to acquire too. He was to become a very typical product of this new England, counting his cost, and then forgetting the prudence of figures in the delight of adventure. The pattern of his future life was laid very early.

Death hit hard, and constantly; the Barnes and the Carleills took their share of suffering with other London families. Nothing in this world was sure, only the love and justice of God. The young Christopher saw many funerals before he was ten years old; that of his grandfather Sir George Barne in 1558, the following year that of the widow, Dame Alice. The eldest son of the Carleill family, that other Christopher, also his two sisters, were dead before 1561;[11] in 1561 'that good Alexander Carleill' was buried in Whittington College. Machyn reported the funeral with a careful wealth of detail; Alexander had given twenty black gowns, some frieze gowns and mantles to poor men, 'and there were the clerks of London singing, and Master Crowley did preach, and then to the place to dinner and a dole and two dozen escutcheons of arms and the livery of the Vintners'.

The hearse-cloth of the Vintners' Company was brought out for its Master; his bier lay in Whittington College covered with a cloth of gold and purple velvet pile, and on it was embroidered St. Martin sharing his cloak with the beggar and again holding his crozier as Bishop of Tours. The Virgin Mary, as Our Lady of Pity, sat with the dead body of the Saviour in her lap, and to the right and left of her were two jaunty skeletons holding in their claws a spade and a coffin, and round them the grape growing. These words were written in Latin, *So die that you may live. The death of sinners is most wretched*. And then with sudden intensity, *Learn to die because thou must die*. There were words of comfort at the last, *The death of the just is the life of souls*.

Kneeling beside the bier, Christopher must have thought of the words he knew so well, '*Learn to die because thou must die*'.

Fit words to guide a soldier's life.

Alexander Carleill lay under a marble slab in St. Michael Paternoster, or Whittington College, and his two daughters, Elizabeth and Anne, lay with him. He had divided his goods and chattels and debts according to the laudable custom of the City of London into three equal parts, one-third for his wife, Anne, the second part for his two surviving children, Christopher and Alice, and one-third for his executors.[12] There was a brother, William, in the city of Carlisle and William's sons, and 'Alexander Carleill who lately dwelt with me'; there was his sister Cecily Ashendon, wife of a haberdasher in the City of London. The Sign of the Saracen's Head at Bagshot and its land went to his wife Anne, as well as the messuage or tenement where he had been living in the parish of St. Michael's. After her death they were to go to his son Christopher, and to Christopher's heirs, and if he should die without heirs, then to his daughter Alice Carleill and to her children. The poor belonging to the company of the Vintners were not forgotten, and twelve poor people of Whittington College and others in the parish of St. Michael's were also helped.

He was not a rich man according to the standards of his father-in-law Sir George Barne, but he had been comfortable and secure. Perhaps 'that good Alexander Carleill' indicated a certain generosity with his money.

His widow faced life with her two children; Christopher was about ten years old, his sister Alice considerably older.

In 1564 Anne Carleill married again,[13] and this marriage was to affect the lives of her children most profoundly. Her husband was Francis Walsingham, then about thirty years old, member of a family of Kentish merchants holding land in Scadbury, Rokesbie, Footscray and Chelsfield. The family had risen with discretion, step by step, from craftsman to gentleman;[14] there had been no sudden eruption into prominence as in the case of the rich Tudor wool families. In the fifteenth century a certain Thomas Walsingham was an importer of wine and an exporter of cloth and a member

of the Vintners' Company, owning property in London. He bought
the Manor of Scadbury in Kent, and his son, also a Vintner, was
describing himself, in 1462, as a gentleman. James, his son, was to
bear arms, to become High Sheriff of Kent and to represent his
country at the Field of the Cloth of Gold. The next generation
produced a prominent personality, Edmund, who became Governor
of the Tower of London, passing to the block Henry VIII's un-
fortunate wives. He was young Francis Walsingham's uncle and
held an important place in his life, for Francis's own father had died
when he was an infant. This father had been an able man too,
Common Serjeant to the City of London, which included being
legal adviser to the Lord Mayor. He had bought land in London
and the Manor of Footscray in Kent, near his grandfather's land at
Scadbury. But Kent was to mean little to young Francis, for his
mother, inevitably, married again and went to live in Hertfordshire.

Her new husband was Sir John Carey of Plashey, Royal Bailiff of
the royal manor of Hunsdon, whose brother was to become the first
Lord Hunsdon and Elizabeth's Lord Chancellor; he married the
Queen's maternal aunt, Mary Boleyn.

This was a lucky event in the life of the young Francis Walsingham. Not only did he have a link, through his father, with the City
of London, but through his stepfather a link with the wider life of
Court and of politics.

Certain factors in Walsingham's youth must have moulded his
character into the severe form that it took. He went to King's
College, Cambridge, where he was tutored by a strong supporter of
the Protestant Reformation in a college that was alive with the new
ideas and in a University where Martin Bucer, newly arrived from
Strasbourg and appointed Professor of Hebrew, was its eloquent
exponent. The young Walsingham was to carry the influence of
these men with him throughout his life.

Later he went abroad to escape the Catholicism that Mary had
brought back to England. He studied at the University of Padua,
where he was chosen Consularius of the English nation in the
Faculty of Civil Law, a responsible position for so young a man to
hold. Padua was renowned for its school of Roman Civil Law, and
Walsingham read this subject.

Perhaps the most profound influence on his life during his sojourn
in Italy was the new method of Machiavellian diplomacy which was
being discussed freely in Italy. Machiavelli's *Prince* was being studied

by the small Italian states who needed to rely on cunning since they lacked material force. Machiavelli offered strength to the weak through the use of cunning, teaching them to find the chink in their foes' armour, to speak fair and to work foul, and to tunnel beneath the enemy's defences by employing spies. Venice was the school for Machiavellianism, and statesmen and potential statesmen went there to study the new methods. This detestable subtlety was perhaps less useful as it came to be understood and accepted; in its early days its effect must have been startling and deadly.

Walsingham accepted the necessity of running an efficient secret service; many years later, as the Queen's Secretary of State, he was to ruin himself by conducting this service at his own expense. The man who felt so keenly about his religious principles that he could not tolerate life in England under Mary, learned that in public life there could be no principles, that the end justified the means. At Padua the new Society of Jesus was adopting just these methods; Walsingham was able to study them at work and in later life 'to out Jesuit the Jesuits', as was said of him.

So a curious break in his personality began, all too common in sixteenth-century men; the private Walsingham was staid, responsible, trustworthy, his promise sure, good to his friends, labouring heavily for the cause in which he believed, highly intellectual, a good linguist and a most excellent stepfather. In public life he was a deadly foe who would stop at nothing. The two personalities were quite distinct.

He watched the doings of his two stepchildren, Christopher and Alice, as if they had been his own children. His first wife had left the young Christopher to his care 'to be by him virtuously brought up'.[15] He never ceased to help his stepson; all through his life he would be behind him, supporting him in all his enterprises.

At the time of Walsingham's marriage to the widow, Anne Carleill, he transferred the Manor of Footscray in Kent, left him by his father, to his two brothers-in-law, George and John Barne. And in 1563 he leased for thirty-one years from his cousin, Henry Denny, the estate of Parkerbury near St. Albans in Hertfordshire, and here he made his home. Perhaps, looking at the young Christopher, he may have thought of his own life with his stepfather in Hertfordshire; the strong relationships of life are often based on these identifications.

There in this Hertfordshire countryside he was surrounded by childhood friends, his cousins, the Dennys, and nearby at Brockett Hall, more cousins;[16] Theobald's Park, where William Cecil lived, was not far away. He described himself, when he wrote, as 'of Parkerbury'. And so did his wife Anne, for in her will she was Anne Walsingham of Parkerbury. Alas, they lived there together for barely a year. And then Anne died.

So young Christopher had lost seven members of his family before he was thirteen years old. Even for the sixteenth century this was excessive.

His sister Alice was the only one left him. By now she was married to Christopher Hoddesdon, a man a good deal older than herself, an active agent in Russia for the Muscovy Company. He had been apprenticed to Sir George Barne, and was described in Dame Alice's will as 'my servant Christopher Hoddesdon'. But he was the Barnes' friend too, for after their death the Muscovy Company wrote that 'for his service and pains he shall be considered as reason is, as friendly as if his friends were living'.[17]

When he returned to England from Russia he found that the Barnes' granddaughter, Alice Carleill, had grown up, and he married her, thus prudently reminding the Muscovy Company of its obligation towards him. He was to prove a firm friend and supporter of his young brother-in-law, Christopher Carleill, in all his later dealings with the Muscovy Company.

In 1566 Walsingham married again. His second wife was Ursula St. Barbe of Ashington in Somerset, the widow of Richard Worseley, Captain of Carisbrook Castle in the Isle of Wight. He had been 'a brave, stout and worthy gentleman', and had died young.[18] Ursula was a prim and decided-looking lady with a pursed up mouth. Indeed she had some reason to close her mouth over her pain, for her story is a sad one. Hardly had she received her new husband and stepson in the lovely valley of Appledurcomb, near Godshill, which her first husband had left her, than a terrible tragedy took place. Her two Worseley sons, aged eight and nine, were being tutored in the gate-house where some barrels of gunpowder were drying in preparation for the musters. A spark fell on a barrel; the explosion was fatal, both boys were killed. That same year she had Walsingham's daughter, a gleaming and tragic creature, who married first Sir Philip Sydney, and after his death in battle, the Earl of Essex, who was beheaded for high treason. Her third marriage was less dramatic. Ursula had another daughter too, Mary, who died in 1577.

There is no record that Ursula's life was in any way linked with that of her stepson, Christopher Carleill; Christopher was about fifteen at the time of her marriage to Walsingham, and already in the world of men.

Ursula's first brother-in-law, John Worseley, took possession of Appledurcomb on the death of his two nephews, and Walsingham and his wife had to console themselves with the Priory of Carisbrook and the Manors of Godshill and Freshwater.

They must have lived principally at Carisbrook, where the great Castle towered above the village. Walsingham pulled down the chancel of the church and inserted a new East window, and that is the only trace left of his life there, for the remains of the Priory which he restored are now incorporated into a farm-house.

For a while he could combine a life at Carisbrook with his work as member of Parliament for Lyme Regis, and must often have sailed from the white cliffs of the Isle of Wight past the golden cliffs of the Dorset coast into Lyme Bay.

In 1568 he bought a house in London, a large and luxurious affair near St. Mary Axe, formerly a dwelling for poor priests. In all likelihood this now became his headquarters, and so Christopher Carleill, after several changes of scene in a very few years, found himself once more in the home of his childhood.

There is some evidence that he was sent to the University of Cambridge,[19] where his stepfather had studied. Certainly Walsingham would have chosen it for him, rather than Oxford, where Catholicism lingered. We learn in Stow's *Annales* that Carleill 'was in the University where he attained unto perfection of good letters and understood many languages'. In later years he showed all the signs of having received an excellent education.

There was once a document, which was afterwards destroyed by fire, purporting to be a letter of advice given by Walsingham to a nephew who was going abroad to study.[20] This reveals the training that Walsingham considered essential for a young man; some such advice must have been given to Carleill in his time.

Walsingham wrote that some part of each day should be set aside for prayer and reading of the Scriptures; no day should pass without translation from one tongue to another; Roman history should be studied, also philosophy. In the reading of history the student should note how methods of government in the ancient world could be applied in modern times, and he should modify them accordingly.

All should be brought under the rule of Tully, which Walsingham described as the rule of honesty, without which no man could serve his country well.

The student must join himself to some company, 'for books are but dead letters'. This company should be both godly and honest, and he should avoid lewd youths of wanton and dissolute dispositions.

French, Spanish, Italian and Latin should be written and spoken fluently; mathematics came next in importance, especially that part concerning cosmography, so that when travelling in foreign countries he should observe them correctly, and in this manner serve the commonwealth of which he was a member. He should be civil and companionable to all, but reject advances. As much as possible he should acquaint himself with men of state, in order to learn 'whether they appertain to civil government or warlike affairs'. All the details that he had observed he was to enter into a diary kept for that purpose.

There was no doubt that Walsingham was trying to establish in this young man the qualities that would produce a newsagent for his own use, for as Secretary of State he had many correspondents overseas who kept him supplied with information.

The letter must have come as a chilling douche to a young man about to take his first step in life; in it there was no allowance for the warmer qualities, for love or for laughter.

Fortunately for Carleill he was too direct and impetuous a character to take his stepfather's advice literally.

So the days of his boyhood passed. The little Tudor princes and princesses pass clearly before us in their stiff clothes, their faces pinched with a certain apprehension, their eyes wary, but the children of lesser men are not often seen in any detail. Then, as we examine the panoply of life that surrounded them, accepting not too critically the standards of their time by first forgetting our own, we may draw close to these children, closer in fact than had we known a few humdrum details about them, that they had caught the measles on a certain day or had fought with their school-mates. We can examine the London that Christopher saw, so strange to us from where we stand in our own century, and see it with something of the freshness and surprise of his own youthful vision.

2

FIGHTING FOR THE
PRINCE OF ORANGE

DURING THE year 1568 Walsingham was employed doing secret service work, sifting information gleaned from agents in Scotland and the Continent and passing it on to William Cecil.[1] After this period of training he was chosen in 1570 to go on his first diplomatic mission to France to help the Huguenots in the peace treaty that was being hammered out between them and the French King. As a keen Puritan it was a mission after his own heart.

France was bringing its Third Civil War to an end, wars of ambition between rival factions enflamed by differences of religion. On one side there was the ultra Catholic party, highly aggressive, led by the Guise family; against it were the Huguenot Bourbons in an uneasy alliance with Catholic Montmorencis, dedicated to a policy of toleration in religion and peace in France. These parties competed for control of the weak King Charles IX, who left public affairs largely in the hands of his mother, Catherine de Medici.

The Huguenot leader, Admiral Coligny, was an able soldier, prepared to ally himself with Protestant England and Protestant Germany against the Guises, who turned to the Pope for support, to the Emperor and to Philip II of Spain. A vast game of power politics was being played, with religion thrown in to enflame passions. The young and innocent fell into the trap and prepared themselves to die for their respective faiths. Catherine de Medici stood in the centre between the opposing French parties, caring only for the advancement of her sons, Charles IX, the Duke of Anjou and the Duke of Alençon. She practised expediency in the conduct of public affairs, irrespective of principle, for she was incapable of a sustained policy. Because of the Crown's weakness France passed from one war of religion to the next, and at any given moment it is hard to tell which political combination had the upper hand.

The Netherlands

NORTH

SEA

GRONINGEN

FRIESLAND

DRENTHE
Steenwijk

Meppel

Alkmaar

OVERIJSSEL

Haarlem
Amsterdam

Leiden
UTRECHT
The Hague
Delft

GELDERLAND

ZUTPHEN

Brielle
Rotterdam

Rhine

Schouwen
Veere
ZEELAND
Walcheren
Flushing
Middelburg

Bergen op Zoom

B R A B A N T

Maas

Ostende
Bruges
Ghent
Scheldt

ANTWERP

Alost
MALINES

LIMBURG

FLANDERS
Courtrai
Brussels
Louvain

A R T O I S
Gembloux

Lille

Mons
NAMUR
Namur
BISHOPRIC OF LIEGE

Valenciennes
HAINAULT

Arras

LUXEMBURG

▬ ▬ ▬ ▬ ▬ **Boundary of the United Provinces**

0   20   40   60
└──┴──┴──┴──┘ miles

By the year 1570 she had joined the Montmorenci policy of toleration of religion and peace in France, and with the Huguenots they made a powerful combination against the Guises. At St. Germain the Huguenots were given freedom of conscience throughout the country, and the exercise of their religion in public in two cities in each province and in the houses of Protestant nobles who exercised high justice. They could garrison the towns of La Rochelle, Montauban, La Charité and Cognac. Their allies, the Prince of Orange, who was Stadtholder of Holland, Zeeland and Utrecht, and his younger brother, Louis of Nassau, were formally recognized as friends of the King of France.

Here at last was a certain stability of outlook, pleasing to Walsingham.

William of Orange was a powerful figure in that ancient and civilized land which for generations had been governed by the Dukes of Burgundy, and now was part of the old Hapsburg Empire. The Netherlands was a collection of seventeen countries, duchies and seigneuries, each with its own Stadtholder, administering its own laws; there were also more than three hundred independent towns, having their own guilds, charters and municipal councils. French was the language of some of the states, Dutch of others, and there was little national unity between them. Each sent its delegates to the meeting of the Estates General in Brussels, but this body had little power save that of appointing the Stadtholders. In Brussels also was the Imperial Court, and this vied in elegance and wit with that of Paris. The nobility of the Netherlands regarded themselves, both in blood and in wealth, as the first in Europe.

This varied land was bursting with energy and creation; stained glass, church music, Flemish painting, tapestry and lace, came from those walled cities, Bruges, Ghent, Valenciennes, Arras, Louvain and Malines. In the north were rich farms, producing cheese and cattle; Middelburg, Amsterdam, Dordrecht were fishing ports; Amsterdam was the corn-staple for Europe, Dordrecht for Rhine wine; Antwerp, that huge town, was the money market of the world, where each nation had its own concession; every financial loan in Europe was negotiated here.

We see the donors in those masterpieces of Flemish religious painting, their bare foreheads crowned with caps like vessels in full sail, fur round their necks, their beringed fingers curved round book or scroll, their shrewd little eyes betraying no tenderness. The painters had not romanticized them, but had presented them to the world as grave, responsible people, civic elders, aware of their fortunes and of how to keep them. Even the Madonnas in the triptychs were made of the same flesh and blood as the donors, showing little of the ecstasy expected from the mother of God. Peter Breughel the Elder knew the stuff of which the peasants were made; never had such earthy clods lumbered through painted landscape before. The signs were all there for those who could read them . . . these were no people to trifle with.

Charles, Duke of Burgundy, had inherited the crown of Castile and Aragon from his mother, also the duchies of Austria, Styria and Carinthia, the county of Tyrol and all the land that had made up the Hapsburg Empire. After this he was no longer just Charles, Duke of Burgundy, but the Emperor Charles V. At his abdication in 1555 the estrangement of his son Philip from the Netherlands became yet more pronounced. Philip II, King of Naples, became King of Spain, and through his marriage with English Mary, was also King of England. The centre of his Empire was in Madrid, and he had the riches of Mexico and Peru at his disposal. He left his half-sister, Margaret, in Brussels, as Regent of the Netherlands. Under her were three powerful nobles, the Prince of Orange and the Counts Egmont and Hoorn, all loyal to Philip, yet watchful lest the liberties of the Netherlands be infringed. Ranked against them were Philip's men, later to become an inner clique who were to decide all the important internal problems of the Netherlands.

For Philip's handling of the Netherlands was the work of a bigoted and unimaginative man. Spaniards were put in official positions, loans were extorted to pay Spanish troops on Netherlands soil, till the clamour against them grew so violent that even Philip was forced to remove them—though only temporarily.

There was an uneasy period when William of Orange, loyal to his Prince, tried to interpose himself between Philip and the angry Netherlanders, but this ended in 1567 when the Duke of Alva came as Governor, and bound the country in one of the most horrible tyrannies that Europe has ever known.

Catholicism in the Netherlands had been pliant, and the teachings of Luther had not met with serious opposition. Some heretics had been burned in the days of Charles V, but the Duke of Alva was instructed by Philip to carry out a policy of total extermination of heresy, a very different matter. William of Orange had a horror of torture and of burnings, whether performed by the Inquisition in the Netherlands or by the Calvinists in Geneva. And he saw in the policy of Alva not so much the extermination of heresy as the extermination of the Netherlands. He himself was one of those pliant Catholics of the old school, and he feared that the uncompromising young priests of the Society of Jesus introduced by Philip into the Netherlands would stiffen the Protestant opposition, and so call forth more of Alva's fury.

In 1566 the Calvinists of Antwerp had risen and had insisted on preaching outside the town, since they were forbidden to preach inside it. The fury had spread into other cities, church windows were smashed, images broken. William of Orange had quelled the riot by giving the Calvinists the right to hold their own religious meetings, a concession he had wrung from the frightened Regent. But crowds of refugees flocked into England and Germany; the country was being deprived of its best weavers and cloth-workers, and of many of its rich burghers too. This was a serious loss for such a highly industrialized country; the Spaniards, by their persecution, were losing the riches they desired.

In 1567 the fury became a Spanish one, for the Duke of Alva set up the Council of Blood, composed of three Spaniards. It seized and tortured members of the nobility and all the important men in town government. Next year fifteen hundred prominent citizens of the Netherlands were imprisoned, whatever their religion; Philip was using Catholicism as a cloak under which he could exterminate the Netherlanders. One day the Duke of Alva was to claim modestly that he had slaughtered eighteen thousand six hundred people in this unhappy land.

The resistance grew. In the woods guerrilla fighters lurked, *Gueux de Bois* they were called, while on the high seas the *Gueux de Mer*, the Sea Beggars, fell upon Spanish shipping and upon everything else that came their way. The Spaniards looked on these men as rebels, and when captured they were killed. *Gueux*—beggars— had been the name contemptuously given to the protesting nobles and gentry. Now with beggars' bowls slung round their necks, they brought gusts of merriment to the Brussels mob, and *Vivent les Gueux* was the popular cry. The excitement grew, hatred of the Spaniards whipped through the Netherlands. Everywhere the people were humming or whistling the song of Wilhelmus van

Nassouwe,[2] a password at dark street corners or thick woods. Years later the tune, heard suddenly, would bring the same old tingling of the flesh, a yearning maybe, for the heroic days.*

William of Orange fled from a charge against him of high treason. In Cologne he raised an army of German mercenaries, and helped by French Huguenots and by his brother Louis of Nassau he crossed into Friesland where the Sea Beggars victualled him.

These outlaws with patched sails and ragged clothes were the terror both of their friends and of their foes; later the Prince of Orange was to hew them into the beginnings of the Dutch navy, but now they were pirates.

Louis of Nassau won his first victory in Friesland, but the Prince's army was forced back to Strasbourg through lack of money to pay his troops. Lack of money, that was his continual tragedy.

In the violence and toughness of the Calvinists of Holland and Zeeland the Prince saw his great hope. He and Louis eventually became Calvinists, a political expedient rather than an act of conscience. Even in this manner, years later, would the Huguenot King Henry IV change his faith, with his *'Paris vaut bien une messe'*. Religious toleration was still the Prince's ideal for the Netherlands, but fanaticism on both sides was abroad, and toleration was not the spirit in which to win battles.

During the last year of the Third Civil War in France, the Prince of Orange and Louis of Nassau fought on the side of the Huguenots, as did the Catholic Maréchal de Montmorenci in Languedoc. After St. Germain in 1570 they hoped that the Huguenot policy of attacking Spain in the Netherlands would be adopted by the French King. For only with the financial help of France, England or Germany could the Prince of Orange ever prevail over Spain. This he knew, and for the next decade his policy was to provide himself with allies, any ally who would give money and men would do, but an ally he must have.

Elizabeth reacted to these events with her usual caution. She could never approve of subjects who rebelled against their rulers, and she

* See page 132.

did not feel very strongly on the subject of religion. But the fate of the Low Countries was of great importance to the English who exported cloth through Antwerp. Elizabeth was afraid of French influence there, for France with possession of the Netherlands would become unbearably powerful and close to England; Spain on the other hand was weakened by the possession of the Netherlands, so far away from Madrid. It was better for England, she thought, that Spain should retain the Netherlands, the base for English trade. The balance of power in Europe was an old problem, and Elizabeth tried to hold the scales. The contortions she performed in the process were often incomprehensible, even to her ministers. So against the advice of Walsingham she did not at first encourage the Dutch Calvinists, nor lend money to William of Orange, though she allowed Dutch refugees to crowd into East Anglia.

Then events were suddenly twisted. The arrival of Catholic Mary Stuart in England, chased out by her infuriated Scottish subjects, and her polite imprisonment in England, supplied a focus for Catholic ambitions at home and in Europe. The Spanish Ambassador in London sided with English Catholics in the Rebellion of the North, the Pope excommunicated Elizabeth and relieved her Catholic subjects of the necessity of obeying her. Here was Catholicism pronouncing Elizabeth to be a bastard and Mary Stuart the rightful heir to the throne; it was revolution and the threat could not be ignored.

The old Anglo-Spanish alliance was no longer valid, and Elizabeth was forced to turn towards England's traditional enemy, France. After St. Germain the Huguenot cause flourished; this was a France with which she could negotiate. She toyed with the idea of a marriage between herself and the Duke of Anjou, and when this fell through, as the Duke would not abandon the practice of his Catholicism in England, she and Catherine de Medici played with the alternative, a marriage between herself and his younger brother, the Duke of Alençon.

Walsingham with his deadly realism knew that a war was inevitable; the French Huguenots, helped by England, could fight Spain; alternatively, Catholic Guisean France in league with Spain could launch an attack upon England, using Mary Queen of Scots as a weapon. Of these two wars he preferred the first.

Now he saw a third opportunity presenting itself and wrote to Leicester, 'If God had not raised up the Prince of Orange to have entertained Spain, a dangerous fire ere this time had been kindled in our own home. To assist him, therefore, is to assist ourselves. . . .'

He would have liked Elizabeth to adopt a policy, to make a choice in favour of Orange. But this was what she was incapable of doing, unless some fearful crisis forced a conclusion. Her behaviour, which to some European observers seemed to be based on Machiavellian principles, was the result of her devious nature: what some politicians did by choice, she did by compulsion. Fortunately for England, the results, on the whole, were beneficial.

Walsingham, soaked in the technique of Machiavelli, used such methods as he dared in handling the Queen, but he could never disguise from her the force of his Puritanism. He would give her a rational reason for an action which in reality had been dictated by his faith, but Elizabeth knew the strength of his faith and disliked it. Puritanism was as grave a challenge to her authority as Catholicism, and less attractive. Perhaps his religion was the great bar that divided them; she respected her Secretary of State, but she never loved him.

Philip II was also changing his tactics, and turning from his old alliance with England; his attitude hardened in 1568 when Elizabeth seized Spanish treasure ships in English harbours as a reprisal against the attacks of Flemish pirates on her merchant ships. English merchants, preferring a climate of peace, began to shift their centre from Antwerp to Hanover.

The outcome was inevitable; in 1572 came the Treaty of Blois, a solid defensive alliance between England and France to bridle the greatness of Spain, a triumph for Admiral Coligny and the Huguenots over the Guises. Negotiations were also beginning for the marriage of Marguerite de Valois, the French King's sister, to the Huguenot Prince Henry of Navarre, whose Court was at La Rochelle. Walsingham saw his policy flowering.

Then in the Netherlands the flood broke, as though a dike had been cut. Louis of Nassau was established at La Rochelle, headquarters of the Prince of Condé, and with a fleet of Dutch privateers was attacking Spanish shipping off the coast of Biscay. Some of those pirates under a brilliantly successful ruffian, the Count de la Marck, sailed up the Channel and based themselves at Dover, to the consternation of English merchants, for their acts of piracy fell on all alike. Finally in February 1572, Elizabeth, fearing reprisals from

Spain, expelled them from her ports, ordering that no one should supply them with food.

The result took her and the whole of Europe by surprise. For on April 1st de la Marck with a small fleet of Sea Beggars fell on Brielle, a Spanish-held town in Zeeland, literally in order to feed themselves, and captured it without a blow. At this the whole Island of Walcheren rose in sympathy, with the exception of Middelburg, and declared for the Prince of Orange.

From Flushing de la Marck wrote to Elizabeth asking her to send over her Flemish refugees to help him; he also asked for arms. Elizabeth feared that the French might act before her, and for the moment she conquered her dislike of assisting rebels against their anointed monarch. She consented that a force of armed men should leave England, between four and five thousand of them, Flemish refugees and English volunteers.

With them went Christopher Carleill, abandoning the education that his stepfather had planned for him. It was an action that Walsingham would have taken had he been a younger man. One answered the other during the next ten years of war in the Netherlands, the older man striving in the world of diplomacy to help the Prince of Orange, the younger man offering his sword; they were like the reverse sides of one medal.

On May Day 1572 the Queen reviewed the volunteers before her Palace at Greenwich, and there, with a summer breeze floating from the river and the May Day revels somewhere over the hill, she watched the soldiers in their red and blue cassocks marching and wheeling and even skirmishing before her. She, who had but recently turned de la Marck out of her ports, had performed one of her characteristic somersaults, and was now helping him. But not very much. For the volunteers were being equipped by the Protestant merchants of the City of London, who did not relish the state of affairs in the Netherlands nor the loss of Antwerp, their staple town.

Many of the soldiers in their bright cassocks had served before in Ireland, or perhaps in Scotland, or in the wars of religion in France, and were now penniless and hoping for gain in the Netherlands; others, like Christopher Carleill, were aflame with crusading zeal to help the Dutch, Protestants and Catholics alike, against the hated Spaniard. For England had suffered the Spaniard in her own home barely fourteen years before, and the tradition of their insupportable pride lived on. 'You people are of a sort that wherever you set foot, no grass grows, and you are hated everywhere', Burghley was to say to the Spanish Ambassador in England, with more candour than tact.

Captain Thomas Morgan, Commander of the English volunteers, was a Welshman and a keen soldier. Under him was Roger Williams, also a Welshman. He admired the modern methods of warfare practised by the Spaniards and was to write a tract extolling the use of the arquebus over the bow, and this was to give offence to some old soldiers tied to a conventional past. His valour in battle was great, and he had a happy gift of indiscretion which gave punch to the narrative he was to write of the Netherlands war, the narrative which we shall use. There could be no better account of the fighting of those early years, as far as the volunteers were concerned, the muddles, the miseries and the follies of an untrained force tackling the finest army in Europe, seen through the eyes of an intelligent and critical soldier. The truth springs up before us, rich with the little details that convince us that this was the way things happened. In this hard school the young Christopher Carleill was to receive his training; from this watery battlefield he was to emerge a man of action, able to command either a fleet of ships or a regiment of soldiers.

The province of Zeeland was composed of islands, which appeared or disappeared capriciously, for in the high spring tides the drowned land—Verdronken, the Dutch called it—was engulfed by water. These islands formed the delta of three rivers, the Rhine, the Maas and the Scheldt. The high dunes kept the sea from drowning the polders, tracts of land lying below sea-level. Where there were no dunes, dikes protected the land. This was to become the last desperate defence of the Dutch, to cut their dikes and drown their land, leaving the towns like boats floating on the waves.

On the Island of Walcheren was the port of Vlissengen—Flushing, the English soldiers called it with a superb indifference to pronunciation—while a few miles inland was Middelburg with the high tower of its church ringing the *carillon* as the hours passed by. These sturdy little towns with their crowding roofs were protected by fortified walls and the ever present water. The Ramelius Fort on the Scheldt guarded a canal which opened into Middelburg Haven, and ships could sail to the gates of the town.

The land, this first summer, was as yet unscarred; a shining light seemed to flow from the earth to meet a sun in a huge sky, and together they illumined the town till the tiles on the roofs winked like rubies, and the distant trees on the horizon bent all one way with the wind in a delicate fringe of green and gold; on the flat land a ditch would catch the light suddenly, like a knife turning. All was held in a sea of light, and all about them a sea of water, and the mast of a ship rising suddenly, so it seemed, from a green field. Later soldiers would trample this civil land into a black bog.

To the east of Walcheren lay the Island of South Beveland with the town of Tergoes—Goes now—and to the north the island of Schowen with the splendid town of Zierikzee. Both were to play a great part in the struggle. War was fought here as much on sea as on land, and here the Beggars' Fleet sailed, or was shoved, through the shallow waters, carrying men or provisions to the besieged towns. These Beggars were outlaws, some for religion's sake, some for crimes against the Spaniards, some for crimes against their country's laws. Most of them were nobles or country squires, all were patriots. They would be starving men without the raids on the Zeeland villages or on passing merchant ships, and their deeds were as black as those of the Spaniards; they burned the Zeeland abbeys, raped nuns, strung up monks, broke altars and images, then appeared on the decks of their ships wearing the gorgeous cassocks of their victims, using the golden chalices as their drinking cups. De la Marck himself with tangled hair and beard robbed and raped in company with his men. This was the Beggars' answer to the horrors of the Spanish persecution—but where the Beggars killed in their hundreds the Spanish were killing in their thousands. Both sides were curiously unselective in the choice of their victims.

The Prince of Orange was a humane man who deplored excess. He knew that great national movements could not be led by ogres such as de la Marck, but having as yet no other Admiral, he was forced to uphold him. But he was only biding his time.

George Gascoigne fought in the Netherlands with Christopher Carleill, during those early years. He was a poet, though not a very subtle one; but he recorded his experiences, and Carleill, not being a poet, was silent. Later Carleill was to write fluently to his step-father, and his letters were to reveal much of his life. But now George Gascoigne and Roger Williams must speak for him, Williams the older and more responsible man, Gascoigne a 'young blood', like Carleill.

He wrote a poem called 'Gascoigne's voyage into Holland, 1572'.[3] Through the trivial jingle of words the truth stares out with the unblinking realism of a soldier's vision. He reveals a world of brutality which must have astonished the early volunteers.

For the English ship in which he was sailing to Brielle with a contingent of armed men stuck on a sandbank at the entrance to the harbour, through the incompetence of a Dutch pilot. Twenty of the volunteers were drowned; the rest fired their big guns to attract the attention of the townsmen. But the Dutch did not stir. Only one hoy came out to take a look at them, but returned at once. The reason? Most of the townsmen were drunk.

> Well, at the Brill to tell you what we find,
> The Governor was all bedewed with drink,
> His trulls and he were all laid down to sleep,
> And we must shift and of ourselves must think
> What means was best and how we best might keep
> That yet remained . . .

Gascoigne, not unnaturally, was very angry, and wrote disparagingly of the Dutch:

> Methinks they be a race of bullbeef born
> Whose hearts their butter mollyfieth by kind,
> And so the force of beef is clean outworn
> And eke their brains with double beer are lined
> . . . .
> Inwardly they be but hollow gear
> As weak as wind, which with one puff upgoeth.

The English were at first disgusted with the drinking habits of the Dutch; later they learned to do the same.[4]

> Well, drunkenness is here good company
> And therewithall, *par conséquence*, it falls
> That whoredom is accounted jollity.

And he goes on to describe how the nuns acted as messengers between the English volunteers and the whores of the town. Strong meat, but evidently not too strong for Lord Grey of Wilton to whom the poem was dedicated.

After the capture of Brielle came the revolt of Flushing and the ejection of its Spanish governor. The Sea Beggars offered their help, but it was accepted with a certain reserve. The Zeelanders were quiet country folk, mostly Catholic, and to rebel against Spain did not mean that they would also rebel against their religion and join the Calvinists. Not yet; that final rebellion was to come, thanks to Alva's ferocity. Now they were shocked at their new allies.

At this stage the English volunteers under Morgan arrived, and with them Roger Williams, eager for battle, and Christopher Carleill.

To the help of Flushing came many outlaws, Walloons and Flemings, who had been hiding in the woods, and from La Rochelle three companies of French Huguenots.[5] The men of Flushing repaired their ramparts and mounted ordnance on them.

The Spaniards at Middelburg launched an attack, and there was much skirmishing on the flat land intersected so treacherously with dikes. But Flushing held. This was the volunteers' first rough taste of battle.

The English were at first received with the extravagant hospitality which is usually accorded to liberators, but which rarely endures. Morgan became an important person in the town.

He wrote to England for reinforcements, and made no objection when Sir Humphrey Gilbert arrived with one thousand four hundred men, and was put in authority over him. Gilbert was a poor soldier, relying on his personal bravery rather than on his brain; the Walloon Governor, Tseraerts, was also a poor soldier. With these two in charge, defeat was inevitable.

Their attempt to relieve Mons failed, for Bruges stood in the path, and Bruges was for Alva. Roger Williams was contemptuous of both sides, writing that Gilbert 'in a great choler and swearing divers oaths ordered the town to yield', but Tseraerts, hearing that Spanish reinforcements were on the way, persuaded him to retire. The Walloon governor of Bruges was a 'lily-livered soldier', and instead of sallying, contented himself with executing the burgesses who had had intelligence with Tseraerts.

So there, in that town of spires and churches, where the narrow gables of the houses dangled their placid reflections in the canals, and the *carillon* from the belfry called the citizens to prayer, the men of Bruges were dangled over fires till their feet were frizzled off or hung head downwards from the gallows till their ear-drums burst. The Spaniards thought of the most ingenious methods of slaughter.

The English were forced to retreat to Flushing, for a fine Spanish general was on his way to the help of Bruges. Now the Spaniards were the best soldiers in Europe; war was a science which they studied, and as yet the English did not. And this was to count very damnably against them in the field.

Another rather foolish English expedition occurred, this time to attack the important Spanish garrison of Tergoes, on the Island of South Beveland. Through this route the Spaniards passed supplies from Antwerp to Middelburg. The Sea Beggars carried the English troops in their vessels, and it must have been with mixed feelings that the inhabitants of Tergoes saw the arrival of the rakish fleet. Which was the most terrible to endure, Spanish fury or Beggars' victory?

Skirmish followed skirmish that day. Roger Williams wrote with his wry pen, 'You must think that in those days few of us or of the enemy knew the war so well as since', and then he makes a charge against Gilbert that he did not know the country he was fighting over, that he had no guides, that he had no good intelligence. The Spanish Governor in Tergoes was 'lily-livered', and presently as no conclusion was reached in the fighting, the volunteers re-embarked in their pirate ships, 'not unwilling for anything I could perceive . . .'.

At Flushing they found the town gates shut in their faces, their credit was gone. Liberators must never quail; if they do they find themselves reduced from heroes to scamps. And these scamps were obliged to retreat to the village of Southland, on the west coast of Walcheren, out of reach of the angry men of Flushing.

The Walloon Governor of Middelburg thought this was the moment to attack. He prepared to defeat the volunteers with a *camisado*, and 'to do it more terribly' the soldiers were issued with halters with which to string up their prisoners. Some two thousand of them, Walloons and Spaniards, marched on the sand-dunes between Flushing and Southland where the volunteers were lying by the lively grey waters of the North Sea. But despite their numbers they were finally thrown back 'at the push of the pike' and chased half-way to Middelburg. 'This piece of service', wrote Williams, 'was one of the best and worthiest encounters that our men had from that time to this hour in all the wars of the Low Countries.' What more could he write? Many of the enemy were captured, creeping up the ditches, and were strung up on their own halters. 'Chief praise, next to God,' wrote Williams, 'ought to be given to the English ensigns and armed men.' After the shame endured at Flushing, this triumph must have been balm to his soul.

Unfortunately Gilbert and Tseraerts were also elated, and they decided to attempt Tergoes again. The Sea Beggars landed them once more in South Beveland, this time in two places. Morgan and the volunteers were sent to attempt the fort which stood at the head of the haven of Tergoes, and six batteries were landed to bombard it. All day long there was skirmishing. Then at night a shameful and absurd incident occurred. 'So great a pick and jealousy' had grown up between Sir Humphrey and Tseraerts 'that each would fain disgrace the other'. A *scalado* was attempted on the parapet, two thousand volunteers sallied from their quarters at night 'all in *camisadoes* with scaling ladders, God knows like ignorant soldiers or we would never have attempted a *scalado* on such a troop . . . nevertheless ambition and courage so pushed us on . . .'

Sir Humphrey and Tseraerts were up their ladders, the gleam of their armour hidden by their shirts, and besides them many other men on ladders. The enemy lay low, then as the climbing men rose, suddenly discharged a volley in their faces. Whereupon the English fled. Others 'at push of pike' attacked the volunteers still on the ground. 'At which terror we retreated without commandment', wrote Williams. 'And not without reason.'

Help was sought from the Prince of Orange, who sent some two thousand Netherlanders and Germans, 'simpler men' even than the volunteers. And the undisciplined rabble settled down to wait outside Tergoes.

It was all very foolish, and there was no hope against the expert Spaniard. For Alva sent Mondragon, a fine general, with a regiment of Walloons and Spaniards, about three thousand strong. And here in this world of water he was to perform one of the famous military feats of the war.

For he arrived at Bergen op Zoom on the eastern Scheldt to find the Beggars masters of the seas, and he had no way of crossing the water to South Beveland to relieve Tergoes. But by the intelligence of spies he found there was a shallow channel where the sea was only four feet deep at low water. This was the 'drowned land' made fifty years ago when a tempest had caused the dike of the island to burst.

On a warm autumn night Mondragon led his men across, and before dawn they were lying, black with mud and exhausted, on dry land. And the volunteer guards had not seen them. In the morning the Spaniards rose and marched on Tergoes; the town opened its gates. The disorder was great as the volunteers escaped and tumbled into the Sea Beggars' ships; many were drowned, many were slain, many yielded. 'Thus ended our poor ignorant siege', wrote Williams dryly.

But Gascoigne was kinder and praised his fellow soldiers:

Yet surely there without brag or boast
Our English bloods did there full many a deed. . . .

Quite certainly these deeds were done. But battles are not won by individual men acting in isolation, but by trained troops. This fact was never really accepted by Sir Humphrey Gilbert, who always believed in the power of the individual to sway events. He clung to the old tradition of the hero, and was not adjusted to the new methods of warfare.

The defeat was too much for him, the blow to his pride hard to endure. He decided to return with his men to England. The Prince of Orange 'made large offers' for him to stay, but he refused. Morgan, however, with some of the volunteers, including Carleill, remained.

Then came the siege of Haarlem, 'the tediousest, dearest, painfullest of any of these days'. It lasted from December 1572 to July 1573, with Alva's army of thirty thousand men encamped outside the gates. The Prince of Orange with his small army was in the south, Dirk Sonoy, his general, in the north.

Morgan was there with ten English companies, fortunately minus Gilbert. They arrived when the siege was at its height, but though the service required haste the English soldiers refused to march without pay, which they had been promised at their landing. Morgan, however, and Roland York and their bands and Richard Bingham, already a fine soldier who had fought at Lepanto, and Roger Williams, offered their services to the Prince without pay, and with them went the young Christopher Carleill, too young as yet to count the cost of the action which in the end was to lay waste his life with poverty.

There was a naval battle, in which the Beggar' Fleet, now no longer under de la Marck, was defeated. The hoys holding Morgan and his company were burned.

When the Spanish troops at last entered the famished city four executioners set to work on an organized massacre. But the carnage was perhaps too slow, for presently three hundred men were tied together, two by two, back to back, and chucked into the mere. And it was all done in the name of God; the Spaniard prayed first, and then the killing began. When a massacre was taking place, the peasants in the fields, leagues away, would hear a great cry, like the deep note of an organ, break from the anguished town.

Roger Williams reacted with a certain grudging admiration to these massacres. 'To say truth,' he mused, 'if there can be any good order in massacres, the Spaniards do theirs in good order.'

But Alva had his troubles. He lacked money to pay his troops, a permanent source of difficulty in both armies. The men mutinied. The siege of Alkmaar, a town in the north, proved a Spanish defeat. Here the cutting of the dikes flooded the land, and the Spaniards fled before the rising tide. There were English in Alkmaar, two hundred of them.

After Alkmaar the tide began to turn rapidly against Alva. He attempted to advance into the heart of Holland to relieve his troops in the rich villages between Leiden, Delft and the sea-coast as far as Brielle. Williams wrote that 'there were many hot skirmishes' between the volunteers and the Spaniards, who held The Hague, 'the fairest village in Europe'.

But diplomacy was at work in Madrid. The Spanish priests, according to Williams, had persuaded Philip II that Alva was too proud and high. It was also clear to the King that Alva wanted to spend a great deal of money, and there was little to spare in Philip's large and unwieldy Empire. Philip decided that the endless wars of the Netherlands should cease; since violence had not succeeded, milder methods must be used.

Orders came from Alva to return home; Don Luis de Requesens was to replace him, 'a soldier of great reputation for counsel, but no body for execution', wrote Williams, 'but belike in respect of his wit and mildness the King sent him into the Low Countries, being persuaded that a mild captain would win the hearts of the people better than Duc d'Alva with all his cruelty'.

Then Williams went on to reason with a terrible sixteenth-century realism. 'To say truth, fury and resolution well used or executed had been the only way to suppress that nation. . . . God help the prince or state that must be forced to compound with such a people by any means but the sword, which had been far more easy in the hands of the Duc d'Alva than of the poor commander.'

Indeed it was far too late to win over the Low Countries with mildness; but Philip was always an adept at bad timing.

*

Meanwhile the Island of Walcheren was being besieged by the Prince's ships led by de Boisot, Governor of Zeeland, with his kinsman Louis, Admiral of Zeeland. They would let no reinforcements reach Middelburg, which was still in Spanish hands. Before the governor had time to send for help, the Netherlanders had seized the fort at the mouth of the haven.

The Spaniards, now that they had lost the fort, sailed round the Island of Walcheren to land their men east of Campfeer—Veere now —a little town north of Middelburg. Two hundred of the Prince's men marched from Flushing to meet them, including Morgan and his company.

The Prince's navy also arrived at Campfeer and anchored within half a league of the Spanish ships. Mondragon's men were moving with munitions and victuals between the coast and Middelburg, and the Governor of Campfeer with de Boisot, Governor of the island, sallied to confront the Spaniards and entrenched themselves on a dike set in a country cleft with ditches. There they fought their enemies 'with push of pike' till they were beaten back, and during the night, exhausted, they began to withdraw their ships to Antwerp. Seeing this, Louis de Boisot and his Beggars attacked them as they sailed past Campfeer. Morgan and most of his company and many of the English volunteers were aboard the Dutch Vice-Admiral when she boarded her Spanish counterpart, and the fighting was fierce. The Spanish ships fell back before the wind, and cramming on all the sail they could, made for the river at Antwerp. About thirty-two sail were taken, burned or forced to run on to the sands, while others were towed into the town of Campfeer.

A curious scene followed in that prim looking little port, complacent in its prosperity, the prosperity brought by wool. On its quay stood a row of narrow fronted, richly ornamented houses, like small provincial councillors dressed in their civic finery and hung with medals. One of them was the wool-staple of the Scottish merchants, a florid grey and gold affair, swelling with its own importance. Here the Scottish wool was received to be worked by local weavers; not so long ago many commercial transactions had taken place in this house, ships' captains, merchants, money-lenders and farmers had bustled in and out. But slowly the life had been ebbing away; chaos in the Netherlands was spoiling the trade, and many of the weavers had found refuge in England where they could practise their religion in peace. A quietness was settling on the house in Campfeer; it stood fixed in the light that poured out of a huge sky like water from a glass bowl.

Then out of the mists came the Sea Beggars, with their patched sails and raucous crews, pirates all of them. They pushed their Spanish prisoners into the town gaol, and then fell to looting the houses, as if the people had been their enemies instead of their friends. At night the feasting and the singing began and the swilling down of drink, while the poor citizens of Campfeer hid their daughters and said their prayers.

The Prince of Orange was now master of the seas and was sure that he would win the whole island in time. A few months later Middelburg again fell into distress through want of victuals. The Prince sent de Poyet, his Lieutenant-General, into the Island of Walcheren with most of his soldiers. But Colonel Morgan's regiment remained behind in Strinland 'standing on terms for pay and leave to return to England, by reason of some discourtesies that fell out betwixt the Prince and the officers of the said regiment'.

Nevertheless there were some gallant souls who stood by de Poyet, despite lack of pay. And these, wrote Roger Williams, were Captain Walter Morgan, Master Anthony Fant and Captain Christopher Carleill. He did not mention George Gascoigne, but Gascoigne was with them too. The choice had been a hard one for the young Carleill to make in the face of his elders' advice. The results of his choice would be with him till the day of his death, for he was to work for the Prince of Orange for five years without any pay at all;[6] slowly the small fortune that his father had left him was to melt away in the waterlogged cities of the Netherlands.

It was not easy, receiving no pay. George Gascoigne gives an ugly picture of the hunger and the bickering that went on. His poem *Dulce Bellum Inexpertes* reveals the lack of discipline in the English camp;[7] hungry men will not be ruled. The ideals they had followed were wearing thin; personal considerations came first now, how to eat, how to live, how to keep one's own share of food, how not to be robbed, how to rob . . . soul-deadening occupations.

> And God he knows the English soldiers' gut
> Must have his fill of victuals once a day
> Or else he will but homely earn his pay.
> . . . .
> They neither gave us meat to feed upon

> Nor drink, nor powder, pick-axe, tool nor spade
> So might we starve, like misers woe-begone,
> And send our foes with blows of English blade.
> For shot was shrunk, and shift could none be made:
> Yet more than this we stood in open field
> Without defense from shot ourselves to shield.

Of course the English began to quarrel among themselves, that was inevitable. Morgan, a temperamental Welshman, fought with Gascoigne, as years later he was to fight with Carleill.

> And in the broils (a beastly broil to write)
> My Colonel and I fell at debate
> So that I left both charge and office quite
> A Captain's charge and eke a martial's state . . .
> . . . .
> Yet stayed I still, though out of pay I were
> And learned to live as private soldiers do,
> I livéd yet, by God, and lackéd too.

Gascoigne stayed because of the Prince of Orange. He loved and admired him, and defended him from the angry attacks of many of his followers, for the Prince came in for his share of insults too, in that desperate land.

> Oh noble Prince there are too few like thee,
> If Virtue wake, she watcheth in thy will,
> If Justice live, then surely thou art he,
> If Grace do grow, it groweth with thee still.
> Oh worthy Prince, would God I had thy skill
> To write thy worth that man thereby might see
> How much they err that speak amiss of thee.

Here for a moment Gascoigne wrote from the heart. Carleill, too, shared this feeling, at one with his stepfather in loyalty.

Roger Williams, a professional soldier, was sick of war in the Netherlands, and very bitter about the military ignorance of his leaders. When he arrived in England he watched Morgan and some four hundred of his best men go to Ireland: 'They were the first troops that taught our nation to like the musket', he wrote, and that was about as much credit as he would give them.

Then, hearing that the Huguenot Prince of Condé had escaped into Germany to raise an army, he decided to join him. But in Germany he learned that the rumour was false. On his way home to England he was captured by the Spanish and brought before

Julian Romero, the Master of the Camp, who 'earnestly requested him to try the courtesy of the Spanish army'. And Williams accepted; 'Having spent all my crowns and being loth to return to England without seeing something, I promised to stay. Also in those days there was no dispute betwixt her Majesty and the Spanish King to my knowledge.'

That, of course, was a splitting of hairs. Although Elizabeth was not at war with Philip, yet she was allowing English volunteers to assist his enemy. Williams was taking full advantage of his position as mercenary. 'We know of good experience', he wrote, 'commonly they follow the best purse.' An easy choice for him to make in this instance; no purse could be lighter than that of the Prince of Orange.

His service with the Spanish army was to prove very useful; sixteen years later when the Armada was expected off the English coast, Roger Williams was summoned as one of Elizabeth's military advisers.

Meanwhile Carleill and his two English fellow officers were by the Ramekins dike on the Island of Walcheren, with de Poyet and his troops.

Of the great naval battle for Middelburg Williams was to write, 'But in troth I heard divers reports . . . that the fury [at Lepanto] was nothing comparable to this, number to number. . . .'

Williams was still fighting for the Spaniards and must have encountered some of his compatriots fighting for the Prince of Orange. No one, however, seemed to resent his disloyalty—or so to us it seems, with our twentieth-century standards. So his narrative continues from the Spanish angle, and it is thus that he describes the Battle of Romerswaal.

Mondragon, inside Middelburg, asked for help, and one hundred and twenty sail, crumsters and hoys were put in readiness; many lay anchored against the Island of Tergoes, the rest across the water at Bergen op Zoom in Brabant. Brave soldiers there were aboard among the Spaniards, but few mariners who knew the shoals and shallow waters. The Commander himself, Don Luis de Requesens, with his nobility and a great troop of soldiers, put himself on a high bank near Bergen to view the battle, and doubtless to enjoy the Dutch defeat.

The Spanish ships near Tergoes advanced towards Romerswaal

where the Sea Beggars lay. The Dutch policy was to draw the Spaniards on to the shoals, for their vessels drew deep water and could not sail towards the rest of their fleet lying at Bergen op Zoom. Before long the small Spanish vessels were in hot skirmish with the Beggars, many of the bigger vessels being run aground. De Boisot and Julian Romero, master of the Spanish camp, boarded each other, and the Vice-Admirals of both fleets were hot at work for two hours with push of pike and blows of swords. De Boisot and his fellows were the better seamen and better furnished with supplies of gunpowder to blow up the enemy ships.

The moment of defeat came, and Julian Romero fled, and with some of his men 'with wonderful hazard' leaped into the skiffs and rowed ashore, landing at the feet of the Commendator who was watching the destruction with little relish.

The smaller vessels were grounded, many were burnt and the rest made sail for Antwerp. The Dutch followed them up the river, slaying or taking prisoner about six thousand soldiers and mariners. Many taken that night were drowned by the conquerors, and corpses floated down the river like logs. About sixteen hundred Dutch soldiers and mariners were killed and Admiral de Boisot lost an eye.

Thus in February 1574 ended the Battle of Romerswaal, and Middelburg fell. When the Prince's troops entered the town they did so in good order, no looting or violence took place. For negotiations as to the treatment of captured towns and prisoners of war had been going on between the Prince and the Spanish general; Alva's ferocity was giving way to Requesens's 'milder manners'. No longer were Dutch prisoners to be exterminated as rebels, they were to be accorded the honours of war. The Prince made the first gesture, causing the Middelburg garrison to be escorted to their boats by his own soldiers to guard them against the attacks of the peasants, and he waived the indemnity he could have forced upon the besieged town. It was no mean gesture to make in that time and age, with the horrors of the Spanish occupation burning in men's minds, and it needed a big man to make it.

The young Carleill took part in this honourable action, guarding the Spanish prisoners with his sword as they were marched to the ships. He had been defiled by contact with the Sea Beggars; what man could have fought on their side and remained intact? Spanish massacre, Beggars' revenge, these he had come to accept as part of the order of things, for the human heart, hit too hard, makes its own adjustment to pain. But hope was not quite gone; years ago, or so it seemed, in England, he had read books of military science, setting out the rules of war. At home he had been brought up to guard his own personal honour as something precious; honour was a value of paramount importance to sixteenth-century men, something to which they could dedicate their lives, avowing it openly, for there was still something of the medieval chivalry left in Europe, though it was fast slipping away. But in the revolt of the Netherlands Carleill had seen no discipline and very little honour; only the Prince of Orange blazed like a star.

Now a new world was opening for the young Englishman, and he would never look back. All his life he was to be seen disciplining his men, putting 'some sharper punishment' on those who were 'forward and stubborn', than was often employed by captains in Ireland;[8] using tact and magnanimity in his parleys with rebel chieftains in Ulster.[9] He was to become a stickler for discipline and honour. Ubaldino, the historian, was to write of him that he was 'careful of his military honour'. This was in 1588 when he had refused to execute Spanish survivors of the Armada wrecks who had surrendered to him, asking for mercy; he was to send them to Scotland, in face of the orders received from the Lord Deputy.* His action then was the direct result of what he had seen at Middelburg in 1574.

Unaware that this was a turning-point in his life, the young Carleill marched the Spanish prisoners of war to their ships, while the Dutch peasants, clamouring for revenge, jibed at their persecutors.

At some stage of the fighting the Prince transferred Carleill from land service to the Beggars' Fleet, where he was to make his name as a sailor. Gascoigne, so he himself tells us, was given a hoy that the Prince had equipped for him. There is a story, published fifty years later, that Admiral de Boisot himself consulted Carleill before going into action.[10] This may be an exaggeration when one considers the difference in age and status between the Admiral of Zeeland and this very young man. Here is the translation from the Latin of Henry Holland's account: 'Boisot, indeed, Admiral of the Prince of Orange, esteemed him so highly that nothing discussed in the Estates General was to be executed unless he had been told about it and his opinion first sought.'

* See page 103.

Of one thing we can be sure, Carleill learned to be a very skilful seaman in Holland and Zeeland, for in 1577 he was to be sent with a fleet of ships to help the Prince of Condé at the siege of Brouage near La Rochelle, and in 1582 Walsingham was to choose him to escort the Muscovy merchants in their hazardous voyage to the Russian port of St. Nicholas.

Then, in 1574, came the famous episode, the Relief of Leiden, a town that had held out for months against the Spanish army. Here, as at Alkmaar, the dikes were cut by the Dutch, and the river Maas flooded the land and bore the flat-bottomed boats of the Beggars with alarming suddenness towards the enemy. They were shoved, punted and sailed by mud-stained Beggars; the sight of them threw the Spanish soldiers into confusion and they fled.

But once again, as at Alkmaar, there was mutiny for lack of pay: Spanish deserters marched through the countryside plundering the peasant, more dangerous as marauding bands than as serving soldiers. Requesens was no more able than Alva to control hungry men.

Gascoigne with his sharp pen wrote of the differences between the Dutch and the English:

> But what I said I say and swear again
> From first we were in Holland sore suspect,
> The State did think that with some filthy gain
> The Spanish peers us Captains had infect,
> They thought we meant our ensigns to erect
> On King's behalf, and eke the common sort
> Thought privy pay had made us leave our fort.

This was unfortunately true, but the deception did not lie with the private soldier, but much higher up, with the politicians. According to William Camden, both the French and the English 'cunningly went about to possess themselves of Flushing, but being disordered by grudgings and heart burnings one against the other, kindled between them through the cunning practice of the Prince of Orange, they could not effect it'.[11]

Always Gascoigne excluded the Prince from his strictures on the Dutch; men have a deep need in them to find a hero,

> Where good Guillam of Nassau bad me be
> There need I none other guide but he,

It was against this very unsympathetic background on the part of his native land towards the Netherlands that Carleill continued to help the Prince. Elizabeth was resuming a pro-Spanish policy and turning from her first gesture of co-operation with the Dutch rebels. She had gone back to her old belief that a stable Netherlands under Spain would help the English wool trade. The Council of Nymegen in 1573 re-established commercial relations between England and Spain, and then Elizabeth offered herself as mediator between Philip II and the Dutch, a favourite rôle of hers that enabled her to play for time. Her next move was to ask Philip to drive the English Catholic refugees out of the Low Countries, where they were stirring up trouble against her, and in return she proclaimed that the Dutch settlers should be ejected from England, including the Prince of Orange—should he be rash enough to go there. This was a personal stab that the Prince could not ignore.

So England and the Netherlands settled down to play a game of mutual reprisals; the Prince blockaded the Scheldt as far as Antwerp and the Beggars attacked English ships in the Channel; Elizabeth, in reply, seized Dutch ships in English harbours; in 1575 the Dutch put the Merchant Adventurers' fleet bound for Antwerp in detention at Flushing.

In 1574 Walsingham became Elizabeth's Secretary of State; his sympathies still lay with Orange in the Low Countries and with the Huguenots in France; his distrust of the Catholics was growing; Christ and Belial, he said, could hardly agree.

But Elizabeth did not see eye to eye with him. She would adopt any policy that would buy peace, if only temporarily. Dangling before her were two horrible alternatives; if she did not help the Dutch, the French would; if she alienated Spain, England would lose a good customer and gain a bitter foe.

The young Carleill had made his choice. His world was a simple one; in it you fought and lived, or you fought and died.

3

SAILOR AT LA ROCHELLE: SOLDIER IN THE LOW COUNTRIES

DURING THE early seventies the relationship between France and England, which had been growing kinder, was twisted into a new direction by two startling events, the revolt of the Netherlands and the Massacre of St. Bartholomew.

The appearance of a Huguenot General with an army outside Mons during the early days of the Netherlands war showed both Elizabeth and Philip that the French were prepared to fight for their ambitions there, a situation which alarmed both of them.

In France there was every sign that the King was turning towards the Huguenots, and the marriage of his sister to the Huguenot King of Navarre was to be celebrated in Paris in April. But the Queen Mother, Catherine de Medici, was personally jealous of Navarre and feared that his influence over her son might lead to war. She planned the massacre of St. Bartholomew to take place two days after the wedding. On that ghastly night Coligny and many of the Huguenot leaders were murdered; Navarre and Condé, being of royal blood, were spared. Protestant countries received the news with horror, Catholic states rejoiced. It is hardly possible to overestimate the emotions roused in England by the event; Elizabeth went into mourning, and the French Ambassador was received at Court in an atmosphere of freezing disapproval.

Walsingham, who was acting as English Ambassador in Paris, barricaded himself into his house, giving shelter to English residents. As the morning light revealed the cobble-stones splashed red with blood and corpses huddled in grotesque positions, he must have rededicated himself to the cause with renewed strength: he had seen with his own eyes, and that is worth more than many written words.

In France Gascony was in arms and the Huguenots barricaded into the fortress of La Rochelle. If the Treaty of Blois was to be observed Elizabeth could not help them, but privately she did so, and English volunteers joined the Huguenot forces, both from England and from the Netherlands.

A period of confusion in the diplomatic world ensued. In France the King's younger brother Alençon had been associated with the King of Navarre and Condé and the Catholic Montgomery to force *politique* doctrines on the French Court, an alliance with England and a Protestant League, leading to war with Spain. After St. Bartholomew, Alençon was imprisoned, and Elizabeth's marriage with him, an extension of the Treaty of Blois, had to be dropped.

Then the French King died, and his brother Henry III, a very devout Catholic, inherited the French throne. Walsingham's fear of the union of a Catholic France and Spain and renewed religious strife in France seemed justified; Elizabeth's own horror of French ambition in the Netherlands flared up, and she was on the point of sending financial assistance to Condé, who was raising an army in Germany.

But Catherine de Medici and her son were anxious to remove the ill effects of St. Bartholomew on their relationship with England, and they angled for the marriage negotiations between Elizabeth and Alençon—now the Duke of Anjou—to be opened again. When liberty of conscience had once more been established in La Rochelle and in three other towns, the Treaty of Blois was finally ratified in 1576. At once Elizabeth agreed to talk about her possible marriage with Anjou, her pock-marked 'Little Frog', as she called him, and for some while this diplomatic flirtation bewildered and entertained the French, Spanish and English Courts, and Elizabeth succeeded in holding—for a time—the balance of power in Europe.

The next incident in Carleill's career was connected with the Huguenots in France. Norroy, King of Arms, records it in the Grant of Arms given to Carleill in 1593. Here is a translation of it from the Latin, 'In the year of salvation 1577 as commander of eight ships [he] helped the Prince of Condé near Rochelle at the siege of Brouage, attacking the royal fleet of France with fire in a terrible battle . . .'[1]

This is the only reference to the incident of which we can be sure, a small incident in a wide and protracted war. Other stories from English sources connecting English ships with Brouage contradict each other and cannot be proved, as uncertain as rope-ladders in a wind.

'L'année des mauvaises nouvelles' was how the Huguenots described the year 1577. That summer they lost Brouage, which according to the French King was one of the strongest fortresses in his kingdom, with great walls built by the Huguenots. It was also an important port on the Ile de Ré, guarding the entrance to the harbour of La Rochelle. It was famous for its export of salt.

Early in 1577 the Prince of Condé seized La Rochelle and Brouage, which the previous year had been granted freedom of worship again. The inhabitants of both towns were divided, those who welcomed Condé, those who feared he would exploit them.[2] The religious differences, of course, were fanned by both parties, for there were Catholics as well as Protestants here. In Brouage the hereditary Seigneur had been ousted by Condé and replaced by a Governor who exploited the citizens and withheld the garrison's pay. Condé had much ado to establish order.

The King of France sent two armies to besiege the town, and a fleet to attack it by sea: in May another royal fleet arrived commanded by young Lansac. The men of La Rochelle had twenty vessels, and these challenged the royal fleet as it lay at the entrance to the harbour and tried to burn it—Carleill's 'fire and terrible battle'—but there was lack of discipline among the Huguenots; they tried to grapple and board the enemy, failed, and were forced to withdraw.

Meanwhile in the town, food, munitions and medicines were running short, for Lansac had sealed up the mouth of the harbour with masts, making a 'palisade', or boom, which prevented ships from entering. A second fleet, hastily formed by Condé, tried to relieve the town, but owing to contrary winds, it failed.

Meanwhile, the Duke of Anjou, the 'Little Frog', arrived with three hundred horse. At the end of April, starving and without hope, the garrison surrendered. It was agreed that the Protestants should leave in safety and go to La Rochelle or elsewhere. But Condé temporized, hoping to gain time in which to form a third fleet. Finally, the Protestants left on August 27th, and the Royalists entered; one thousand *écus* of salt were found, and the King divided it up between Lansac and his generals.

These are the bare bones of the story. It is interesting to watch the skirmishing that went on in the diplomatic world while these hard facts were taking place at Brouage.

Sir Amyas Paulet, the English Ambassador in France, had been writing to Walsingham in July[3] that 'those of La Rochelle were stronger on sea than the King'; young Lansac, for the King, was demanding the help of ships and soldiers as he lay in the Channel before Brouage; there was no time to lose, the French King was sending the Swiss Guard to help the besiegers.

Daniel Rogers from the Netherlands wrote in the same vein to Walsingham;[4] the Prince of Orange had told him they were rigging five or six ships in Zeeland, and suggested that the English should supply five or six more to convey Colonel Chester and Colonel Morgan and other Englishmen to France.

On August 6th the Queen Mother, who could not have been ignorant of the happenings at Brouage, was suspiciously questioning Paulet about the English ships that had been seen on their way to La Rochelle—possibly the third fleet for which Condé was waiting.[5]

They made a strange couple, Catherine de Medici, with her shifting ways and her shifting religion, and Sir Amyas Paulet who nine years later was to preside as Mary Queen of Scot's keeper at that last scene of high tragedy at Fotheringay Castle. He was a stiff Puritan, upright and austere, a man of the new world which was coming so painfully into being. He reported this conversation in a letter that he wrote to Elizabeth.

The Queen Mother had raised some awkward questions; what were the seven or eight ships 'equipped in warlike manner' lately seen passing Brest for Rochelle? And more, there were four ships and eight or ten English hulks arrived in the Isle of Wight in the name of the King of Navarre, captained by Englishmen and provisioned by England; four of the Queen's ships had been sent to the seas containing one thousand two hundred men bound for Rochelle; and lastly, were not three other ships with small barks being equipped for a further enterprise?

Paulet expressed amazement; he knew nothing of this; his Queen was not at war with France. And then with a flash of spirit he added: 'Concerning the other three ships and small barks supposed to be sent to the seas, if it were indeed true, she ought not to find it strange, and that considering the practice of Fitzmaurice and the preparations made by La Roche, your Majesty had good cause to arm by sea'.

And finally, while the Queen Mother set her square jaw, looking like an angry landlady, he began to defend the English volunteers,

'I told her if it were true . . . she ought not to find it strange that young men finding themselves at good leisure would seek their advantage'; some of these young men in fact served the King of France too, as well as the Prince of Condé.

The conversation was a long one. It was continued that night in Paulet's house when a representative of the Queen Mother arrived with many grievances to discuss.

But time, as usual, was the enemy. On August 27th Elizabeth at last consented to help.[6] Walsingham was instructed to write to the Prince of Orange that she could not openly support him because of her alliance with France; nevertheless she would send ships and money to the value of £2,000, though for obvious reasons she could not sign the letter.

She was too late: the following day, on August 28th, the Protestants left Brouage and the Royalist troops entered.

There is an amusing end to the story. After Brouage had fallen Paulet and the Queen Mother were sparring again; this time she was accusing the English of sending money to Germany where Condé was trying to raise an army; Paulet replied that this was just as untrue as the story of English ships sailing to La Rochelle.[7]

There is more confusing evidence; Henry Holland in his *Herologia Anglica* of 1620 wrote that Carleill was at Brouage with one ship and a frigate of his own, and that the Prince of Condé committed to him English ships carrying English soldiers and French sailors. The date he gives however is 1572, which does not speak well for his accuracy.

Taking everything into account it would seem likely that the English ships reported by the Queen Mother in August could not have reached Brouage in time: Carleill's eight ships were privateers under his command, and were there in the spring, active during the first naval battle.

For the rest of his life, he would always own ships; it was a taste he had acquired in the Zeeland fighting.

In Holland, during the year 1576, a new and sinister complication had arisen, the appearance of the Malcontents. These were the Spanish soldiers who had mutinied for lack of pay and who had imprisoned their officers in Ziericksee which they had besieged for nine months and had finally gained. Then they had swept the Island of Schouwen bare and had eaten their way towards Brussels. There were two thousand of them, perhaps more, mostly experienced soldiers, and by September the whole Spanish army had joined them and many Germans and Walloons as well. The Castles of Antwerp, Valenciennes, Ghent and Utrecht, among others, fell into their hands. They ravished the countryside and performed every outrage upon the inhabitants.

The benign land of the Netherlands was gone: in Holland and Zeeland the fields lay half-drowned in muddy water, while here and there the roof of a house pushed itself above the flood; the towns, protected by their walls, were like floating boats with church towers instead of masts; refugees struggled towards them, dying of hunger or drowning on the way; men robbed and killed to live; storks and herons flapped great wings over the shallows.

Antwerp, the richest city in Europe, fell to the Malcontents. And then followed that horrible event known as the 'Spanish Fury'; eight thousand people were slaughtered and thousands tortured to make them reveal their wealth. The poet George Gascoigne wrote of the massacre done 'when the blood was cold', that 'they neither spared age nor sex, time nor place, person nor country, profession nor religion, young nor old, rich nor poor, strong nor feeble'.[8]

At this moment Catholics and Protestants were united in their desire to eject the Spaniard from the Low Countries. At the end of 1576 the Pacification of Ghent was signed between the Estates; the new religion was to be established in Holland and Zeeland, while in the fifteen Catholic provinces its practice was not to be prohibited; the Inquisition was to be abolished. Thus for a short while the Prince of Orange united the country in a toleration of religion in which he himself believed so profoundly. But it was to prove a toleration of convenience, not of conviction, and was not to endure.

But meanwhile the Spanish hold was weakening. Don John of Austria, the new Governor-General, consented early in 1577 to send his soldiers back to Spain. But their departure was delayed, and even after they had gone German mercenaries remained at large, looting and destroying. Terror is a habit, easily established and hard to break.

The peace between Spain and the Estates was an uneasy one. Holland and Zeeland held aloof under their Stadtholder, the Prince of Orange. Don John thought that only by holding these states could the Netherlands trade be controlled, only thus could he rule. But the Dutch were repairing their dikes, and the Walloon Catholic nobility, always fickle, began to desert him. Fearing for his life, he seized the citadel of Namur and tried to seize Antwerp; he called for the return of the Spanish army under the Prince of Parma. At that the citizens of Antwerp and Utrecht pulled down their citadels, emblems of Spanish tyranny, and declared for the Prince of Orange. Don John had wider ambitions too. The Spanish army might serve him well in his design to free Mary Queen of Scots from prison, and make himself her husband: the Low Countries was a springboard for England, a fact which Walsingham was impressing upon the harassed Elizabeth.

Then the Estates declared that Don John was no longer Stadtholder and Governor of the Netherlands, and war with Spain broke out once more. Twenty thousand Spanish soldiers arrived under the Prince of Parma; the first clash between the two armies revealed the military supremacy of Spain, for the Walloons were badly defeated at Gembloux, and Orange and the Estates General were forced to withdraw to Antwerp; the defeated Walloon army went over to the Malcontents, and ravaged the countryside.

Religious strife between Catholics and the Reformed religion began again, fiercer than ever. In Ghent, that hotbed of militant Calvinism, images were smashed and Catholic clergy attacked. Orange was no longer able to sustain his policy of toleration. The Catholics began to look to Spain for protection against their Calvinist neighbours, and the Malcontents became the champions of Catholicism; in the north the Protestant states held to Orange.

During the month of October, worn out and broken-hearted, Don John died, and Alexander of Parma took over the government.

The rift between Flanders and the Walloon provinces grew, and in 1579, the Union of Ghent, Gelderland, Friesland, Holland and Zeeland was to be signed, the foundation of the Dutch Republic. Gelderland was the natural bulwark of Holland and Zeeland, commanding the four great rivers of the country, and under the government of John of Nassau. These states did not challenge the sovereignty of the Spanish King, but bound themselves together against Spanish militarism. Not till 1581 did the Estates General depose Philip II from dominion over the Netherlands.

The Walloon provinces, full of Malcontents demonstrating against the insolence of the Spanish soldiery, now made their peace with Parma; the unity that Orange had struggled so hard to gain was broken.

But no peace came. In southern Flanders the Malcontents advanced, and Parma's troops overran Brabant. And now there were the horrors of civil war to add to the war against Spain.

The previous year foreign actors had appeared in the Netherlands, eager for power which they hoped to wrest out of the confusion around them. The young Archduke Matthias, brother to the Emperor, and nephew to Philip II, was welcomed by the Prince of Orange for the foreign army he would bring. He became Governor-General, and the Prince his Lieutenant-General: but it was the Prince who held the power.

In April the Commissioners of the Duke of Anjou had entered Brussels to treat with Orange, and his four thousand arquebusiers were on the move; it was decided that should the Estates General accept another sovereign other than Philip, Anjou was to be the first choice; meanwhile he was styled 'Defender of Netherlands Liberty'. He had an army, and for that reason Orange supported him.

During the summer yet another potentate had appeared, Duke Casimir of the Palatinate, a zealous Calvinist from Germany with his 'reiters' to join forces with Orange. He was acclaimed by the Calvinists as their saviour, whereas Orange, with his policy of toleration, was losing face with the extremists of both religious parties. These foreign princes who came ostensibly to support the Netherlands against Spain, did very little and their armies overran the unhappy land.

Orange now turned to France because of the uncertain and grudging help that Elizabeth had offered him. She had held the Duke of Anjou in a scintillating flirtation, dangling before his eyes marriage with herself. But as the marriage proposals revealed themselves to Anjou in all their uncertainty, his interest in the Netherlands had grown. When he entered Brussels to negotiate, Elizabeth's jealousy of France flared up, and at last she offered help to the Estates. But Orange received these offers now with lukewarm interest; the English would not be welcome in the Netherlands, he said, unless the French were to enter in warlike manner. He distrusted the English, he hated the French, but help he must have; 'No great account is made of our nation', wrote Walsingham to Davison, in his bitter disappointment.[9]

Leicester, the Puritan, and a keen soldier, was anxious to bring over six thousand English foot and a thousand horse, but the Estates suspected this was but a move to bring in more.[10]

The Queen offered her troops to Casimir, six thousand soldiers and a loan of £20,000, to be followed by another £20,000, and we read of Christopher Hoddesdon carrying £20,000 to Casimir, during September, in the form of ingots packed in barrels.[11] The sum was not enough. Casimir was no soldier, but for no one will an army continue to fight without pay, and soon it was living off the land, while Elizabeth reviled him for his insufficiency.

By April 1578 some arrangement with Orange had been reached, for among the Estates troops were to be found English soldiers under Norris and Morgan, and Scots under Colonel Stuart.[12] Ever since January Morgan had been struggling hard to bring English troops to the Low Countries, had even offered to provide 'their furniture' himself. He had been 'so importunate here that the Prince has been wearied to hear English soldiers mentioned', an informant had written from Antwerp.[13]

And then in May, Leicester—who was not allowed to leave England after all—was busy recommending Norris to the Archduke and to the Prince of Orange for Colonelship of the English soldiers; he had every gift apparently, birth, skill, courage, wisdom, and modesty, faithfulness to the Prince.[14]

And from that moment English soldiers—as distinct from the early volunteers—come into the story of the Netherlands fighting. Norris had asked that the English should be removed from the Estates army, where they had been for the last few years, to be put under his command and so swell the number promised by Elizabeth.

They were a very different force from the three hundred volunteers who had gone to Flushing six years before, and had later been joined by Sir Humphrey Gilbert's rabble of one thousand two hundred men.

The English army now modelled itself on the Spanish pattern. At its head was the General, who according to Digges in his treatise, must be 'religious, temperate, sobre, wise, valiant, liberal, courteous, eloquent, of good fame and reputation'.[15] Below this heroic figure came the High-Marshal, responsible for the administration of justice and for the organization of the camp, then the Generals and Colonels of infantry and of cavalry, the Master of Ordnance, the Treasurer-at-War, finally the Sergeant-Major whose job was to 'draw the men up into battle'.

This position of Sergeant-Major, a rank soon to be given to

Carleill, was of great importance.[16] He was one of the public officers
of the army, his authority spreading over the whole force and not
only over a regiment, as was the case of the Colonel. He must have
an exact knowledge of military tactics, and be able to put an army
into battle formation; to help him he had four corporals of the Field
to pass instructions to the captains of the companies; these were
experienced men whose rank was higher than that of a captain. Late
in the eighties the pay of the Sergeant-Major was higher than that
of the Colonel, but in 1580 when Carleill was in the Netherlands,
the Colonel received half as much again as the Sergeant-Major.

The main unit was the company, varying from one hundred to
two hundred men, under the command of a captain. During the
early days in the Netherlands private persons had raised their own
companies to serve with the Dutch, but after the year 1578 this
became less common.

Next in rank to the Captain came a Lieutenant, then the ensign-
bearer, two sergeants, two drummers, a surgeon-barber and six
corporals.

The companies were divided, according to the Spanish pattern,
into *camarados*, groups of seven to ten men who messed together and
were encouraged to be brothers to each other.

Early in Elizabeth's reign the companies were not grouped together in regiments. But the force that went to the Netherlands in
1572 with Sir Humphrey Gilbert was described by Roger Williams
as 'the first English regiment', and was composed of ten companies
under a Colonel.

As to their arms, this was a subject of constant dispute. The use
of the bow was on the wane, but it had its strong protagonists, and
certainly those who upheld the use of firearms were looking, full of
hope, into a future in which the arquebus would develop into a more
effective weapon. The new firearms were more expensive to produce
than the bow; moreover, the soldier was put in the extraordinary
position of having to pay for his allocation of powder out of his
wage of eightpence a day, and this 'made cowards' of the men in
the interest of their purses. What with a levy put on them for
the surgeon, the clerk, the muster-master and the priest, and the
constant defrauding of them, performed by the captains,* the
soldier's lot was a poor one, and the great difficulty found in recruit-

* See page 154.

ing men in the shires is explained. The willing volunteers were interested in war largely for the opportunities it offered for adventure and loot.

There was a variety of heavy guns, the falconet, the falcon, the minion, the saker, the demi-culverin, the culverin and the cannon. These were mainly used to batter walls during a siege and the projectiles were of bronze or iron, and for the larger guns, stone balls.

Pikemen carried a pole about eighteen feet long, tipped with metal, a sword and a dagger; they were big heavily armoured men, but as the reign went on the armour tended to become lighter. Mobility was an end now considered important; in the cavalry the demi-Lance was also on the wane in favour of the Light Horse. In 1575 the national muster revealed the number of two hundred and seventy demi-Lances as against two thousand four hundred Light Horse.

The study of military tactics was a new requirement for officers of the Elizabethan army; to a generation fed on Machiavelli, science was becoming an important factor in all walks of life. Not till the eighties did military textbooks make their appearance in any numbers; then several important ones were published. But in 1578 the keen soldier must study the wars of the Roman generals, or read about the Battle of Crécy, or better still, learn by bitter experience how skilfully the Spaniard fought in the Netherlands.

Carleill appeared from his adventure at Brouage during the summer of 1577, saddened by the Huguenot defeat.

After his return there was a savage encounter at Rymenant, near Mechlin, of Matthias's army with that of Parma. The Archduke's force contained English, Scots and Flemings under the Count Bossu and the Huguenot leader, La Noue—*Bras de fer* his men called him— for he had lost his arm and wore an iron hook. There were fourteen thousand of them against thirty thousand Spaniards, including their *Tecio Viejo*, their finest troop.[17] The August sun blazed, and the English threw their armour off and fought in their shirt-sleeves. A miracle happened, the Spaniards were defeated. After Gembloux this was a triumph indeed for La Noue and Norris.

Carleill soldiered with great success during this year in the Netherlands, for in 1580 he was elected as Master of the Field and Sergeant-Major of the English force. His early experience in the Netherlands was useful to Norris; he had studied the Spanish art of war, and his lively mind had acquired a knowledge of French, Spanish and Flemish necessary for the Master of the Field in that Tower of Babel. His personal knowledge of the Netherlands army and of Orange was invaluable, and as Walsingham's stepson he had ready access to the Prince.

During those last years of the seventies his name appears often in the State Papers. In December 1578 we read of him carrying letters from Walsingham, then Secretary of State, to Davison, the English Ambassador in Antwerp.[18] Two years later he is to be found carrying more letters.[19] Certainly he and his brother-in-law, Christopher Hoddesdon, both kept their famous relative supplied with news. Hoddesdon rather touchingly confided the care of his son Francis to Walsingham 'with his poor patrimony', during one of his dangerous expeditions abroad.[20] And in 1580 Hoddesdon was writing to Walsingham about a debt of Christopher Carleill's of £100, which Walsingham had met;[21] 'My wife thanks you for having her in remembrance, imputing the chief cause both of my greater credit and her own estimation in those parts to the good countenance which we receive from you; acknowledging also no less on behalf of her brother, whose estate of late so greatly relieved and advanced by your means, that she cannot but confess you to be a very loving father to both. . . .'

So Christopher and Alice had kept in touch with each other during the stormy fighting in the Netherlands. Hoddesdon was busy in his capacity as merchant, either in Antwerp or in Bruges, during these years, and later in Hamburg as representative of the English merchants there. At times he negotiated loans with the Prince of Orange, for he possessed the financial flair that his brother-in-law lacked. His letters to Walsingham would make a book in themselves.

At this stage in Carleill's life we have the first description of him as his contemporaries saw him. In 1581 a book was published,[22] purporting to be a dialogue between two soldiers, Geoffrey Gates and William Blandy, and dedicated to Sir Philip Sydney. The two soldiers were contrasting Captain Corne, an officer who had recently been killed in the Low Countries, with Carleill who had survived. 'In feature and limbs of body something inferior to Captain Corne when he lived, in proportion of mind, if you respect therein prowess, equal; if policy, attained by learning and study, his superior far. These two principal gifts of a noble mind are in this Carleill beautified with other two in kind and nature not so excellent, yet most fit and necessary to be resident there, where true nobility pleaseth to harbour—affability and liberality.'

As Captain Corne had previously been described as small, presumably Carleill, being 'inferior in limbs and body', was smaller still. Beneath an engraving of him in Holland's *Herologia* is written, *Par mer et par terre, l'art de la guerre?*[23]* Latin words encircle him, among which we read *Carlellus Gallus*, a curious description of him and entirely without foundation as his family had never come from Wales.

Another engraving of him by Robert Boissard, now at the Royal Library, Windsor Castle, has the word 'Steenwick' [*sic*] written behind the figure. A similar print, also at Windsor, has been cut down and has an inscription:

> Captain Christopher Carleill Esquire
> At any time if Carleill had a fleet
> Neptune would lay her trident at his feet
> And when by land his powers he did advance,
> Mars himself would be glad to bow at his lance,
> Let them both Land and Sea his fame forth tell,
> Who both on Sea and Land deserved so well.[24]

These engravings reveal an alert and pleasant face, that of a responsive man, quick to make personal contacts. He had lost an eye, probably in battle.

As early as 1572 Carleill had shown his interest in military strategy by writing commendatory verses in Latin for a translation by Sadler of Flavius Vegetius—'a martial work'.[25] The verses are quite unremarkable in themselves, and show that he was less proficient with a pen than with a sword. But they are a record of the way his mind was turning.

Treachery against Orange grew in this land where most things could be bought with Spanish money. Count Egmont's treachery was dramatic and the first account of it that we have in English comes in a letter written by Carleill to his stepfather.

Count Philip Egmont was the son of the Count of Egmont, the great friend of Orange and hero of the early Netherlands revolt against Spanish militarism. He had been declared a traitor by the

* See note 23 in References for Chapter 3, page 185.

Council of Blood under Alva and he and Count Hoorn had been executed in Brussels. His son, a staunch Catholic, now plotted, with the help of the Walloon Malcontents, to seize Brussels and hand it over to Spain, for since Don John's flight to Namur it had been in the hands of the Estates. He began by selling himself to Spain for twenty thousand crowns and a pension of ten thousand florins a year.

Christopher Carleill was at Antwerp, the headquarters of Orange and the Estates General, when a principal burgher of Brussels arrived to seek help from the Prince.

Carleill wrote[26] that Egmont with some twenty horse had 'made semblant' to go out of Brussels by La Porte de Haws*, where he had planned that some carts should be waiting, laden with hay in which soldiers were hidden. The gate was opened for Egmont, who with the help of the soldiers seized it; they were soon joined by seven ensigns and some of the burghers. Then, leaving a guard at the gate, he marched to the Market Place and captured the King's House. But the Governor had most of the burghers on his side, and accompanied by the Estates soldiers they won back the gate from Egmont's people, then succeeded in trapping Egmont in the Market Place, forcing him to parley.

Here Carleill's account ends. He did not describe how Egmont had stood, hour after hour, in that flamboyant Grande Place where the grey and gold masonry seemed to flow like waves in a small harbour, trapped by his fellow countrymen. In this same place, eleven years before to the very day, the Spaniards had executed his father. So enraged were the burghers that it was with great difficulty that deputies of Orange and Matthias prevented them from burning the houses in order to suffocate the traitor; they cried out that should he move a paving-stone or two he would see the stains of his father's blood.[27] Egmont wept with rage and shame; finally he surrendered.

Carleill did not dwell on the drama of the situation; his reports were always factual and precise.

There is, however, a short and lively account of Norris written by him to Walsingham in June 1580.[28] Here he was not tied to a discreet statement of public events and he explained with a certain raciness that coming back from the surprise of Alost, Norris's men

---

* In *Cal. S.P. Foreign June 1576–June 1579*, no. 687, this is described as Porte de la Halle, an incorrect rendering. It is however still called Porte de Hal —Hal being a village to which the road leads.

'fell out with a drunken waggoner or naughtily disposed man'. Norris's soldiers had rebuked the waggoner, who 'answered them with vile speeches, that one of the Colonel's servants, not able to endure them, struck the waggoner with his sword in his scabbard'. Swords were then drawn on all sides, 'and in this broil . . . someone struck Mr. Norris with a great staff over his nose and one eye, whereupon his nose was beaten flat to his face and his eye somewhat bruised. But the eye is already well recovered, and the nose so raised up again that it will be no disfigurement at all'. Mr. Norris was, however, driven 'to keep his bed for better ease'. The Prince and all the better sort seemed very sorry for the mischance and 'make semblant that they will have justice done in the matter'. Norris, the wise soldier, knowing how easily men rebel, had decided to take no action.

There were other traitors to the Estates' cause as well as Egmont. The Governor of Mechlin was one; another was Count Renneberg, a noble belonging to a great Walloon family, whose brother had been a personal friend of Orange. The young Renneberg was Stadtholder of Friesland and Drenthe, an elegant and accomplished person, who had been described—but ill-described—as the Dutch Sydney. For although he was a classical scholar and a lover of music and poetry, he wrote no immortal poems as Sydney did, and unlike Sydney he died an inglorious death. He sold himself to Spain for twenty thousand crowns and a pension of ten thousand florins a year. Such sales were common amongst the nobility. His excuse lay in the fact that, as an ardent Catholic, he feared that the Reformed religion of Holland would grow so strong that suppression of the Catholic mass might follow. His case would have been strong enough had it not been for that bribe.

Groningen in Friesland was part of the Union of Ghent, Gelderland, Friesland, Holland and Zeeland that had been formed in 1579. Now Renneberg in 1580 made a *coup d'état*, seized the Catholic town of Groningen and withdrew from the Estates General. But the provinces did not follow the city, and the peasants of Drenthe and Friesland calling themselves the Desperates and opposing both the Spanish and the Estates armies, marched through the land burning and looting. An Estates force under Sonoy and Louis of Nassau besieged Groningen, but was defeated by a small force of Parma's men: Groningen fell to Spain.

Hohenlo, the General of the Estates army in Friesland, was a drunkard and a poor soldier. Renneberg had only eight thousand men, but his strength lay in his opponent's weakness. In 1580 he laid siege to Steenwijk, the key to the province of Drenthe. And it is here that Carleill appears again clearly defined as a very proficient soldier.

Steenwijk was an old town on the little river Haa, with three gates, one where boats came, in that flat easily flooded land.[29] Ramparts encircled the town. Orange had sent Captain Cornput with a garrison of soldiers to help the Burgomaster, and together they governed. The men of Steenwijk wrote to the Prince that they could only hold out for eight weeks against Renneberg, but Cornput in his pride set the period at six months, and he was very nearly right. Renneberg had six thousand foot and twelve hundred horse, but the garrison only consisted of six hundred soldiers and the untrained burghers. Cornput quelled the opposition of those who wanted to surrender, by the force of his buoyant personality. Certainly they had reason on their side, but Cornput had passion.

The Estates army under the incompetent Hohenlo was encamped in the country offering help. The winter set in, hard and cruel, and Renneberg pounded Steenwijk with red-hot cannon balls, a new invention. In November news was sent from Antwerp to England; 'Mr. Norris has been chosen Master of the Camp and has accepted conditionally that the States will pay his soldiers monthly. He is now gone to the relief of Steenwijk with all the power he can make.'[30]

He must have remembered Morgan's trouble with the unpaid English soldiers in 1572; he was not risking this again.

Walsingham received more news;[31] three companies of men had been left behind at Swart Sluys while Norris went on with his men to Campen to join ensigns fighting against Spain. Renneberg charged, and the English, who were defending the place stoutly, came out of their trenches to fight. During the skirmish the Colonel arrived with the rest of the men and put the enemy to flight; but owing to an insufficiency of horse Renneberg was not completely overthrown. 'The Colonel and his men are held in great honour', added Walsingham's informant.

December came and the town starved; Norris could not use chariots to carry in victuals, for the rattle of their wheels on the ice could be heard in the still cold nights.[32] But he did succeed in sending in forty men with sacks of gunpowder slung round their necks.

The English were ill-fed too, eating horseflesh. It was not till Sonoy came to relieve Steenwijk and held the fort a league away, that Norris's camp at St. Jean could be victualled. Nevertheless the English fought on.

Hoddesdon wrote to Burghley: 'News has come from Friesland that Mr. Norris has not rested, but by alarms and excursions has kept the enemy busy.'[33]

The besieged town shot lead bullets weighing two pounds into their rescuers' camp which contained messages. Throughout the siege messengers penetrated the enemy lines to collect food, despite the fact that Renneberg had ringed Steenwijk with fires. Their safe passage was regarded as a miracle.

Indeed the desperate men lived on the hopes of a miracle taking place. Three partridges were picked up by hand in the market-place in February, and the gift of prophecy suddenly descending on Cornput, he proclaimed that as God was of three substances, so He would feed the town, 'but not till three weeks were passed because of the citizens' lack of faith'.[34] His words were to come true; three weeks passed and the food came.

Norris and his men were fighting gallantly. In February he defeated three cornets of the enemy cavalry and took one of the sconces outside the town. He and his men were forced by the cavalry to lie up in an orchard, but they broke out, killed four hundred of the enemy and retired in safety to Meppel. They were to return and this time 'to give the enemy a great overthrow'.[35] He himself was wounded in the shoulder.

Meanwhile in Steenwijk much hoarded food had been discovered, enough to allow six loaves a head for a week. This came just in time to prevent the garrison from mutiny.

Renneberg tried to break the besieged men with insufferable baiting and jeering. At Easter he asked if the town had eaten all its horses, and in reply sixty starving men on sixty starving nags processed round the ramparts, a frieze of black skeletons against a pale sky.

The garrison made daily sorties against the enemy forts with straw and tar. At one stage Norris conveyed one hundred and fifty cheeses and three hundred and fifty loaves into the town with powder and match, all strung together, in charge of five men. Another time he engaged the enemy in a hot skirmish, while other soldiers rushed the bridges with supplies of food, and Cornput attacked the forts. Steenwijk was indeed 'a place of small force or importance, and yet for the value of them that defended it worthy to be cared for': so thought the Prince of Orange.[36]

Easter came and a slow thaw began. Renneberg realized that his sullen soldiers could no longer be kept there, knowing that they were still unable to prevent food from reaching the besieged town. So one dark night he withdrew to a place some eight hours' march away.

Out came the burghers, cautiously at first, into the abandoned camp; there was meat, there was wine and venison for starving men, and they carried them back to Steenwijk, rejoicing. And so on the very last day of the three weeks prophesied by Cornput, the town was fed.

But there was no happy ending to this story; death was not to be cheated; before the year was up the Plague was in the town, and men died, for they were weak. A reason was found, in itself a comfort, in the days when God's avenging hand was seen everywhere; men said that the dried blood and the unburied corpses were reason enough for the disease.

Once more we meet the English involved in Friesland. In 1581 they were outside Groningen which was still in Renneberg's hands. William Blandy described the action with gusto. 'The English held Fornecloister against the Malcontents', he wrote, 'then marched to Upslaught and beset the place so strongly that the enemy could not escape, and sent a herald to crave mercy.' The soldiers wished 'to destroy so hellish a brood', but Norris let them depart, their lives saved and their arms taken.

Outside Groningen there was 'hot and bloody bickering', and then Roger Williams—now once again with the English—drew his horsemen under the side of the mountain and pointing to the dead carcasses covering the plain 'exhorted them with many fine words to charge'. They charged, and killed a hundred of the enemy.

Though Roger Williams earned great glory that day 'there were others also no doubt which did win at that present, if not the like, yet great praise and honour—Captain Carleill, now Sergeant-Major of the English regiment' and then follows a list of six names. Thus wrote William Blandy in 1581, the year of the incident, when all was fresh in his mind.

The Malcontents, he continued, sent querulous messages to the army of the Estates General: 'Dismiss the English brood with their great ruffs'; and trying to avoid the English they wandered to and fro in the countryside.

Norris and his men were popular after their triumphs at Steenwijk. The Prince held him in such high favour that he put him in command of the Estates army in Friesland, a mixed force of Dutch, Flemings, English, Germans, French and Scots. And Carleill, as Sergeant-Major of the English force, was swung into a position of greater power than ever.

But he was to be given a wider command than that. Holland recounts the story that the Prince of Orange set him over the garrisons in the castles, for it was felt by the different nationalities that they should have one man over them, in the confusion of tongues and temperaments that prevailed; a tribune of soldiers elected him and he held this high office during the absence of Norris.

Not only must he be a fine linguist, this paragon, but he must be a diplomat and a disciplinarian as well, a surprising combination in a soldier who had passed his youth in the brutal wars of the Netherlands.

Holland also has a story of his prowess at the defence of Swart Sluys, which seems to have taken place before Christmas 1581. With two thousand infantry and six hundred cavalry he routed the enemy and killed eight hundred of them. It is not entirely clear from this statement if this incident took place before the Siege of Steenwijk or after it, as Swart Sluys featured twice in the Friesland fighting.

In February 1581/2 Norris was writing to Walsingham, and there were words of praise for his stepson, 'No man has won more honour near to Captain Williams, both in our camp and in the enemy's.'[37]

He had spent nine years of his life, from youth to manhood, in the most savage war of his time. It is significant that Boissard, in his engraving, put the word 'Steenwick' [sic] behind the figure of Carleill, not Cartagena or San Domingo, episodes in Drake's West Indies voyage that brought him fame in his own country. Perhaps because the rank he attained in that many-tongued army of the Netherlands revealed him not only as a proficient soldier, but as a man of wide attainments. He had blossomed into that romantic and versatile figure so dear to the sixteenth century, of the fighting man civilized by the gift of poetry, the knowledge of classics or the practice of diplomacy, sometimes by all three together. Sir Philip Sydney—later to become Carleill's brother-in-law—was the shining example of this much admired man.

4

MERCHANT ADVENTURE

MAN CANNOT live on deeds of valour alone, and Carleill had to consider how he was to remain in the Netherlands with insufficient money. For five years he had served the Prince of Orange for no pay at all; for the past four years he had received pay, but only intermittently. He had broken into his own 'poor patrimony', which was disappearing rapidly. By the end of 1581 he realized that he must move elsewhere.

There had been trouble about pay in the Low Countries ever since the time when Morgan and his men had walked out of Holland in 1573. In 1580 the situation in Ghent was tense, and the treacherous mayor had offered the Scots troops, who were in a state of mutiny, arrears of pay and six months' pay in advance to yield the town to the Prince of Parma.[1] To their honour they refused. At the same time the first echévin of the city of Ghent received a despairing letter from a compatriot, 'Once more I beg you will attend to the matter of the English by action and not by words or excuses, otherwise I shall certainly believe that you care neither for me, nor the keeping of the town.'[2]

In Friesland English companies were in mutiny too. Hungry men will not fight; some of them even joined the Malcontents who were pillaging the countryside. They were 'marvellously discontent', wrote Morgan to Walsingham in July 1582, adding that there never was a 'greater disorder or discredit to our nation than has fallen out at this time'.[3]

Carleill's account with the Estates was still not settled in April 1582,[4] when his friend Abraham Ortelius, the famous cartologist, was looking into the matter for Walsingham. At the same time Fremyn, who kept Walsingham supplied with news from the Netherlands, was writing to him rather bitterly about the Dutch, 'They want to be served with soldiers without paying them, and

that they should come to their help and requite them with insults.'[5]
He went on to explain that the foreign soldiers were being excluded
from the towns as much as possible, which were being garrisoned by
Netherlanders; if it should become necessary to admit the volunteers, they were to enter in small numbers only, so that they could
be quickly thrown out again.

It was all very sad, distrust on both sides, and with justification.
Every soldier knows this phenomenon, when the military struggle
grows less, enthusiasm wanes, and allies rend each other; the tide
was running out and all was bitterness and disillusion.

Carleill and Bernard Mayor, a merchant of Melcombe Regis, had
owned a ship called the *Samuel of Weymouth*, alias the *Golden Hind*.
She may have gone with Carleill to Brouage in 1577, that expedition
cloaked in rumour. In 1579 he seems to have had some litigation
with Mayor about her;[6] he went to law as easily as most sixteenth-
century men. In April 1581 the *Samuel of Weymouth* was involved
in piracy, for she spoiled a Spanish ship,[7] but by then Carleill was
no longer part owner, for she belonged to Luke Ward,[8] and in 1583
Edward Hayes took her with Gilbert to America. This connection
with piracy of a ship once owned by Carleill is worth noting; his
name was to be connected adversely with piracy in later years, and
this incident may have started the rumours.

The collaboration with Mayor in trade could not have been a great
success, for by 1581 Carleill was turning his attention to adventure
in the New World. All his family connections lay in that direction;
in his childhood he had listened to talk of sea voyages and of the
riches of strange lands, his grandfather and uncles, grave men with
long beards, debating with the mariners who came into the Muscovy
merchants' house in Seething Lane. Now his stepfather, Sir Francis
Walsingham, owned this house, and from the latticed windows the
masts of ships anchored in the Thames could be seen gently swaying
against the sky. In London the life of the sea was never far away.

Carleill's friendship with Abraham Ortelius affected him profoundly. To return from the jungle of warfare in Overijssel and to
talk to this detached scientist with his maps and charts and his
knowledge of the New World, had given hope to the soldier with
dust in his mouth. There was much for Carleill to learn; there was
much that Ortelius had to tell Walsingham.

In England Carleill had strong kinsmen to give him practical help; his uncle George Barne, who had been Governor of the Muscovy Company in 1580, and was to be so again in 1583,[9] Christopher Hoddesdon, who was a veteran of the Company; finally his stepfather, who had a double interest in mercantile adventure, both as a private trader and as the Queen's Secretary of State. He sifted the information with piercing exactitude brought to him by the two Richard Hakluyts, and by Dr. Dee who was a mathematical genius as well as magician and astrologer. And it was among these brilliant and practical men that Carleill found himself on his return to London.

The merchants of the Muscovy Company were no longer entirely satisfied with the Russian trade, and were looking elsewhere for outlets. There were two routes to Russia, the first to St. Nicholas, the northern port on the White Sea which the English merchants had originally used, the second to Narva, a Baltic port on the borders of Estonia, which had suited them better in later years, as the journey overland from Narva to Moscow was shorter than that from St. Nicholas. But to reach Narva ships had to pass through the Sound, that narrow arm of sea lying between Denmark and Norway, and here the King of Denmark collected toll, a profitable occupation. In 1581 Russia had lost Narva to Sweden, and now the English merchants were forced on to the northern route to St. Nicholas by way of the North Cape, and the King of Denmark lost his toll. But he would not accept this deprivation, and he declared that he had the right to collect toll in the northern seas too, where they passed between the Danish possessions of Norway and Iceland. He complained bitterly that the English merchants on their way to St. Nicholas were trading on the coast of Lapland, where he claimed sovereignty. In 1581 there had been an encounter between the Danish fleet and the Muscovy merchants near the North Cape and the Danish ships 'put to the worst'.[10]

Two years later Carleill was to write his 'Brief and Summary Discourse',* addressed to the Muscovy merchants with the intention of interesting them in a voyage to the 'hithermost parts of America' and colonization there. In it he was to condemn the Russian trade as having fallen 'to very ticklish terms', the chief troubles being the interference of the King of Denmark, the possibility of performing only one voyage a year, the Emperor's dealings

* See pages 79–81.

which were 'very fickle', and the great cost, which always fell on the Muscovy Company, of conveying ambassadors between Russia and England; finally the competition of Dutch merchants in the north.

The voyage to the Moluccas and to China by way of the North West Passage—as yet undiscovered—had been interesting the Muscovy merchants during the late seventies and early eighties. Frobisher had tried to find it on three separate occasions without success. In 1580 the Muscovy merchants had launched an attempt to discover the North East Passage by way of the North Cape, but that too had failed.

During the year 1581 different combinations of men were being suggested to the Privy Council, and plans discussed. In April Walsingham and Leicester had consulted with Drake, Hawkins, Frobisher and Richard Bingham.[11] In October Leicester had bought a ship of two hundred and fifty tons for Frobisher to take to the Moluccas, and Drake had agreed to send mariners and to join in the risk. Leicester would be the chief promoter, putting up £2,200; Oughtred, a Southampton merchant, followed him, and then came members of the Privy Council, the Muscovy merchants and the adventurers themselves, Frobisher, Fenton, Luke Ward and Carleill, putting up £300 each.[12]

But matters dragged; next year in February there appears to have been a quarrel about Frobisher's second-in-command;[13] the Muscovy Company had wished to thrust a lieutenant of their own choosing—Edward Fenton—on to the expedition, and Frobisher had walked out. These adventurers were exceedingly temperamental and had no shame about exposing their feelings.

Then Henry Oughtred intervened;[14] he was not happy that Fenton was to be in command; he would have preferred young William Hawkins to lead the expedition, he who now was to sail as Fenton's lieutenant. He suggested that Hawkins and Carleill would make a good combination instead; the men would agree well and the merchants and mariners would welcome the choice; Fenton had small experience at sea, was choleric and stubborn, and would make 'great discord in the company'.

If only this wise advice had been followed at the time.

But Leicester, Burghley and Walsingham had a different rôle planned for Carleill. They put Fenton in command of the four ships, and Carleill under him as General of the land forces. He was 'to acquaint himself with the language' and to be put ashore in China with some of the members of the company, in order to trade with the inhabitants. We catch the flattering remark, 'Mr. Christopher Carleill is by us thought a meet man for this purpose.'[15] The affable linguist was to be used in a rôle that would suit him.

He was to sail in the *Galleon Leicester*,[16] in which would be Edward Fenton, William Hawkins, Nicholas Parker and Richard Madox, a preacher, and one hundred and twenty mariners. A number of specialists were to go with them, among others a surgeon, a jeweller, a distiller of fresh water, a shoemaker, eleven musicians, an apothecary, and two or three serving men to each officer. How they were all to fit into the ship is not very clear. The *Edward Bonaventure*, Vice-Admiral, was to be commanded by Luke Ward, the *Bark Francis* by John Drake, and the *Elizabeth* by Thomas Skevington.

Carleill did not appear to be very happy with the Privy Council's instructions to Fenton. But that was because he did not trust Fenton. Earlier in the year the Spanish Ambassador, Mendoza, had been stirring up trouble between Frobisher and Fenton in order to delay the voyage, and his sinister practices had not been in vain.[17] Perhaps he continued to stir up trouble, for trouble there still was, this time between Fenton, Hawkins and Carleill.

Carleill's position under Frobisher had been a strong one; he was one of Frobisher's assistants in the voyage, and there was as yet no mention of young William Hawkins.[18] He was also chosen to keep the 'true note of the voyage' for the Council. Three coffers were to go with them containing the names, secretly written down, of the General's successor, should the General die on the voyage; the keys were to be held by Frobisher, Fenton and Carleill. These instructions were issued to Frobisher on February 11th.

But after Frobisher had taken himself off, new instructions were given to Fenton on April 9th,[19] and Carleill's position was considerably weakened. He was not chosen to be one of Fenton's assistants, but William Hawkins was there instead. The 'true note of the voyage' was to be kept by the preacher Richard Madox; the keys of the coffers were to be held by Luke Ward, William Hawkins and Madox. Small irritations for Carleill, perhaps, but signs which way the wind was blowing.

Carleill, stepson of Walsingham and nephew of Alderman Barne, the Master of the Muscovy Company, was being edged out; the Earl of Leicester, chief promoter of the voyage, favoured Fenton and Hawkins.

In Fenton's Instructions of April 9th was this phrase: 'On all occasions and enterprises that may fall out to be upon the land, we will that Captain Carleill shall have the general and chief charge thereof.' But in Frobisher's instructions there had been an additional clause, referring to Carleill's command, 'and therein to dispose as by him shall be found most expedient'. Now it was withdrawn. Who withdrew it?

Certainly the Instructions of April 9th showed the Privy Council's desire to tie everyone up, so that neither tyranny nor indiscipline was possible. 'You shall not remove William Hawkins, your Lieutenant, Master Captain Luke Ward, your Vice-Admiral and Captain of the *Edward Bonaventure*, nor Captain Carleill in his charge by land who we will not to refuse any such service as shall be appointed to him by the General and Council.' These officers named could only be removed with the consent of Fenton's four assistants and then only with just cause. It was clear that the Privy Council was not entirely happy about the situation.

Oughtred, Alderman Barne and Towerson, the three Muscovy merchants who were members of the Commission, did their best to improve Carleill's position. They wrote strongly to the Privy Council urging it to order Fenton and every member of the company to help Carleill and his company with arms, provisions, powder, shot and merchandise in every way, short of depriving the two great ships of the fleet of those necessities. 'Direction, command and authority as in the like affair is ordinarily prescribed', was asked for Carleill.[20] The note was endorsed at the back with the words, written in another hand, 'A note of certain defects in the instructions and preparations for the voyage to China to be supplied.'

There may have been an answer, but if so it could not have re-assured Carleill. He had a heavy responsibility before him, and his position was not sufficiently defined.

We have some indications of the merchandise needed for the China trade, for two years earlier Richard Hakluyt had given instructions to a couple of men sent by the Muscovy merchants to discover the North West Passage and to trade with Cambalu or China.[21] Woollens and materials of all kinds were to go, felts, taffeta hats, capes for mariners, quilted caps, gloves, girdles; one's mind reels at the thought of the small vessels, heavily laden, in angry seas; there were to be shoes, English and Venetian glass, goggles, on and on the list goes, and then in Richard Hakluyt's

Captain Christopher Carleill.
Engraving by Boissard

Sir Francis Walsingham. After J. de Critz the Elder

English volunteers
at Brielle, in Zeeland.
Engraving in
the Delft Museum

Sir Francis Drake.
Attributed to Hondius,
finished by G. Vertue.
About 1858

Sir John Perrot,
Lord Deputy of Ireland

delightful prose, 'All the several coins of our English moneys to be carried with you to be shewed to the governors of Cambalu, which is a thing that shall in silence speak to wise men more than you can imagine.' These two Englishmen had to observe details of the Chinese navy, of their ordnance, of their army, of their methods of harvesting, and of the growing of grain. They were to entertain men of note, and to take with them for the purpose perfumes, marmalades, suckets, sacks, prunes and sugar, and many other delights.

In fact Carleill, had he gone to China, would have needed to be diplomat, spy, merchant adventurer and perhaps fighting soldier. He would have carried out these duties well, even to learning the Chinese language. But something happened and he did not go.

As early as March Richard Madox, the preacher, in his private diary,[22] written largely in cypher, safe, as he thought, from prying eyes, reported that he had been dining regularly with Carleill in London; they were making friends rapidly, recognizing in each other a common honesty; they had dined at Mr. Secretary's lodging at Court, another day at Christopher Hoddesdon's house, and yet again at Carleill's own table when Fenton and Parker had also been present. The diary at this stage breaks into cypher, 'Here Fenton feareth lest William Hawkins should outmatch him.'

This jealousy of young Hawkins was to become an obsession with Fenton, causing scenes of violence on the voyage. As early as October 1581 there had been signs of it. William Hawkins was impetuous and dashing, 'open and glorious but very childish', as Madox was to describe him, one to be held in check. But Madox had worse things to say about Fenton, writing that Alderman Barne thought him but 'a foolish, flattering, fretting creeper'.

When the *Galleon Leicester* sailed from London to Southampton in April she carried with her a little group of visitors, there to make merry, and Carleill was mentioned in their company, with George Barne and Towerson. Perhaps Carleill left the ship with them at Gravesend, for when the *Galleon Leicester* anchored at Hampton Wood on April 20th Madox wrote in his official diary: 'News came that Captain Carleill was kept back by an ague whereof very many were sorry, but especially the tidings did trouble me because I reposed more comfort of the voyage in the hope of his good company . . . and had determined myself also to have remained with him wherever he had stayed while God would give me leave.'[23] Thereupon Mr. Alderman Barne and Fenton had 'appointed

Nicholas Parker to all the preferments and charges which by commission had been assigned to Carleill'.

But Madox gave another reason, besides the ague, for Carleill's disaffection. 'Captain Carleill upon some discourtesy taken would not go, which was a great grief to me, but the Lord's will be done in all things.'

This was the reason that Fenton hoped would be believed, for no one would accept the ague version. Fenton himself expounded the theory in a letter written to Leicester on April 22nd: 'Carleill's [discontent] grows chiefly by placing before him in the instructions young Mr. Hawkins . . .'[24]* He went on to say that Carleill had been aggrieved with Fenton for not having taken action with the Privy Council to amend this, that he had tried to content Carleill 'according to an agreement set down between Leicester and Walsingham'. And so on, declaring his love for the 'virtuous gentleman'.

It was a typical Fenton performance; he was able to give one more kick to the hated Hawkins.

Looking into the future and examining the events of this disastrous voyage, one must conclude that Carleill left in the nick of time. The voyage was not what the promoters imagined it to be, for Fenton had no intention of trading in cloves in the Moluccas, nor of leaving behind a colony in China; he intended to be the captain of a pirate ship, and to make his fortune.[25] Madox revealed that he had the mad idea of installing himself as King of St. Helena with the ship's crew as colonists, and then he would fall upon the Portuguese carracks coming from the East Indies. Other wild schemes were suggested or tried; Fenton was neither a good seaman nor a successful pirate. The crew seemed to have shared his taste for piracy, except for the two chaplains who were deeply shocked at the proposals made to them. Perhaps fortunately for Madox he died on the voyage.

Parker, who was in the rôle that had been allotted to Carleill, was roughly handled by Fenton. Early in the voyage he asked if he could choose his own lieutenant and corporals for the 'better performance of his service'; Fenton replied that 'there would be no land service, and as for the lieutenant he would suffer no other in the fleet but his own'.

Before the expedition left England, Mendoza had heard rumours

* See note 24 in References for Chapter 4, page 186.

that it was not bound for the Moluccas, as was supposed, but was to sail down the coast of Brazil to Port St. Julian and the Straits of Magellan:[26] someone must have talked. If Mendoza knew this, how much more must Carleill have known or suspected? What would his position have been on that lawless pirate ship, shorn of his powers as General of the land forces? He would have had to submit to the change of plan, or else to have overthrown Fenton.

So on May 3rd when George Barne and Towerson mustered the company of the *Galleon Leicester*, and Madox prayed for a safe voyage, Carleill was not there.

On April 20th Madox had reported the rupture between Carleill and Fenton in his 'Book'. On April 28th a certain officer in the Netherlands army, one Fremyn, sat down to write a letter to Walsingham. For several years he had kept the Secretary of State supplied with news from the Low Countries; he was a man of standing, and can be classified more as a news agent than as a spy. He wrote in French and his letter can be translated thus;[27] 'I have heard that Monsieur de Terlell [*sic*], your stepson, has sent his portrait and ring to the beautiful seamstress—with a letter telling of the affection and friendship he bears her, with a view to marriage. It is not handsome nor honourable of a gentleman of his quality to fall in love with a courtesan and do this disgrace to himself and his relations. For this reason I have told you that you may remedy it without saying who sent you word, so that he may not get himself laughed at.'*

Coming at this moment in Carleill's life the question obviously occurs, was this exceedingly unconventional proposal of marriage an act of desperation after the rupture between himself and Fenton in April? Or had it precipitated his decision to leave the expedition? Either action would be comprehensible to a contemporary mind, but a sixteenth-century man would not react in these ways.

In that striving century marriage was as practical an arrangement as a deal on the Stock Exchange is today; first and foremost it brought land to those who hungered for it, and secondly a partner in life's battle. The trappings of finery, the ceremonial that surrounded marriage, the poetic discourses and the romance deceived no one about the hard facts that lay beneath the surface.

* In the *Calendar of State Papers Foreign 1581–82*, 'la belle lingère' is incorrectly translated as the 'pretty milliner'.

It was no bad thing for these people to throw up a jewelled glitter, like a fountain in spray, for when death presses close it is wisdom to beautify life. In a land where the Plague struck regularly, spouses tended to lose each other after a few years of marriage, their children budding and falling like leaves; a husband would lay his partner in the grave with all the elaborate shows of grief, then away in search of a replacement, more land, more children, there was no time to waste, soon he too would be gone. Conjugal love grew in these fleeting partnerships, and the voices of affection that reach us are real enough.

The sport of love was different, and had its own set of rules. Adoration was often lavished by a young man on a lady of rank, usually his superior in station, and this provided an outlet for poems of passion, for every gentleman wrote poetry, and the pangs of unrequited love was a conventional theme. This fashion of love was the remains of the medieval tradition of chivalry that had produced the troubadours. The existence of a Virgin Queen in England had revived a way of life which had been dying, and now the game of love was played at Court with a hectic vehemence, and often feigned passion was twisted by jealousy into something approaching the real thing. For the prize was high, no less a reward than the Queen's favour.

It is inconceivable that Carleill, in his considerable position as Sergeant-Major of the English forces in the Netherlands, should have contemplated marriage with a Flemish seamstress. His career would have ended, his powerful relations would have deserted him. This was the age when patronage was essential, and men would stoop low to obtain it.

But when his mind began to turn to adventure in the New World, and he saw himself as a planter administering large tracts of land in the 'hithermost parts of America', he may have realized the difficulty of finding an English woman of his own station who would accompany him. Here at hand was a woman whom he knew and loved, a hard worker and beautiful into the bargain. She would not disgrace him in a New World, not yet bound with the conventions of the world he was leaving.

As to her being a courtesan, surely Fremyn's imagination must have run away with itself. The sixteenth-century trollop was an unlovely creature. In London she lived in 'the stews', a bawdy quarter on the south bank of the river set aside for her by the law that punished her severely at times, but on the whole tolerated her existence in exchange for the appropriate payment. Memories of Sir John Falstaff and Doll Tearsheet at the Boar's Head Tavern rise in the mind; the very name explains her. A man might take a seamstress with him to the New World and still be a wise man, but only a lunatic would take a trollop.

Whether '*la belle lingère*' said yes or no, we have no means of finding out. Carleill was married by 1586, but before that date he never mentioned a wife in his letters to his stepfather. As soon as his part in the Fenton expedition had fallen through, he was busy preparing a new adventure.

Mendoza, the Spanish Ambassador in London, had to keep Philip II up to date with information. His method was to present him with every rumour that he had heard, whether true or false, and to leave his master to sift them for himself. The man in black, sitting alone at night in the Escorial, a bundle of documents before him, examined each story with patient industry, writing tart little comments in the margin. He was like a spider devouring very small flies.

Our difficulty with Mendoza's information is obvious; it must be regarded with great caution unless corroborated elsewhere. Often it is.

During the summer of 1582 he was busy reporting the Danish trouble. He was delighted at the insults that Elizabeth was receiving, and was explaining to Philip[28] how the King of Denmark had written to her about a certain expedition that the English merchants were making to Muscovy by the way of the Frozen Sea; the King intended to sink all ships using this route in the future. That same month he had written demanding that the Muscovy merchants should pay him their dues.[29]

Mendoza also spied into the doings of adventurers to the New World, watching the movements of ships in English ports with the gravest suspicion. But the information he gleaned about them was curiously composed of truth and falsehood.

Then on June 29th he wrote to Philip that the King of Denmark had sunk the English ship *Mignon*[30] on her way to St. Nicholas, that the Queen had instantly ordered the arming of two fresh ships to guard those that were about to leave for Muscovy. 'These are the ships that I wrote were going to plunder on their way to the Indies, the captain of them being a son of Walsingham.'

And this is the only reference we have to the small expedition that Carleill had been planning. He may have been helped by his uncle George Barne, for Mendoza also reported that an alderman of the City of London and a certain Winter were fitting up two ships to plunder on the coast of Brazil.[31]

But the Queen stopped this little fleet from going, and for a good reason. For in July Mendoza had reported more trouble to his master;[32] two merchant ships had appeared in the Thames on their way home from Russia. They had gone ahead of the eleven armed Muscovy merchantmen and now had come flying back from pursuit with all their cargo aboard, having 'discovered' a fleet of eleven Danish ships and thirteen armed galleys with 'eight bronze pieces' each. These ships had chased them, but they had escaped. In London the merchants feared greatly for their ships already on the way north, as there was news from their factor at Hammerfest that eleven Danish ships were awaiting them at St. Nicholas.

That same month the Tsar was writing to Elizabeth, assuring her that he would send men-of-war to assist her against the King of Denmark, and urging her to send armed ships to 'waft' her merchantmen to St. Nicholas.[33] The Tsar had good reason to distrust the Danes.

The Queen at once ordered Carleill to take her ship the *Tiger* and to escort the Muscovy fleet, now due to sail to Russia, nine ships and one bark. The *Salomon*, the biggest of the merchant ships, was appointed Admiral, and the *Thomas Allen* was Vice-Admiral. The master of the *Prudence* was to confer with the Admiral and Vice-Admiral upon courses and directions and they were instructed to defend themselves if attacked.[34]

And so Carleill's second attempt to reach the New World failed.

The *Tiger* was a ship that was very much connected with Carleill,[*] for he took a *Tiger* to Russia in 1582, and a *Tiger* on the West Indies expedition in 1585. Henry VIII had built a *Tiger* for his navy in 1546,[35] and she had been 'reformed', or rebuilt, in 1570.[36] Another rebuilding of the *Tiger* took place in 1585,[37] and finally a *Tiger* fought against the Armada in 1588. Just to complicate matters further, there was a London privateer called *Tiger* in 1591, and it is

---

* See note 3 in References for Chapter 6, page 189.

recorded that a *Tiger* was converted into a lighter during Elizabeth's reign.[38] We must examine which *Tiger* went with Carleill in 1582.

The word 'reformed' meant literally what it said, made into a new form.[39] The material of which a ship was built would be the same, and that was very nearly all. In 1546 Henry VIII's *Tiger* had been an innovation, one of four galleasses which broke with the tradition of the old floating fortress, propelled by oars, from which guns shot, aiming to destroy men rather than ships. The new vessels had low freeboards and no cage-work or high superstructures; they were swift and easily manœuvred and they carried heavy cast metal guns that could aim low, at the enemy's hull. Henry still continued to build great ships, unwieldy and over-gunned, to puff the prestige of the monarch. But the new galleass was his stroke of genius, the ancestor of the Elizabethan navy.

A number of Henry's ships were in dock to be rebuilt in 1570, including the *Tiger*, and she must still have been a sturdy ship when she sailed on the month's voyage to Russia, eleven years later. By 1585 she was again in dock to be reformed, and then she was described by Burghley in a marginal note as 'New Tiger'. She was almost certainly used in 1588 in Admiral Seymour's squadron against the Armada, but it is extremely unlikely that in 1588 she sailed with Drake to the West Indies.

Carlellum Sarmata laudat is written under Carleill's portrait engraved in the *Herologia*. Sarmata was the original name given to Russia, wrote an ambassador that Elizabeth was to send there in 1591, adding that after A.D. 800 its name was changed to Russia.[40]

And so to Sarmata went the little fleet, leaving Ratcliffe upon the ebb and passing the great cuckold's horns which reared themselves derisively on the river bank making a mock of the married men of London. Thence to Greenwich, where the larger ships were towed past the Palace by little boats. There must have been a crowd to see them go; never before had the Muscovy merchantmen been armed in this manner.

They carried, as usual, a full cargo of kerseys, cottons, broadcloth, copper, lead for roofing, and pewter vessels. There were also gifts for the Tsar, Ivan the Terrible, for good relations with him were vital; scarlet cloth of tissue, violet and azure—the Tsar appreciated brilliance. These ships usually returned laden with wax, tallow, train-oil and furs. But this time the risk was too great; they would not be fully laden because of the Danish 'pirates'.

At Harwich they took to the open sea, and the one month's voyage began. Carleill knew the angry grey water dividing England from Holland, but the coast of Norway and of Finmark were strange lands to him. All his life he had listened to stories about this voyage, as a little boy admiring his adventurous elders. He knew that once a rainbow had been seen there, in the form of a semi-circle with both ends turned upwards, that the whirlpool between Röst and Lofoten called Maleleand would make a terrible noise and would shake the iron handles on the doors of houses on the island ten miles away, while a whale caught in that eddy would 'let out a pitiful cry'. In time the little fleet would pass the hills of Finmark, high and always covered with snow; Vardö Huis was a castle on an island, two miles from the shore and subject to the King of Denmark. This was a dangerous place for English ships to linger.

He was prepared for it all, but perhaps no one is prepared for the clear mirror that is the northern sky. The thick light of the west was gone, drawn back like a curtain from before a window, and instead 'there was no night at all, but a continual light and brightness of the sun shining clearly upon the huge and mighty sea'. It was a silver sun, not golden as our sunshine is, and as the hours passed and midnight came, the ship's mast would cast a longer shadow on the water, and a smudge of gold would quieten the silver world, and this was the only night they would have. There was little need of sleep, but the eyes grew tired of staring into that bright emptiness, and a craving for darkness grew.

Round the North Cape they sailed, sometimes meeting 'heaps of ice'—the icebergs. They prayed for a wind that would deliver them from these perils. Here they met the 'King of Denmark's pirates', sailing near the English ships to see their strength before attack.[41] But there was ordnance mounted on the English ships, and the Danes altered their course.

More alarming than the faint-hearted Danes were the many monstrous whales crying terribly, as it was 'the time of engendering'. Some were as great as sixty feet long and their amorous antics near the small ships must have caused big surges of the sea.

At the mouth of the enormous Dvina river, they found themselves sailing among low wooded islands and passing a great stone to which incoming ships made offerings of butter, meal and other victuals, so they could pass in safety. For this was the land of witches and of witchcraft. Fish there were in shoals, haddock and cod and multitudes of seals. These seals produced the train-oil which the Muscovy merchants took home; there had been the usual annual massacre in the spring before the fleet arrived. Moose and white bear moved on the land.

As the English boats sailed up the river they were surrounded by little flat-bottomed craft, and the peasants offered them food. They saw the alabaster cliffs, slashing through the dark firs that seemed to stretch away for ever, muffling the land, and by the water's edge the lean white trunks of the silver-birches and the trembling of lemon-coloured leaves.

There were forty wooden houses at St. Nicholas—even the street was made of wood—and one house for the use of the English factor. The monks of St. Nicholas came from their monastery with great solemnity, bringing gifts of fish, rye loaves and butter. The Russians regarded St. Nicholas as 'the porter of heaven's gate', rather as the Catholics thought of St. Peter. In 1568 Thomas Randolph had written critically of these black-cowled monks that they 'were given much to drunkenness, unlearnéd, write they can, preach they never do, ceremonious in their church, long in their prayers'.[42]

It was hot that summer, hotter than an English July, and the moujik had thrown away his gown of cow's hair and put on his shirt and buskins. His wife was with him, her face painted with bright colours over the dark smears made by the wood fires, a heavy silver necklace and a great cross at her neck. When a merchant passed in the street, the moujik would grovel before him, lying prostrate on the ground; he would also cast himself down before the holy images set over the gates of the houses. Carleill was expecting this, but like most contemporary English travellers, he must have reacted unfavourably to the constant signs of self-obeisance. He knew all about the drunkenness of the Russian, he had seen heavy drinking in the Low Countries, but he now saw drinking and dicing in this little port that distorted the Russian appetite for pleasure into a veritable gluttony. A man was capable of gambling away everything he had and of walking stark naked, his clothes gone.

A messenger went upstream to Kholmogory, and thence by road to Moscow to tell the Emperor that the Muscovy merchants had arrived. Gradually the dark firs would give way to the rich cornlands around Moscow, and he would be riding through a golden world towards the many-domed capital. A certain chill of unease would be on him; heads rolled swiftly in the neighbourhood of the Tsar, this little genial man with a hooked nose, a high forehead, a shrill voice, and a perverted lust for cruelty. His private pleasure was to see monks torn to pieces by bears; the sufferings he had imposed on his people were astonishing; the town of Novgorod had been wiped out with little concern, a morning's entertainment. . . .

For many years he had had a terrible notion in his head of marrying an English wife—Elizabeth herself had been considered, secretly, in this rôle. He had already had six wives, and so many concubines that they ran into thousands. Their children were strangled at birth. The previous year, in a fit of rage, he had hit his son and heir on the ear, and 'he had taken it so tenderly that he had fallen into a burning fever and in three days he was dead'.

The grief of the Tsar had been immense, like all the movements of his spirit. But now he was more determined than ever to take an English wife. His interest in the English trade was strong; he himself was a great private trader. And he was a statesman and knew that trade was the doorway to contact with the west. In 1567 he had even gone as far as suggesting 'a perpetual friendship and kindred' between the Queen's Majesty and himself, and that they might be 'friends to each other's friends and enemy to each other's enemies'.[43] In a secret treaty he had asked for asylum in England should his subjects turn against him—the lurking fear of the autocrat. Elizabeth did not find these suggestions congenial; she continued to deal with him on practical matters, but avoided the wider diplomacy. And this the Tsar resented.

In 1581 she had sent, at his request, physicians and surgeons to his Court, and one of these had recommended the Lady Mary Hastings to him as his wife. She was a kinswoman of the Queen, and daughter of the Earl of Huntingdon. So when Carleill's little fleet was due to return to England it was joined by an Ambassador, Andreevich Spisemskie, 'a very discreet and aged counsellor of his accompanied with a secretary named Neodalzo Gawreto'.[44] He was to see the Lady Mary Hastings and make a report to the Tsar on her beauty.

This carrying of a Russian Ambassador to England was surrounded with pomp. Many noblemen went with him, bringing with them cases of elegant apparel, long robes richly embroidered with gold, and high fur caps; they also had presents for the Queen, sables, ermine and black fox, Persian carpets and hawks—in 1562 we know that Persian horses were also taken.[45]

Spisemski sailed with Carleill in the *Tiger*, and it is with a certain relief that we read Jerome Horsey's description of him, that 'he was noble, grave, wise and a trusty gentleman'.[46] The two men, understanding little of each other's language, were to live in cramped intimacy on that long voyage home.

They sailed on August 11th and reached England on September 16th. As the ships did not carry much merchandise the Muscovy merchants described the expedition 'for defence upon doubt of some force as very chargeable'.[47] Clearly the Ambassador and his train must also have been the cause of lack of merchandise.

In England an epidemic of smallpox was abroad, and the Queen and her Court were living at Windsor. Spisemskie was moved about the country from one great house to the next, while the Lady Mary Hastings recovered her good looks after an attack of the disease.[48] After much diplomatic dalliance he returned to Moscow with a description of her; but we hear no more of the marriage, and this is not surprising when we learn that the reigning Tsarina had given birth to a child while the negotiations were in process.

A year later the Tsar was dead.

At home in England Carleill found himself once again poring over the delicate lines of nautical charts and discussing the new navigational instruments. He also watched his opponents narrowly.

Sir Humphrey Gilbert's projected expedition to America was still being formed, but not consolidating with any rapidity. The patent was to run out at the end of two years, and time was passing. He had hoped to take with him a large number of Papists led by Sir George Peckham and Sir William Gerrard;[49] these saw in immigration to the New World a way of escape from the crushing fines imposed on them in England. Between June 1582 and February 1583 Gilbert had assigned, out of his patent, at least 8,500,000 acres on the mainland and seven islands off the coast to these Catholics.

But Mendoza, resolute and meddling as usual, seems to have prevailed on the majority of them to withdraw, warning them that Florida and the Island of Novembergia belonged to Spain.[50] He feared that the priests coming to England from Rheims would lose their support, and that the Catholic faith would suffer. In the end, some Catholics formed their own expedition.

Walsingham and his stepson were watching the uncertain progress of Gilbert's adventure with a personal interest. Carleill knew Gilbert's shortcomings, his temper, his lack of military knowledge, his obstinacy; all these he had seen in the Low Countries. How could he, of all people, put faith in such a leader, however brilliant his external appearance? Now he saw Gilbert's followers falling away, one by one. By November, both he and Walsingham had schemes turning in their minds.

A mercantile corporation in Southampton was to have the privilege of trade with the territories under Gilbert's patent, and Southampton was to be the sole staple port.[51] Members of the corporation were to provide money or goods for their adventurers on a joint stock basis, and to have shares in the goods taken during the voyage. Those adventuring in the first voyage would be given land as well as a return on their stock. Two groups of people were to be excluded from membership, Southampton men and their issue who had not adventured in Gilbert's earlier voyage to the New World, and the Muscovy merchants and their issue. Fierce rights of forfeiture of the goods and fishes of these two groups were laid down. This exclusion of the Muscovy merchants seems to have aroused an enmity in them; they were to counter-attack very soon.

Then the Queen, exasperated perhaps by the delay, announced that she wished Gilbert to stay at home and not to lead his expedition 'because he was a man noted of not good hap at sea'. He pleaded that bad weather had held him back all the winter, and reminded her that she would have the usual one-fifth of the metals found on the voyage. In March she relented and sent him, by his half-brother, Sir Walter Raleigh, the token of an anchor guided by a lady.[52] But even then he did not go. If he had been ready then, Walsingham and Carleill could never have put forward their own scheme.

The previous autumn, in November 1582, Walsingham had received a letter from the Mayor of Bristol offering a ship or two barks to go with Gilbert, to be furnished by the Bristol merchants.[53] Thoughtfully Walsingham had put the letter aside, and it had remained unanswered. Here, close at hand, was his stepson who had recently returned with success from Russia; here, too, were the Muscovy merchants, excluded from Gilbert's voyage and ready for their revenge; and finally here were the Bristol adventurers, and they amounted to a great deal more financially than the Southampton adventurers. A shrewd man would add all these factors together; and this was what Walsingham did. There remained only the difficulty of Gilbert's sweeping patent from the Queen.

In March 1583 Walsingham decided to take action, and he wrote to the Mayor of Bristol advising that the two barks should be made ready to accompany Gilbert, who was due to leave in ten days' time; if they were not ready to go with him, they could follow later.

Richard Hakluyt, the younger, carried this letter to Bristol, and spoke warmly to the merchants of the coming exploit. He was a friend of Carleill's; indeed there is some evidence that he intended to join Carleill's little fleet himself, following in the wake of Sir Humphrey Gilbert.[54] In reply the Bristol merchants wrote to Walsingham that they were pleased at the prospect of furnishing a ship of three score tons and a bark of forty tons, to the sum of one thousand marks.[55] The ships were to be left in the New World 'under the direction and government of your son-in-law, Mr. Carleill, of whom we have heard much good, if it shall stand with your honour's good liking and acceptance'. Thus wrote the Mayor of Bristol to Walsingham in March 1583, adding that they meant not to delay departure later than the end of April.[56]

They did not depart at the end of April, but neither did Sir Humphrey Gilbert.

That same month Carleill wrote his well-known *Discourse* to induce the Muscovy Company to put up money to increase the sum raised in Bristol.[57] It had a lengthy title, 'A brief and summary discourse upon the intended voyage to the hithermost parts of America, written by Captain Carleill in April 1583, for the better inducement to satisfy such merchants of the Muscovy Company and others as are disbursing their money towards the furniture of the present charge do demand forthwith a present return of gain, albeit the said disbursements are required but in very slender sums, the highest being £25, the second at £12. 10s. od., the lowest at £6. 5s. od.'

He began by summing up the failing advantages of the Russian trade,* went on to comment unfavourably on that of the Levant and Barbary, ending with the trade of Spain and Portugal; this last had great social dangers, as the factors and merchants living in these lands were forced to deny their religion. And then he began to enumerate the good points of the voyage to the latitude of 40°, in the hithermost part of America; the shortness of the journey, the fact that it could be performed at all times during the year, the favourable wind, and no other foreign lands touched at on the way, the good English and Irish harbours from which the ships could sail, and lastly that the factors and their children could practise their religion in peace. To every ten ships, he continued, now going once a year to Russia, there would be twenty ships going to this part of America twice a year. In the north of the zone the fishing was as good as in Russia, and the land would produce pitch, tar, hemp, masts, hides and furs without interference from the Danes, while in the south and west, wine could be made from grapes, and olives planted. The country people could be drawn into producing wax and honey; there was salt in great abundance from a lake. By civilizing the inhabitants the settlers would be producing a market for English cloth. A passage by fresh water into the East-Indian sea might be discovered in this northerly part of America.

To the objection already raised that the merchants alone could not provide the money, since the hundred men 'to be planted' would cost £40,000, and therefore that a greater number of men would cost more, with slow return, he replied that on the success of the first colony other private individuals would offer more money. As now the time was short and he himself was ready to try his fortune, this was not the moment to teach ignorant men. A good work would be done by Christianizing and civilizing the ignorant savages, and by providing occupation for the many Englishmen who in England had none. He himself had seen in the Low Countries how 'evil and idle livers after they had joined the volunteers had become industrious, which I can assure you was a more painful manner of living than in this action was like to fall out'.

He then went on to describe the growth of French activities in the region and the necessity of prompt English action. If the

* See pages 3–4, 73–4.

northern trade were to flourish in two years' time, then hope might be found in the southern part which might be yet more profitable. He ended with a personal statement: he himself had ventured more than anyone else had been asked to give, 'beside the hazard and travail of my person, and the total employment of my credit'. It was a fine performance, clear and convincing, with no frills. It revealed the new colonial policy, outward-looking, challenging Spain. The brains that launched it were the brains of Hakluyt and of Walsingham, but Carleill translated their thoughts into practical terms; the thinker and the adventurer were working together. This document holds a place in England's colonial history, and Carleill's name with it.

The Committee of the Muscovy merchants that considered it included Towerson, who had been so active in preparations for the Fenton voyage the previous year, also Christopher Hoddesdon.[58] It was agreed that the City of London should add £3,000 to the £1,000 already provided by the Bristol merchants, but Carleill was asked to procure a Privilege from the Queen: first, the Adventurers who advanced the £3,000 should have the half of all lands, towns, silver and gold and other metals that were discovered, giving the fifth of all metals to the Queen; secondly, the Enterprisers, those who adventured personally, should have the other half of these benefits, also giving up one-fifth of their metals; thirdly, all the trade that ensued should belong only to the first Adventurers, and prohibition to be made to all others of the Queen's subjects to deal in those parts; seizure of them and punishment of their persons or imprisonment would be their portions should they disobey. No other subject of the Queen, nor of any other monarch, should inhabit or traffic within one hundred leagues of the place where the General should have made his chief residence.

This is a puzzling document, considering the Queen's patent to Sir Humphrey Gilbert. He was forbidden 'to go to any land not actually possessed by any Christian prince or people', and as the Muscovy Company was not entitled to any trade as far south as 40° N. in America, the two expeditions might overlap each other. The fact that Walsingham was himself a member of the Muscovy Company makes the merchants' attitude harder to understand. Had there been a break between them and the Secretary of State, and were they foolishly trying to force his hand? Or was he working with them—which is more likely—and they were all hoping that once more the Queen would forbid Gilbert's departure and that his patent would run out? Her uncertainty of temperament was worth a gamble. There was a great deal, too, to be said for Carleill's expedition; Gilbert's was under-capitalized and the Southampton merchants would never be able to finance a colony in the New World as would a combination of London and Bristol. Above all Carleill was no waverer; he would go ahead.

There is no record that Carleill asked the Queen for a Privilege for the Muscovy merchants. In May he was turning to private individuals, and tackled Thomas Badwyn, agent to the Earl of Shrewsbury in London.[59] At first the Earl had offered him his own ship, the *Bark Talbot*, in which John Hawkins seems to have had an interest, and when Hawkins objected, £100 was promised to Carleill instead.

The scheme seemed to have fizzled out; Carleill's expedition never sailed, but Gilbert's did. And so ended Carleill's third attempt to colonize in the New World.

The Queen's uncanny premonition about Gilbert's bad luck at sea was proved right. The *Squirrel* with Gilbert aboard her was sunk in a storm. He who had so often blotched his big moments in life was to handle his death superbly; he was last seen sitting on the poop, a Bible in his hand, calling out the immortal words: 'We are as near God on sea as on land.'

Carleill's defeat did not deter him from making another attempt to reach the New World. There is something rather ridiculous about the rapid rise and collapse of these little groups of petulant adventurers, till one realizes how great were the odds against them. Lack of funds, jealousy between the actors, slow methods of communication during the practical arrangements, the irritating wastage of time to men as tautly strung as were the Elizabethans, all these were factors that contributed to failure. It was not easy to interest a group of merchants in some enterprise, every man jealously watching his neighbour, every merchant backing his own adventurer, like gamblers putting money on a horse. Carleill, growing poorer all the time, seethed with irritation during those two wasted years.

After Gilbert's death Carleill corresponded with Richard Hakluyt, that solid researcher into methods of colonization in the New World. In April 1583/4 Hakluyt was writing to Walsingham and his words are worth quoting:[60] 'I know the present enterprise is like to wax cold and fall to the ground unless in this second voyage all diligence in searching out every hope of gain may be used. . . .' He sent messages to Walsingham's 'worthy and honourable son-in-law'— he described Carleill in another letter as 'virtuous son-in-law'. Walsingham had been ill and during this time Hakluyt had written direct to Carleill about the western discoveries, 'If Mr. Carleill be gone it might come in good time to serve Mr. Frobisher's turn . . . seeing as he saileth not forth, as I understand, till the beginning of May.'

That is clear enough.

There is corroboration for this story from a strange source. Thomas Phelippes, Walsingham's decipherer, was at work on two letters in cypher written by one Angel Angelini during April and May 1583/4. They were intended to carry information to Spain, and a phrase runs thus, 'The brother of Raleigh and the stepson of Walsingham have sailed with five ships to the Indies.'[61] The brother of Raleigh was Adrian Gilbert, actually Raleigh's half-brother, who had been associated with Dr. Dee over research on the North West Passage. The second letter written by Angel Angelini reported that the vessels had not yet sailed, and that Hawkins might be going with them, and perhaps their destination was not to be the West Indies after all.[62]

But in July the same informant was quite wide of the mark when he reported from Middelburg that Carleill had been captured off the coast of Brazil.[63]

This was an impossibility, as early in August Carleill was to sail into Cork Harbour, bringing another frigate with him. There had been some change of plan, the enterprise had waxed cold, and we can only guess what had happened by watching Carleill's activities that summer.

Never again was he to try his hand at colonization in the New World. He was to go there the following year, but in a very different capacity.

5

SAILOR AND SOLDIER IN ULSTER

DURING THE summer of 1584 Carleill had been building up
a small fleet of ships by somewhat unusual methods. He was
collecting vessels that were involved in the pirate trade, but for
what purpose is not at first clear. It was unlikely that he would
use them in a colonizing expedition to the New World, perhaps
some raid on an alien coast or patrol work in home waters was
planned.

Lundy Island was a wicked little place that lived by the pirate
trade, for pirate ships were victualled and refitted there. Carleill's
ship lay off Lundy during the summer, in wait for a man-of-war—
the name given to vessels engaged in piracy. He captured Captain
Lewis's bark, set Lewis ashore, then with all the crew still aboard
her, sailed into Cork Harbour with his prey.[1]

There two repentant pirates were due to join him, Thomas
Roche and Thomas Mallarde in their bark the *Falcon*.[2] They had
been pardoned for some minor piracies, and now were atoning for
their sins by working for the Queen. They were joined by a high-
powered member of their profession, William Arnwood, who had
recently been released from gaol after Walsingham had sued for his
pardon.

When Carleill arrived in Cork he applied to the Lord Deputy
for munitions and victuals and leave to chase four pirates who were
lying some dozen miles from the shore. By this action he revealed
the purpose of his mission in Ireland; he had been sent to clean up
piracy there.

But the Lord Deputy Perrot had another project in mind, both
for Carleill and for the four pirates. He was worried about the
probability of an invasion of Ulster by the Scots of the Isles, and
wanted to keep his shipping close at hand. So he said no to Carleill,
and Carleill, who had received his instructions from Walsingham

84

and who did not as yet appreciate the wider situation, fumed with anger.

Piracy had become an international menace. So lawless were the pirates in the Channel that merchants went in terror of their lives and goods. Relations between England and Spain had been badly strained by Elizabeth's inability to control the trade off her own coasts; on shore the complacent Vice-Admirals were in the know and were gaining profits through countenancing it, while in the ports the Queen's Majesty was being deprived of her dues. But during the summer of 1583 she had decided to challenge the scandal, and had sent four of her ships pirate hunting. The result had been the capture of forty-three pirates off the Dorset coast and the execution of seven famous pirate captains, masters of their trade, flamboyant personalities holding much the same place in popular esteem as prize-fighters and film-stars do today. For piracy had been regarded as an indiscretion rather than a sin; the climate of opinion was now very slowly changing, and this had made the cleaning-up operation possible.

After the 1583 executions, a great number of pirates in the 'second or third degree' were pardoned and set free. And for a very definite purpose, for pirates snatched from the gallows by a merciful hand were useful to a government that had few fighting ships to curb the growing menace of Spain. Among these pardoned pirates was William Arnwood, chosen by Walsingham to help Carleill patrol the coast of Ireland.[3]

For the pirate trade on the English coast was declining, since the merchants and landlords supporting it had been severely fined and reprimanded, and had been told to destroy the shipyards and storehouses kept on the coasts for the support of pirate ships. Now the trade had moved to Ireland and Wales, wilder shores, far from the Privy Council's eye, and Carleill and his little fleet must follow.

Ireland was not only the support of the pirate trade, it was also the focus for political trouble. The Papal invasion of Smerwick was still in men's minds, and there was a very real possibility of another striking force of Spaniards being sent to Ireland, a Catholic and hostile country always ready to rebel. Scotland, too, was a danger now that Mary Queen of Scots was held a prisoner in England, the focus of Catholic plots and ambitions. The Western Isles of Scotland were very near the north coast of Ulster, and the two

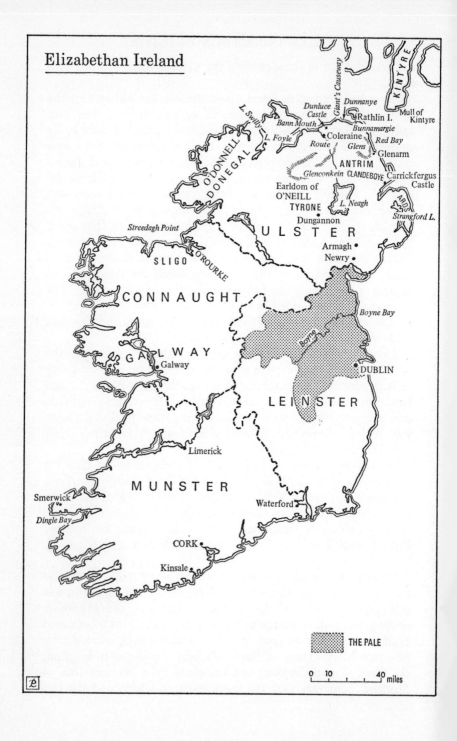

Elizabethan Ireland

KINTYRE

Dunluce Castle
Dunnanye
Giant's Causeway
Rathlin I.
Mull of Kintyre
Bann Mouth
Bunnamargie
L. Foyle
Coleraine
Red Bay
Route
Glens
Glenarm
O'DONNELL
DONEGAL
ANTRIM
Glenconkein
CLANDEBOYE
Carrickfergus
Earldom of
O'NEILL
L. Swilly
Castle
TYRONE
L. Neagh
ARDS
Dungannon
Strangford L.

Streedagh Point
U L S T E R
Armagh •
S L I G O
O'ROURKE
Newry •

C O N N A U G H T
Boyne Bay
Boyne

G A L W A Y
Galway •
DUBLIN •

L E I N S T E R

Limerick •

M U N S T E R
Smerwick
Dingle Bay
Waterford •

CORK •

Kinsale •

░░░░ THE PALE

0   10   40 miles

countries were linked in many ways. The constant raids made on the Irish coast by the Scots of the Isles could not now be regarded as minor incidents, but carried the threat of larger complications; was James VI of Scotland behind these raids, stirring up trouble in Ulster on behalf of his mother as the preliminary to a Spanish invasion? This was the question troubling the mind of the Lord Deputy.

Great numbers of Scots were expected during the summer of 1584, not just a raid, but a Northern Invasion. Perrot saw very clearly, with a statesman's eye, and began to make his plans.

When Thomas Mallarde and Thomas Roche arrived in Cork Harbour, there was no Carleill, for he had travelled overland to Limerick to offer his services to the Lord Deputy. He had heard the story that two thousand Scots had landed in Tir Chonaill in twenty-two galleys; others had it that three great ships full of soldiers had come into Lough Foyle, bringing one of Shane O'Neill's sons whom they meant to set up in opposition to Turloch Lynneach O'Neill, while the men of Waterford had seen six ships off the south coast. Carleill's little sea service in Ireland might well turn into a big adventure.

Arnwood had suffered considerably in Cork,[4] despite the fact that Carleill had recently arrived there with a warrant for his pardon from Walsingham. Sir William Stanley was acting for the President of Munster who was on progress with the Lord Deputy, and he impounded some of Arnwood's crew and Arnwood was forced to depart rapidly before he himself was taken. This he retailed, whining somewhat, in a letter to Walsingham, well larded with the phrase 'your honour'. A sixteenth-century miscreant readily put himself on the side of the law.

In Ireland officials tended to become small tyrants; they would defy the Lord Deputy in Dublin; easier still to defy the Privy Council, far away in England. Sir William Stanley must have known the purpose to which Arnwood was to be put, and must have chosen to ignore it.

So when Carleill returned to Cork from Limerick to collect his small fleet and sail north as instructed by the Lord Deputy, he found all the pardoned pirates gone. He was somewhat disconcerted to learn that Perrot had also drawn into his service all the pirates that were lying off the coast, promising them 'grace for so doing', and furnishing their 'needful wants and every other particular of their entertainment'.[5] Carleill was to write this to his stepfather later in the autumn, angry that the pirates' 'needful wants' had been granted before his own.

Perrot was taking no risks. He sent his fleet to Lough Foyle to intercept the Scots, but it arrived late, for the Scottish vessels had already slipped away.[6] Why he did not put Carleill, with his Sea Beggar experience, in command would be a mystery if one was dealing with any other man but Perrot. Carleill had come to Ireland with a recommendation from Walsingham; that was enough to turn Perrot against him, for the Lord Deputy hated nepotism. Shortly after Carleill's arrival Walsingham received a letter from Perrot, explaining why he did not always answer Walsingham's letters dealing with the suits of various persons, though he hoped to be good to them all. 'Indeed, many of these suitors make such demands as are out of all reason', stated the letter.

Perrot is said to have scorned Machiavelli, and abhorred double-dealing. He must have connected Walsingham with both. A great tall man, so we are told, with auburn hair, who had 'a very terrible visage and look' when he was angry.[7] And this was very often.

So Carleill began life in Ireland on the wrong foot, and it was months before he could win round this violent and prejudiced Lord Deputy, this wild man of moods, tempered by flashes of political genius.

Carleill should be employed to move food and ammunition from Carrickfergus to the north of Ulster, thought Perrot, for the army must be kept supplied. Also Walsingham's stepson must be bridled, and that would increase his own position in Ireland. So, for a political reason, a good soldier was wasted in a country where there were few.

John Meade, who was acting for the President of Munster with Sir William Stanley, while the President was on progress with Perrot, did not object to nepotism. So he entertained Carleill 'for Walsingham's sake', while Carleill was delayed in Cork Harbour owing to contrary winds.[8]

When Carleill with his two pinnaces at last reached Carrick-fergus—Knockfergus as it was usually called—he anchored below the great brown Castle, and learned to know the townsmen, an exercise which was to prove useful in the future. Captain Egerton, Governor of the Castle, and the garrison under him were ready for trouble, 'and the road was very open and the weather very tempestuous'.

Carleill's sea-service lasted for three months. He needed all his seamanship to sail from the 'billows' of Carrickfergus to the billows of Dunluce Castle on the north coast, where Perrot was besieging Sorley Boy, chieftain of the Macdonnells.[9]

The coast of Ulster was a wild place and Ulster the most unruly land in all Ireland.[10] The Scots of the Isles were constant raiders, making a complicated pattern of violence and intrigue which enmeshed both Irish and English. They came from Kintyre, Islay and Bute—Macdonnells, Macleans, Mackays and Campbells—for the Mull of Kintyre was but twelve miles from Rathlin Island off the north coast of Ulster. For hundreds of years they had been coming at their pleasure, burning villages and carrying off cattle, sometimes staying to act as mercenary soldiers to the Irish chieftains in their constant feuds. For these Scots loved fighting.

The Western Isles of Scotland had suffered from Viking raids, and something of the wandering spirit of the Norsemen must have passed into the Scots, for they, too, were to venture in their long galleys across the seas, a restless, roving people who loved to hear the lowing of other men's cattle as they herded them down to the beaches and pushed them into their boats.

The Scots who stayed in Ireland as mercenaries became known as *galloglaich*, or gallowglass as the English called them. This occupation was hereditary, passing from father to son, and the gallowglass formed a distinct class in Ulster, as distinct as the bards and the chroniclers, in this land of caste with privileges closely guarded. The Macdonnells were the gallowglass of the O'Neill, the MacSweenys served the Macdonnell of Tir Chonaill.

Later came the strategic marriages between the Macdonnells of the Isles and some of the Irish families in Ulster; the Macdonnell-Bisset marriage of 1379 brought hundreds of the Macdonnells into the Glens of Antrim, living there still in contact with the head of the clan in Dunyveg Castle in Islay. There were marriages later with O'Cahan, O'Donnell, O'Neill and Savage. The first Macdonnell chieftain to live permanently in Ulster in 1512 recognized James I of Scotland as his sovereign, and in his time Scots swarmed into Ulster.

A third influx of Scots took place in the sixteenth century with the arrival of Scots hired mercenaries to fight for the Irish chieftains. They came from the Isles, fought in the Irish feuds, then returned to Scotland. They were distinct from the gallowglass who had already spent a few centuries in Ireland. Their galleys, evil-nosed as sharks, landed at Glenarm, Red Bay, Dunluce Castle, Bann Mouth, Lough Foyle and Lough Swilly, Tir Chonaill and the Connaught shore, bringing a new threat to both Irish and English.

The Irish in Ulster were constantly at war with each other, feuds between O'Neill and O'Donnell, between Maclean and O'Donnell, between O'Cahan and MacQuillan. In the Isles, English spies plotted to keep the Scots out of Ulster, the Irish spies plotted to bring them in. But this is a simplification; the truth was far more subtle. For nothing in Ireland was constant, except an absence of constancy. The policy of the English in Ireland was to divide and rule; the Irish performed the first part for themselves with little assistance from the English.

Both the Scots and the Irish were withdrawn from the Tudor world of commerce, living in a tribal society that knew nothing of Edinburgh or of Dublin. The world had moved on, the path of money-making growing more intricate and sophisticated, but the men of the Isles and of Ulster lived still by direct robbery and violence, on moonlit nights raiding each other's cattle and murdering their rivals. They would sit by the peat fires and the bards would sing of the great deeds of their ancestors, the words falling like stars in a dark sky, and some new devilry would come of it all, perhaps another raid with hundreds of cattle taken, and the bard would claim his incitement fee. The language spoken was Gaelic, alike by Scots and Irish, and the words could enflame.

England was a state with one queen, a Parliament and written laws. Ireland was inhabited by a series of tribes, the law administered by the 'brehons', but never written down. Elizabeth could only deal with the chieftain of a sept and never with anyone who represented Ireland. The English and the Irish stood facing each other, like men of the moon unable to make contact with men of the earth.

As for the Anglo-Irish, those English families which had been settled for centuries in Ireland, they had become Irish in their way of life, and had made Irish marriages, often forgetting their own tongue. They betrayed the new English settlers to the Irish, and were considered by the government to be more dangerous than declared rebels. They would spin their Catholic plots at the 'tuaths', or public meetings of the septs in the hills, for their religion was only one of the many things that alienated them from the Council in Dublin. They adopted the ancient Irish system of 'coshering', when a chieftain would travel through his lands, billeting himself and his followers on his tenants and picking them clean. They were surrounded in their houses, like the Irish, by men who considered any form of work disgraceful, the profession of fighting alone honourable. They entered enthusiastically into the wild sport of cattle stealing. And like the Irish their words were masked with charm, while their eyes remained wary and withdrawn.

There had been two schemes for planting Ulster with English undertakers during Elizabeth's reign, but both had failed. There had never been enough money to keep the Irish in order by building forts, nor to pay the English soldiers; the life of the planter was precarious indeed.

The system of tanistry was peculiar to the Irish and the cause of most of the disorders in Ulster. When a chieftain died he was not necessarily succeeded by his eldest son, but by the strongest member of the family who could get support from the sept. The sons did not always accept this rule of the strongest, and murder and warfare resulted. During the reign of Elizabeth 'tanistry' caused the McShanes—the many sons of the great Shane O'Neill—to question Turloch Lynneach O'Neill's claim to the title of 'the O'Neill' in Ulster; Donald Gorme Macdonnell and his mother, Black Agnes Campbell, questioned the right of his uncle, Sorley Boy Macdonnell, head of the clan, to the Glens of Antrim.

The Campbell power was growing in the Isles, for the Earl of Argyll, powerful and wily, had made a worldly link with the Council of Edinburgh and was a supporter of Mary Stuart. He played big politics, using the small Scottish chieftains as his tools. His sister, Black Agnes Campbell, had been the wife of James Macdonnell of Kintyre, but he had died, leaving her with a son, Donald Gorme. She had married again, this time Turloch Lynneach O'Neill, and a complicated pattern of claims and feuds was set up, constantly shifting and changing.

Turloch Lynneach in his 'vaunting majesty' had been gathering Scots mercenary forces together in 1581 with which to attack

Macdonnell. At that time he had four thousand heavily armed kern, or foot soldiers, half of them the new Scots mercenaries, the rest the traditional Macdonnell gallowglass; this in spite of the agreement he had made with the English in '67 not to employ Scots mercenaries. Besides these he had seven hundred horsemen. Turloch was described at that time as 'the very root and seedsman of all the rebellions in Ireland'. He was bombastic, constantly drunk, unscrupulous, corpulent—an unattractive figure—yet capable at times of a winning softness of heart.

The English now adopted a new policy, that of supporting the Irish chieftains against the Scots, and in 1583 two hundred English soldiers were sent to help MacQuillan of the Route against Macdonnell incursions.

Then came the news of friendly meetings between Sorley Boy Macdonnell and Turloch Lynneach O'Neill, and that the son of one was to marry the daughter of the other. This was an alarming combination for England, with her policy of divide and rule.

But the arrival of one of Shane O'Neill's many sons with the force that landed in Tir Chonaill in 1584, ready to challenge Turloch's position as the O'Neill, drove Turloch into English hands, and he became overnight an ally of England, which meant—at the moment—an enemy of Sorley Boy Macdonnell.

So the pattern wavered and changed and was remade, heads were chopped off and stuck on pikes outside the contestants' camps, blood-money was set by the English on the heads of rebels, and this was a temptation that some Irish found hard to resist.

In August 1584 while on progress in Limerick, Perrot had commanded all men from Bann to Boyne to meet him in twenty-four days at Drogheda. The Northern Invasion was at hand, and he meant to march with all the power he could make to shock the enemy into submission. The men of Leinster and of Munster obeyed him; Turloch Lynneach came with his wife, Black Agnes, and together the force began to flow into Ulster. With it were the Earls of Ormond, of Thomond and of Munster, the Lord Barry and the Lord Roche, Fitzgibbon called the White Knight, Sir Nicholas Bagenal, Marshal of Ireland, Sir William Stanley, Sir Thomas Norris, Captain Jacques Wingfield, Master of Ordnance, Sir Lucas Dillon, Chief Baron, Sir Robert Dillon, Chief Justice of Common Pleas, Sir Jeoffrey Fenton, Secretary of State, Sir Henry

Bagenal:[11] in fact every man of importance dwelling in the Pale and outside it.

When they arrived in Ulster, the Irish lords made submission to Perrot on their knees, bringing their kerns with them. Perrot, the base-born son of Henry VIII and the half-brother of Elizabeth, had more than a touch of royal arrogance in his character. He must have enjoyed this autocratic interlude.

Dublin, at that time, had been left very much open to attack, always the fate of one part of Ireland when there was trouble in another.

Perrot, with his force of Irish and English, divided his army into two on either side of the river Bann. Sorley Boy, hearing of this great gathering, fled to the fastnesses and woods of Glenconkein with his people and his cattle. John Norris, 'overskipping' Sorley Boy, fell upon O'Cahan and took from him two hundred cows, which gave some relief to the soldiery; there was a skirmish or two, another prey of cows was seized, and coming away from the great woods of Glenconkein at the bottom of the glen, Norris encountered O'Cahan, who submitted. It was usually this way, the Irish submitted rapidly enough, on their knees, but the submission had little significance in the long run. The Scots, on the other hand, would slip away, vanish from sight, make a strategic withdrawal. But they would be back again, stronger than ever when they were least expected.

The method of the fighting had been hard, so Perrot was to write to the Council, referring to the action in the Glens: 'Our people most commonly stepped in mire above their knees when they assaulted the enemy, and some were so deep as they were fain to be drawn out of the bog by their fellows.' It was a small blow on that side of the Bann, he wrote, and the taking of the forts on this side proved sufficient to flatten the Scots.[12]

Then the Deputy marched to the mouth of the Bann and east along the north coast to Dunluce Castle, Sorley Boy's stronghold. With him went Turloch Lynneach and his wife, Black Agnes Campbell. The Castle stood on a precipitous rock with the waves breaking at its feet, and a mile down the coast, that astonishing march of petrified organ pipes, the Giant's Causeway. The Castle is a ruin now, bending crooked black fingers towards the sea, as though holding back the waves.

Perrot could only attack from the land, but that night came

Christopher Carleill in his frigate, carrying the big ordnance he had brought from Dublin, two culverins and two sakers, as well as powder and victuals.[18] He landed them at Skerries, a serrated rocky island not far from Dunluce, useful only for cormorants and marauding Scots; a skilful achievement in a twenty-four ton frigate, for here the waves swung high and it was often impossible to anchor. Fenton, writing to Walsingham from the camp, referred to Dunluce; 'The ward within makes proud shows and seems resolved to defend it to the last man', and added that their captain had called out in excellent English telling them that he was holding the Castle for the King of Scots.

Here was an open admission that James was involved in the troubles, and Perrot must have felt himself to be vindicated. In spite of their bravado the garrison surrendered, though some of them made away with the rapidity of the vanishing Celt towards Rathlin Island, that 'had always been the very bait and staple of the Scots'. On a sunny day the black and white cliffs flashed like magpies on the wing, but during a storm of rain they could retreat into invisibility. The Mull of Kintyre in Scotland was a blunt blue headland jutting into the sea, and to sail from Rathlin Island would only take a few hours.

This was the tragic island where the Earl of Essex in 1575 had ordered the slaughter of all the Scottish women and children sent there by Sorley Boy for refuge; one ghastly massacre, a reprisal for the constant raids. The story had crept into the wail of the bards over peat fires on winter nights, atrocious in its detail, and the listeners vowed revenge and more revenge.

Opposite the island, on the mainland of Antrim, were the Macdonnell forts and the Abbey of Bunnamargie, where the Macdonnell chieftains lay buried. Behind were the Glens, wild hills covered with forest and treacherous bog, the Bisset land which they claimed and where they could hide, for no Englishman would care to fight in that country. And along the coast were the 'little creeks between rocks and thickets where the Scots galleys did commonly land'.[14]

Sorley Boy was heading for Scotland, perhaps to collect some mercenaries, but meanwhile Perrot must return to Dublin, for he feared the waters would rise and hold him prisoner in Ulster. But first he must put the country in strong hands. There were two fortresses he meant to keep, the Castle of Coleraine at the mouth of the Bann, near the salmon fishing, guarding the Route, in a bad state of repair but wardable,[15] and the impregnable Castle of Carrickfergus on the east coast. Between these two fortresses, on the shore, were the landing places of the Scots. If Perrot could garrison these, one could answer the other and together they could make raids into the Glens and clear the Scots away. He put Sir Henry Bagenal and two hundred men in Carrickfergus, making him Colonel of the forces in Ulster. Then he looked around for someone for Coleraine. Everyone refused on some ground or other; 'He hath dealt with Mr. Stafford', wrote Carleill to Walsingham later,[16] 'but he refused to go to Coleraine because he must be married shortly', and of others, 'they, having slender liking to the matter, excused themselves', and again, 'There were other old soldiers and captains who did rather choose to be discharged of their companies than to abide the hazardous service of their staying behind.' He himself had agreed to remain, probably from a sense of adventure; he had seen little of importance during the last three months, except for some very large waves. 'Myself by great chance being at the same time on the shore entreating my Lord for a certain warrant touching sea causes which I was to have had of his Lordship, was upon his curt answers of others demanded by my Lord Deputy what I would say to the handling of this charge, I answered that whatsoever it were that the General of the field should direct me, I would do my best endeavour to perform. . . .'

So it was arranged that Carleill should remain at Coleraine 'with some better force and provision than afterwards was accomplished'. Thus he wrote bitterly to Walsingham, finding himself left in the waste of enemy country with only two hundred footmen and fifty horsemen. He added that the Lord President, at his last departure, said that if he had thought Carleill was to be 'so slenderly cared for', he would never have agreed that he should remain behind.

But stay he did, and on the old pay, which was considerably less than the new rate. Perrot reported the fact with some pride in his letter to Walsingham, hoping to please the Queen with this small economy. He was most careful, he said somewhat untruthfully, 'to regard the well doing of the garrisons under Mr. Carleill and Sir Henry Bagenal, on whose sufficiency I repose greatly'. He had told the captains and soldiers to victual themselves, living on the country, as was the manner of Irish fighting men, and he would lay no cess on them, while the pay he gave them was 'as little as they can have . . . without any charge to Her Majesty's government'. And finally, with a typical Perrot sentence—for he had a lively pen—'And the next summer if I may have maintenance, pinnaces as you wrote, and a warrant to visit the Outer Isles, if I see cause, I hope with God's assistance to establish . . . that [which] is begun, with the paring off of some Scots' heads.'

What he wrote was good sense. But he was to be refused everything he asked for.

Carleill, writing to his stepfather, described Coleraine: 'It is the very barrenest place of all Ireland, and our men, God knows, as poor as men may be, out of clothes, out of money, out of heart and many fallen sick, the place all together uncovered and yet the winter growing upon us.' The forage for the horses was wasted and the feed poor, no trench made for fortification and only eight shovels to begin the work.

As he wrote, he had just heard that Sorley Boy intended to return to Scotland to fetch more troops, and then to invade Ulster again. Indeed by January six hundred Scots were to arrive from Kintyre and the Outer Isles.

Perrot meanwhile was 'making a pacification in the north', up to a point. He entered into an agreement with Donald Gorme Macdonnell that he should have his uncle Sorley Boy's land in the Glens, in return for his submission to England. He arranged with Turloch Lynneach O'Neill, MacQuillan and the Clandeboye chieftains for the maintenance of English soldiers in the north, for the Irish had all submitted to him at the Newry on their knees, 'having grown in hatred of the Scots'.

He had given Upper Clandeboye to Con O'Neill and to Shane and Hugh O'Neill, Lower Clandeboye. He wrote to England begging £5,000 for three years with which to make walled towns, build bridges and erect castles, he would train garrisons of two thousand foot and four hundred horse and meanwhile, at once, could he have six hundred soldiers, from England?

The letter was 'comfortably received' by the Queen and her Council, and he was instructed to find out what part James of Scotland had taken in the uprising.[17]

Carleill had some dealings with Donald Gorme for Perrot.[18] He met him twenty-five miles from Coleraine in the Glens, and Donald Gorme promised Carleill that he would be honest 'and many good words he gave to persuade me to believe his intentions'.

But he refused to help Carleill to find Sorley's people left behind in the Glens, for in marching all over the country the two garrisons could never get at them. Sorley Boy had told his supporters to make their peace with MacQuillan of the Route till he should return again with reinforcements from Scotland, and now they were lying low.

Indeed Donald Gorme proved in the end to be loyal to his uncle Sorley Boy, and considering that the English had just granted him Sorley Boy's land in Antrim, so coveted by Black Agnes for her son, one can only draw one conclusion from his action, that he had no faith in any permanent English settlement in Ulster, and that he hoped to receive some reward from his uncle when he ultimately returned to claim his land. But perhaps Donald Gorme just could not resist the intrigue; and of course, though he hated Sorley Boy he hated the English even more.

Already in November he was showing that his declarations of fidelity to England were thin. The garrisons of Carrickfergus and Coleraine, four hundred foot and a hundred horsemen, with the same number of Irish, marched towards Red Bay under the command of Sir Henry Bagenal.[19] Nicholas Dawtry, who was with them, described the Coleraine garrison as being much out of heart for lack of clothes, and that they were hoping to fill two of the Queen's ships at Red Bay with victuals from Knockfergus to send back to Coleraine, but they had found no shipping there. Then they decided to go into the Glens in search of the Scots.

This time they came on the Scots, and fourteen hundred Scottish bowmen charged the English rear; then the English and Irish broke and ran to within a mile of Red Bay. 'We wanted our Commander, Captain Carleill,' wrote Walsingham's informant, 'whose absence is greatly lamented by all the garrison at Coleraine.'

For Carleill had gone to Dublin to see Perrot. Five weeks he had endured his charge, keeping the garrison under impossible conditions, and then he decided he must take action, or he and his men would perish of hunger.

In Dublin he met the choleric Lord Deputy at his very worst. Perrot had many enemies there, and they had been writing home evil words about his recent journey into the north; he had gone there on insufficient evidence, it had been a vast and useless expense for the Queen, he had achieved nothing, save the taking of Dunluce

Castle; Sorley Boy was still at large; with all that great force at his disposal, Perrot had not even taken Rathlin Island. There was malicious laughter in Dublin, and this was a dangerous form of attack. What damage the Scots would have done in Ulster had Perrot gone north with a lesser force, was not discussed.

The accusations angered the Queen. The thought of all that expense, perhaps for nothing, when more and more money was needed in the Netherlands ... The arrogance and the pomp of Perrot made her jealous, for she could not bear anyone to usurp her authority.

She sent to Scotland, trying to find out if James was involved in the raids on Ulster. The eighteen year old King promised her to restrain the Islanders in future, and neither she nor Walsingham realized then how little he could control them. Davison, the English Ambassador in Scotland, maintained that the large concentration of troops in the Isles that summer was to be used by the Earl of Argyll against Macleod of Lewis, and had not been preparing for the invasion of Ulster.[20] This news stiffened the Queen's opposition to Perrot; she did not openly declare her venom against him, but he felt it there, heavy in the air.

He wrote bitterly to England that if he had the Queen's money and six hundred men he could bring Ulster to contentment. And he ended with a great cry to his God, since his Queen would not hear him, 'I fear me God is angry with our time.'[21]

At this unpropitious moment Carleill arrived in Dublin and told Perrot that he could not live as a Colonel and chief commander of other companies and Governor of a country without having to spend more than his private captainship was able to bear.[22] With no small oath, Perrot answered that 'Sir William Stanley should go there in his place without a penny of allowance more than a private captain of two-hundred men'. And that was two shillings and sixpence a day.

Sir William Stanley, however, was not so obliging, and when he finally consented to replace Carleill at Coleraine his pay was as much as ten shillings a day.

Carleill, in Dublin, sat down and let his feelings fly in a letter to his stepfather: 'Mr. Treasurer' and Sir Edward Waterhouse could not see the reason why he should be given less than others, 'unless it be as they judge that I am no Welshman, I tell your honour their own words which they spake themselves'.

And then Carleill put his second grievance to Perrot, for Carleill was a sailor as well as a soldier, and Perrot was attacking in both these fields, allowing no man other than himself to deal in the matter of Carleill's sea-service 'in the direct way not to pay me but to spoil me'. He wanted to discharge Carleill's ship on two months' pay when she had been used for three months. His two ships had carried a dozen gentlemen soldiers and nearly two hundred men, 'not so slightly entertained as the ordinary sort'. But the Deputy had cast him at eighty men only of the ordinary sort. While riding in rough seas at Carrickfergus his frigate had lost an anchor, and on the way home his small ship had been cast into Strangford Haven, had fallen on rocks and had broken four of her ribs, timber and planks to the cost of £30 or £40. 'To all this extraordinary damage my Lord will not allow one penny of consideration, more than a liberal delivery of monstrous oaths and foul words, in so much none of the Council can tell how to begin to speak any words at all . . . my Lord being wonderfully and furiously opinionated to maintain his own conceits.' Perhaps the Privy Council could arrange for some Commissioners in England who understood sea-service to deal in the matter?

Carleill, during those difficult few days in Dublin, did not know how Perrot was suffering, nor that he had written to Walsingham telling him that he knew his enterprise was 'considered to be of too high charge and small purpose'. He blamed the Queen and her Secretary for bestowing high pensions on worthless people, herein lay the expense in Ireland, not in his own works. He went on, unable to keep his pen from revealing his heart, 'And if I had been your bailiff at Barn Elms and toiled with my body and my mind there about your husbandry, I am sure I should have had at least thanks and a frieze jerkin.' A worse phrase was to escape him, 'I doubt not to receive at God's hands afterward incomparably beyond any that her Majesty gave me.'[23]

He looked around him, his eyes blinded with pain, and there, close at hand, was Walsingham's stepson, a man easy to beat. Perrot beat him.

Meanwhile Walsingham folded the letter and put it carefully away. The pile of treacherous words grew as the weeks passed; one day words such as these would be used against the Lord Deputy and they would break him.

Carleill's pen was also writing to Walsingham, telling him how

Perrot spoke ill of everyone of good quality in England, 'his will so absolute in determining causes that he will make many enemies. I see his reach is to shroud all under the title of being a good husband to Her Majesty's purse.' Nevertheless, he continued, he had decided to go back to Coleraine because service was now growing on again in the north, and he was ready to serve the Queen.

Here spoke the soldier; he could not keep away, whatever it cost him.

Back at Coleraine the garrison welcomed him. But life was fearful. In January the storms raged; 'At Coleraine there is no haven or harbour to favour any bark above fourteen ton, but are constrained to lie at sea in open roads with their victuals, where the ocean raiseth such a billow as can hardly be endured by the greatest ships, and scarce once in fourteen days, this winter, seas will suffice any small vessels to lay the ships aboard to unlade the victuals.'[24]

The other garrison at Carrickfergus under Sir Henry Bagenal also suffered from billows, but less so.

Nevertheless some action was seen in the New Year.[25] Sir Henry Bagenal with his company marched to Glenarm on the north-east coast, and was joined there by Sir William Stanley who was waiting for his victuals to arrive at Dunnanye, that small fort that hung in the mist on a precipitous cliff west of Ballycastle Bay. While at Glenarm they planned to make a joint attack on Donald Gorme and his men who were lurking in the Glens. For that purpose they were to separate and to meet at Dunnanye.

So they parted, but Bagenal on his way there was attacked by Donald Gorme. But he put the Scots to flight and collected some of their heads—a collection of heads was usually made after a skirmish and set up in a grisly row outside the victor's camp.

Meanwhile Sir William Stanley, Bagenal's cousin, began his march through the rough country lying between Glenarm and the Route. Coming down the hill he saw the desolate Abbey of Bunnamargie[26] lying near the shore. Once monks had prayed beneath its stone arches, while the surge of the waves pulling the shingle up the beach had mingled with the deep lowing of their chant. Now they had gone, leaving the dead Macdonnells in possession. For this was their traditional burial place, those huge fair-headed men from the Isles. The last to be buried there was James Ogue, the first husband of Black Agnes Campbell and the brother of Sorley Boy. They had laid him there with a keening and a crying, while the black galleys lay pulled up in rows on the beach. Near them were three round green hills, and on one of them a Macdonnell castle. This was the very heart of the Macdonnell country, on the edge of the Glens, the forest and bog its shield.

But now Captain Carleill and his troop of forty-seven men were in the Abbey, filling it with the clank of arms and the clatter of hoofs; Captain Warren's company too, and soon Captain Bowen and his troop joined them and unhorsed below the Abbey. Most of them slept inside it, and some of the horses were stabled in the church.

It was Captain Carleill's watch night, but his sentries could not have been awake, for they failed to hear the Scots as they crept down from the hills. Suddenly six horsemen rushed the church with wads of flaming wool tied to long staves.[27] Out dashed William Stanley clad only in his shirt, and he and his men drove the Scots away. The horses were caught in the church and many of them burned to death, while the English fought on foot. Stanley was wounded by arrows and had twelve of his horsemen killed, Carleill had one man killed and twelve wounded.

Afterwards they flung water on the flaming thatch, for a stream flowed near the Abbey. Gradually the fire died down and the horses were quietened; then under a bright moon they saw floating on a calm sea, twenty-four Scots galleys from Kintyre, perhaps carrying provisions for their castle at Red Bay. The English stood burnt and black, helplessly watching them pass, for in the windless calm their shipping could not overtake them.

Next day Stanley went on a few miles to the fort at Dunnanye. There in his eagle's eyrie he must have sat staring across the sea at the piebald cliffs of Rathlin Island, bitterly regretting that Perrot had not taken it during the autumn. For it was still the haunt of the Scots galleys. Very sore from his wounds, he sent in his report to his cousin Bagenal, recording a rumour that two thousand five hundred Scots were expected; there, at Dunnanye, he wrote, the winter was rough, the rain beat continually and the men were permanently wet, cold and hungry; the country was very weak through the neglect of the forts; he had sent for two English companies which were now serving with Turloch Lynneach, and he had ordered them off to Coleraine at once to reinforce Carleill.

This was a wise act, for the galleys he had seen were landing at Conandonney, and Sorley Boy, Angus Macdonnell and his brethren were once more in Ulster. Meanwhile Bagenal was returning post-haste to Carrickfergus, for rumour again had it that the Scots were intending to fall upon the town and burn it; rumour and counter-rumour spread by a network of spies. But the Scots did not attempt Carrickfergus; instead they headed for the Route 'which they make reckoning to be their own at all times'.

Carleill was told to make contact with Sorley Boy that winter as well as with Donald Gorme. His skill in diplomacy was by now accepted; the Irish, themselves easy and charming in manner when they wished, appreciated charm in others. In February he received a letter from Sorley Boy thanking him for his courtesy and good counsel at the parley.[28] Sorley Boy wanted Perrot to restore to him the quiet possession of lands, towns, castles and houses which for the past forty years he had possessed, and which Sir Henry Sydney had granted him. He offered to send his son to the Baron of Dungannon as a pledge for his good behaviour. Then, the inevitable ferocity towards MacQuillan broke out—for they were the Macdonnells' hereditary enemies in the Route; 'After his untrue and false behaviour, the said MacQuillan and I cannot be in one country', wrote Sorley Boy.

Another letter to Carleill reported that MacQuillan's horsemen had been killed by those of Sorley Boy 'for using many ill speeches against me and the rest of my name'.[29] He promised safe passage in future for messengers between Carleill and the MacQuillans, and would Carleill seal this letter and send it on to the Deputy?

But the Deputy was not friendly. He continued to chase Sorley Boy in the Glens, and in the end drove him back to Scotland to collect another army. Not till 1586 was his submission accepted.

Carleill, after his decision to return to Coleraine, was finding life very difficult. Perrot continued to beat him for the supposed sins of his stepfather. He was pulled down 'from the chief place of credit in the field to the second, from second to third, from third to fifth, for so often was the Commission altered'. Thus wrote his lieutenant to Walsingham, laying bare the ugly story.[30] His allowance for diet was not the five shillings a day given to Stanley, Bagenal and Berkeley, but only the sum granted to a private captain. But Carleill had resolved to bear this for the sake of adventures to come.

To keep order in his company after the men had seen him being disgraced was an impossible task. He put sharp discipline on them, stronger perhaps than was usually given by a captain in Ireland. But now that he no longer had chief authority and they saw that 'his credit with my Lord Deputy . . . had vanished clean away', they broke into rebellion. When he commanded them to follow their ensign they refused to obey. Carleill struck at one mutineer with his truncheon, but he struck back again, he and his companions, blow for blow, one mutineer even drawing his sword, till Carleill was forced to regain his own company, 'in much ado to save himself from hurt'. The Commissioners did not uphold him, and the mutiny was 'so slightly passed over and so tenderly handled' that the soldiers escaped without punishment.

Carleill, now realizing bitterly what it was to be fifth Commissioner, decided it was time for him 'to retire himself from such confusion . . . and be where order and discipline may take place or never to go to the field again'.

And so, telling the Lord Deputy he was leaving Coleraine for good, he returned to Dublin. For a week Perrot would not see him and showed 'a countenance greatly offended'. At last Carleill managed to speak to him, 'and yielded some reason of his coming as made the weather calm again, and so passified my Lord's pretended dislike as now my Lord speaketh to him very friendly. Whether my Lord will entertain him here in charge or dismiss him is not yet known.'

Thus wrote Carleill's lieutenant to Walsingham, a man called Jones, who also had received some slights at the Deputy's hand. Carleill had recommended him to Walsingham, and it must have been about this time that Walsingham had scribbled a few lines for his own use,[31] perhaps a note of certain points to be used in letters he intended to write; 'Carleill, straight dealing especially such as I favour   like well submission   service not profitable   to come home   meaning to employ him with Drake   Jones   not blame Deputy   sorry for him   return home.'

So this must have been Walsingham's true feeling about Perrot— he could not blame him. He had not read those desperate letters unmoved.

Carleill waited for three months in Dublin for Perrot to employ him. He was ready and willing to accept any service that might stand with his credit, wrote George Beverley to Walsingham.[32] Perrot certainly had promised to speak and write well of Carleill, but on two occasions he had left his charge at Coleraine 'in the time of chief service', and repaired to Dublin to talk of allowances, so the charge there had been given to other men of long service who could not now be removed; Perrot had spoken slightly of Captain Warren who had come to Dublin without permission and as a result he now lay in prison. There seemed a veiled suggestion that Carleill was lucky not to be in prison too.

For a man who had been Sergeant-Major of the English force in the Netherlands, this degradation must have been insupportable.

And financially the service had nearly undone him—even Wallop, that slippery, dishonest Paymaster-General in Ireland, who was capable of any iniquity and injustice, wrote to Walsingham,[33] 'I assured myself his service has been altogether to his hinderance and to the utter loss of all that he brought of his venture into this land. . . .' There had been the long wait, three months in Dublin before Perrot would decide on his future, and Wallop had lent him £30, 'without which he could not have passed over into England'; this was to be treated as a loan 'to be repaid by Your Honour or himself'.

Carleill had written to Walsingham, 'Your honour knoweth that my estate is very poor, and that a small sum of money to be lost groweth to be a great hurt.'[34] Then Walsingham sent him £20, and at last he was able to get away.

Before he left he must have seen, on April 26th, the meeting of the new Parliament in Dublin. There came the chiefs of Kinel-Connal and Kinel-Owen, namely O'Neill, Turloch Lynneach, and Hugh, the young Baron O'Neill, who had title Earl of Tyrone at this Parliament. And O'Donnell, Hugh Roe, son of Manus. Also Con, son of Niall Ogue, son of Con, son of Hugh Boy O'Neill, as representatives of the O'Neills of Clandeboye. Also the chiefs of the Route Third of Connaught, O'Rourke and O'Reilly. The list is given in the Annals of the Four Masters, and one sees them riding into Dublin on their little horses, men with long hair hanging over their eyes, clad in their ragged saffron shirts, wrapped in great cloaks, dirty, lousy, but with a rare and dashing style. Afterwards they were forced to attend Parliament wearing English clothes, their hair cut—the final indignity. Turloch Lynneach begged that his boy might also walk to the Parliament in trousers 'so that the crowd will laugh at him and not at me'. Indeed Tur-loch's fat form was more dignified swathed in the Irish mantle.

The English point of view ran thus: if the Irish were made to adopt a more civilized appearance, they might perhaps change spiritually too. But such a change could only have taken place voluntarily; force would result in an intolerable sense of grievance, that sorrow that gnaws at the Celt, that is hateful to him and yet irresistible too, so that without it he feels incomplete.

The Parliament achieved much; some of the laws were objection-able to the English in Ireland as well as to the Anglo-Irish, for Perrot required the Oath of Obedience to the Queen to be taken by all members of the Government. He also told the Parliament to frame laws against recusants,* as in England, suspended the Poynings Act and proposed the establishment of counties with Sheriffs and Justices, according to the English system.

He was generous and gracious to the defeated Irish. Turloch Lynneach was granted the northern half of Tyrone and the title Irish Chieftain of Tyrone; Hugh O'Neill was given the southern half of Tyrone and the use of his grandfather's title Earl of Tyrone; he was to keep three companies to defend the north for the English. But the English in Dublin could not forgive Perrot for his wise handling of vanquished men and they began, out of revenge, to practise 'dishonourable dealings and intolerable corruptions'.

Perrot was suffering acutely, mentally and physically. He com-plained of the stone and of a swollen leg—one sees his father, one huge rotten leg stuck up on a chair before him. This natural son, so much more like him than the cold little Edward VI had been, was an outsized man in his mind and in his passions. The rages that tore him were greater than other men's rages, the small betrayals drove him into senseless acts of revenge. The instructions from the Privy Council in England had brought him low; not only was he not allowed to choose his own Clerk of the Check, but he was supervised by the Council of Ireland as if he were not to be trusted. So he fought with the Bagenals, with Secretary Fenton and with Sir Henry Wallop; he knocked Sir Nicholas Bagenal down in a brawl; he clapped Secretary Fenton into gaol for debt, and received a slashing letter from the Queen ordering his victim's release.

Captain Nicholas Dawtry made complaints in Dublin about

* See page 165.

Perrot. There had been waste of money in the Northern Expedition, he said, and a needless number of soldiers; all the Commission agreed with him, save Sir Henry Bagenal who had been Colonel of the forces in Ulster at the time. The Ulster chieftains, continued Dawtry, were keeping their soldiers on English pay, ostensibly to fight for England, but in reality were using them in their own private feuds, and Perrot countenanced this. The Deputy had also 'so muddled the war by making peace with Sorley Boy and giving him better conditions than he had before.'[35]

Dawtry not only spoke in Dublin, he spoke also to the Queen, and though his huge Falstaffian shape made him something of a figure of fun, the Queen seems to have listened to him.

In a letter to Walsingham Perrot wrote, 'The Queen will article of my doings, with every mean man as well soldiers as captains. . . . She is carried with many contrarities of her mood, and passions for my northern service.'[36]

Later he wrote that he had received letters which had so stung him as he was 'never so grieved with anything heretofor, finding now that I am but used, not esteemed'.

At times this colossal grief rose to the heights of tragedy, and he escaped from his egotism. 'I pity Ireland,' he wrote, 'ordained, I fear me till a day or two before Doomsday, to be a torn estate.'[37] And this was not just big talk. There was often a warmth about him when he wrote of Ireland and of its people.

A terrible letter came from the Queen, 'Let me have no more such rash inadvised journeys without good grounds as your last fond journey into the north. We marvel you hanged not such advertiser as he that made you believe so great a company were coming. I know you do nothing but with a good intent for my service, but yet take better heed how you use us so again.' They had both inherited their father's temper.

The conditions of pay in Elizabeth's army were very bad.[38] The soldiers received only a proportion of their pay weekly, the balance at the end of six months, the first known as imprests, the second as full pay. If a soldier died, the Crown often saved on this difference between imprest and full pay. It had been agreed in 1562 that captains should draw a hundred men's pay for ninety-five men, and these five surplus pays came to be known as dead pays. In 1585 the dead pays rose to ten per hundred men. After fighting had taken place it was a temptation for a captain to send in a false casualty list and to continue to draw pay for men killed. Another way a captain could cheat was to buy false certificates from the muster-master, thus enabling him to claim more pay, clothing and food for the men under his command. Often, too, soldiers would offer the captain money for their discharge, and the captain would put Irishmen in their place, and these were willing to take less. When a roll-call was made and there were many absentees who had bought their way out, the captain would hire Irishmen to fill the empty places in the ranks.

The captain could deduct fines from a soldier's money for absence without leave, defects in equipment, swearing, or failure to turn up at divine service. As the soldier only had eightpence a day it is difficult to see where his fines came from. The captain who drew two shillings and sixpence a day found the system of fines one to suit his own pocket.

The soldier had to buy his own victuals, and victuallers followed the Army, selling food for high prices, and the men's health suffered. The soldier had also to find his arms and powder, a foolish economy which produced a desire to avoid fighting. In Ireland the captains were to protest at this suicidal arrangement. A flourishing black market existed for the sale of uniforms; these were so badly made that the men would often sell them back at eighteen shillings for a suit, merchants sold the same suit again and again, and the soldier went naked.

The captains were responsible for levying, transporting and equipping a recruit, and were allowed a man's pay for a month out of fines for deficiency in equipment. In Ireland he was forced to keep a full record and send it monthly to the Chief of the province who would in his turn send copies to the Lord Deputy and the Privy Council; links were often missing in the chain.

Not only were captains accused of much abuse, but the Clerk of the Check and the Treasurer-at-war as well. In 1588 in Ireland the Auditor was to complain that Sir Henry Wallop, Treasurer-at-war, kept the books away from his scrutiny. The post of Treasurer-at-war was considered to be a paying one, provided that the Auditor acquiesced.

In 1592 a resolute stand was taken to cure some of these abuses, but in 1584, when Carleill was in Ireland, the system must have been at its worst. Captain Nicholas Dawtry drew pay 'upon his own suggestion' without warrant, reckoning on a certificate from the Treasurer or Auditor, for himself and all his men in Carrick-fergus Castle from September 1588 till March 1591. And all that time he was in England. Someone 'discovered' him, and he was commanded to reimburse the Queen's Majesty.

At Coleraine Carleill and his men had been told to live off the land, a method which soldiers on field service adopted in Ireland. But the country was barren, though the sea produced fish. Probably salmon and bonnaclabbe, a kind of sour milk eaten by the Irish, was their chief food. We have Dawtry's statement that at Red Bay Carleill's company was out of clothes and wanting two or three days' food. After that they mutinied. Continually, men deserted to the Irish or the Scots, and small wonder. The Irish service was immensely unpopular, and deservedly so, and it did not collect the best type of man from England. There is evidence that even good men went to any dishonest lengths to avoid it.

There was to be one last clash between Perrot and Carleill, and it was about ships.[39] Carleill had entered the Irish scene this way, and this way he would leave it.

The Queen had complained that Perrot was not putting down pirates. Perrot felt insulted, 'I still profess to dislike and hate that kind of people', he had expostulated.

The Huguenot Duke of Joyeuse owned a ship that was engaged in a little gentle piracy off the coast of Ireland. Carleill's bark met her, and during the battle the French ship ran herself aground, and the crew 'flew away', leaving her to be brought into Kinsale by Rivers, the master of Carleill's ship. The pirate had little in her but victuals, for she feared capture by the President of Munster who hoped to fit her out and use her against Callice, a famous pirate, who was also off the coast of Ireland.

Even a ship full of victuals was useful to Carleill in his penniless condition. And now that he was about to leave the Irish service for good, the temptation to strike at Perrot was overwhelming; he would rob the Lord Deputy of his dues on the captured pirate ship, even if it meant turning pirate himself.

The master of Carleill's bark, Rivers, was probably his own cousin, for his mother's sister had married Sir John Rivers of Hadlow in Kent, and there were two sons of the marriage.[40] Rivers must have been a careless man, for he landed in the town of Kinsale, and while he was ashore the pirate recaptured the lost ship and sailed triumphantly out of harbour, later plundering a Hamburg merchant.

Perrot, in his letter to the Queen, complained that if only he had sufficient shipping he 'might do something to break that bad haunt of trade upon the coast'. After he had signed his name, a fit of rage prompted him to lift his pen again, and the postscript is there for us to see, full of venom. 'The ship which took Duke Joyeuse's bark doth appertain to Mr. Carleill who never gave me penny out of Duke Joyeuse's bark, nor I vow will never by shipping any way now.'

What furious attacks must Carleill have suffered on his return to Dublin, the word 'pirate' flung at him without mercy. But his time was up, he must leave Ireland, and with the Lord Deputy's unjust and angry words ringing in his ears he mustered his borrowed money and sailed for England.

The ugly year was soon forgotten in the adventure that lay ahead.

6

THE WEST INDIES VOYAGE

'MEAN TO employ him with Drake. . . .' These were the thoughts turning in Walsingham's mind during April 1585, when he realized how ill the Irish service was benefiting his step-son.

Sir Francis Drake was a personal friend of Walsingham's and there is evidence that Drake's devotion to him was very real; both men were bigoted Puritans, both believed with a passionate conviction that God was on the side of the reformed faith against Rome that God fought for England and not for Spain. When Drake was sent to spoil the great Armada which was forming in Lisbon, he wrote to Fox, the martyrologist, 'Our enemies are many, but our Protector commandeth the whole world; let us all pray continuously and our Lord Jesus will hear us in good time mercifully.'[1] In this spirit were his battles fought; he pillaged the Spanish colonies in the New World in the name of God, even as the Spaniards performed their atrocious massacres in God's name, too.

The war with Spain had taken a new turn. No longer was it a cold war, it was now becoming very hot indeed. When in 1584 the Prince of Orange was murdered, Elizabeth had found herself without a champion to fight her battles for her. She had dallied and dallied with the prospect of supplying military aid to the bereaved Netherlands, to the disquiet of her long-suffering ministers, and then Antwerp had fallen. 'That fiddling woman', as Sir John Perrot was to call her, was too late. But by the end of 1585 troops were at last being sent over to the Netherlands under the Earl of Leicester, and the expedition was costing nearly half the annual revenue of the Crown.

It was essential that Drake should make his gesture in the Caribbean, bringing back treasure if he could, and in any case attacking Spain before she was ready to attack England. There was no Spanish naval force stationed in the West Indies, only one vessel lying in San Domingo harbour,[2] but in Lisbon a great Armada was forming.

Plots were being hatched in England to assassinate Queen Elizabeth and to set Mary Stuart on the throne. As long as the Queen of Scots lived, plots would inevitably gather round her, and one day the storm would break. That would be the signal for the Catholic forces on the Continent to invade England.

During the summer of 1585 Philip had issued a curious order, disastrous to Spain in its results; all foreign ships carrying grain to the Biscay ports were to be impounded with their crews and weapons, to be used as transports for the great treasure fleet on its annual journey to the Caribbean and back to Spain; French ships only were to be exempted. Two of the English vessels that were impounded escaped and returned to England with the news. At once Elizabeth issued letters of marque to Carew Raleigh to attack the Spanish tunny fisheries, thus depriving the Spanish treasure fleet of its supplies, while Bernard Drake sailed to Newfoundland to warn English shipping of their danger in Spanish ports and to capture the Spanish cod-fishing fleet. These exploits were successful.

Drake's expedition of 1585 had various aims; first he was to sail to Vigo to release the English impounded ships, and then to seize the Spanish treasure fleet at St. Vincent. If he failed in this last enterprise he was to destroy the enemy ports of call in the Spanish Main, and if possible raid Panama. For this hazardous adventure he had only twenty-one ships and eight pinnaces, carrying two thousand eight hundred men, including seamen, and ten companies of pikemen and musketeers. He held the position of Admiral of the Fleet and Captain General of the troops and sailed on the *Elizabeth Bonaventure* of six hundred tons; with him was Thomas Fenner. Martin Frobisher was the Vice-Admiral on board the *Primrose* of two hundred tons, while Francis Knollys was Rear-Admiral on the *Galleon Leicester* of four hundred tons. Christopher Carleill was Captain of the *Tiger* of two hundred tons, and Lieutenant-General of the forces under Drake. Whether this ship was the same *Tiger* that he had taken to Russia three years before is very uncertain.[3] The subject, when explored, leads to infinite confusions, and has little effect on the story of the West Indies Voyage.

Drake and Carleill were both students of military tactics. This was a science that was suddenly coming into prominence,[4] as many as eighteen books on the subject having been published between 1570 and 1585. Carleill had already in 1572, as we know, written commendatory verses for Sadler's translation of the Four Books of Flavius Vegetius Renatus. He and Drake were well aware that in order to fight the Spaniards a precise knowledge of the science of war was necessary, and Carleill was already versed in mathematics. Together they made a powerful combination.

Their temperaments, so different, complemented each other. Carleill's affability, his tact and integrity, made it possible for Drake and Frobisher, two impetuous and obstinate characters, to work together on the long voyage to the West Indies. It was Carleill's brilliant conduct of the combined operations, the smooth working together of sea and land forces, that made the beach landings so successful.

Under Carleill was a Sergeant-Major or Chief of Staff, Captain Anthony Powell, two Corporals of the Field, Captain Matthew Morgan and Captain John Sampson, who was 'an Irish officer serving long and with distinction with Carleill'. There were ten company commanders, each with his lieutenant, a sergeant and corporals; there was a priest, a clerk, a surgeon and two or three drums. The soldiers were all volunteers.

We have a list of names, and some of them are of interest; there was Captain Edward Winter, who sailed in the *Aid*, and in the *Vantage* Thomas Moore, in the *Thomas* was Thomas Drake, brother to Francis, and in the *Galliot Duck* Richard Hawkins, son of old Sir John. Other ships were the *Minion*, the *Bark Talbot*, the *Sea Dragon*, the *Bark Bond*, the *Bark Bonner*, the *Hope*, the *White Lion*, the *Drake*, the *George*, the *Scout* and the *Swallow*.

The expedition was equipped with arrows, pikes, halberds, black-bills, muskets and bastard-muskets; the pikemen, halberdiers and billmen carried swords and daggers.[5] Drake seems to have been provided with sixty new cannon, culverins, sakers, minions and falcons.

The London contingent of seven ships left Woolwich 'with great jollity', the *Primrose* leading them, to join Drake who was already at Plymouth. The fleet was to remain there awhile to take in ordnance.

The expedition was financed as a Joint Stock Syndicate, the investors paying all the expenses. The Queen contributed one-third of the share with £10,000 in cash and two ships.[6] These, however, were over-valued at another £16,000. If treasure was taken and a profit made, all would share; if there were losses the investors would meet them, not the Queen. Only thus could the Crown afford these naval expeditions at all, but the arrangement must have pleased the parsimonious Elizabeth.

In July Sir Philip Sydney had become Joint Master of the Ordnance with the Earl of Warwick, and now busied himself with the arrangements at Plymouth. While the Queen hesitated, made up her mind and unmade it again, the men waited, impatient and growing rebellious. Then suddenly, at the eleventh hour, Sir Philip Sydney announced his intention of joining the expedition; the Court was stifling him with its intrigues and its luxuries, and the attentions of the Queen kept him from a life of action. But his escape was to remain a secret; we have the testimony of Fulke Greville, Sydney's friend,[7] that Drake and Sydney had agreed that Drake should bear the title of Governor as long as they remained in England, but that once they had safely left the country both should be equal. Nevertheless Drake knew well that Sydney, as aristocrat and Master of the Ordnance, would in practice be over him. Fulke Greville kept his eyes open and observed that though Drake had treated Sydney with feastings on his arrival, yet was he full of 'discountenance and depression' at the prospect of the voyage. In later years Greville was to write that Sydney 'had over-shot his father-in-law, the Secretary of State in his own bow', and this caused Greville a certain wry amusement. He was to write of those difficult days that 'the leaden feet and nimble thoughts of Sir Francis wrought by day and unwrought by night while he watched to discover us'.

Carleill was very much involved in this tangle. Sydney, as husband of Walsingham's daughter, bore a special relationship to him, but ultimately only because both men were related to the Secretary of State. Carleill's military honour and his sense of duty kept him loyal both to Drake and to his stepfather; in questions of honour his code was a simple one.

While Drake's messenger was hastening to Court with news of Sydney's arrival, another messenger arrived at Plymouth from the Queen with orders for the fleet to sail. Drake and Carleill must have lost all their zeal to be away; luckily for them yet another

messenger arrived from the Queen to stay Sydney, and if he
refused to obey, to stay the whole fleet.

As Don Antonio had failed to arrive—the ostensible reason for
Sydney's visit to Plymouth had been to meet him—Sydney was
ordered to join his uncle, the Earl of Leicester, in his expedition
with an army to the Netherlands.

Fate had struck the first blow; two years later Sydney was to be
killed in action at Zutphen.

On September 14th the fleet sailed, the stores crammed in anyhow
for fear the Queen should change her mind again, and two weeks
later was cruising off Galicia on the north-west coast of Spain. This
land was not unlike Cornwall, concealed in a quiet mist, with fine
rain drizzling. It was inhabited by Celts, akin in many ways to the
Bretons and the Cornish; they saw ghosts and they dreamed dreams.
Perhaps the icy cold Atlantic sea had cast its spell, making the sunshine seem effervescent and the mists a reality.

But when the mists lifted they were replaced by a brassy sun
growing hotter and hotter till at midday all was engulfed in its
light, the sea became dark as a sapphire, and the cliffs a hard ochre.
On the road beyond Bayona and Vigo the pilgrims travelled every
year to St. Iago da Compostella with their scallop-shells, their
staves and their great hats. To have prayed in its Cathedral, to have
stood in awe before its magnificent processions, to have watched
the *gigantis* prance on their stilts before the High Altar, these were
the aims of devout Catholics. As Drake sailed into the Road of
Bayona he knew that he was approaching a holy land—to him
unholy. All his Puritan zeal must have risen within him at the
thought, and a desire to smash the outward signs of Catholicism.
He saw himself as God's soldier. And Christopher Carleill, bred
in the same faith, shared his resolve.

On October 4th in the Road of Bayona Carleill sat down to write
a despatch to his stepfather, telling him of the journey.[8] Near
Finisterre, that cape jutting far into the wild waters of the Atlantic,
they had met a ship of seven score tons laden with New Foundland
fish. First Carleill had chased her in his *Tiger*, then Drake in his
Elizabeth Bonaventure, finally the crews of both ships had boarded
her. She had given out that she was a French ship, but her master
had confessed to selling fish in San Sebastian, and the English had
found some Papal Bulls of pardon aboard her. Drake had taken the

fish, and if on his return the ship turned out to be a Frenchman, he would pay compensation: thus wrote Carleill, a little nervously skating round the subject of piracy.

Eight or nine small French ships returning from Lisbon with salt were next encountered. They had taken one, 'and the General shall give order for the payment thereof'. According to Captain Walter Biggs, who recorded the events of the voyage, the ship was empty of her crew and rolling helplessly in the swell of the Bay of Biscay.

But this act had its repercussions in England. The French King was very angry, and wrote to Elizabeth that Drake had stayed *La Magdalena* and taken all her equipment, saying he had need of her for Her Majesty's service.[9] Her value was 2,800 crowns; England was not at war with France, wrote the French King, and the French merchant should be recompensed.

Carleill, in his letter to his stepfather, described how they had seen a St. Malo bark of sixty tons laden with sugar, rolling heavily in a great sea, and out of control. They had boarded her and had found the master and the master-gunner slain, and others 'sore hurt were in their beds unable to move'. Drake's men had presumed her to be a pirate ship, but there was no proof, for the ship's papers had been thrown overboard.

The storm lasted for four days, and battered black clouds raced above a heaving sea, and men clung to ropes lest they be washed overboard. When the wind dropped the sea began to subside, like an invalid recovering from a fever.

Then Drake sent the pinnace and the ships' boats to row towards Bayona. They were met by a boat sent by the Spanish Governor, with some Spanish sailors and an English resident aboard her. They had come to buy corn, for the harvest had been atrocious. Drake sent them back to the shore, and Captain Sampson with them who was to say that the English were there to demand the cause of the imprisonment of Elizabeth's subjects. Captain Sampson 'was of good judgement', wrote Carleill, who had known him well in Ireland.

When Sampson met the Governor he offered him peace or war, just as he wished. But the Governor replied that his commission did not stretch so far that he could make peace or war, and that the English merchants were no longer under arrest; he offered to water the English ships as one captain should with honest courtesy do to another, 'their princes being in league together'.

When Drake received the Governor's reply, he sent the English resident back to say that if the English merchants proved to be no longer under arrest, he for his part would use peaceful methods; he invited the Governor to meet him for a conference.

But by midnight another storm had arisen, and though Drake's ships rode under the lee of the island, the *Bark Talbot* and two other vessels lost their cables, and were forced out of the Road.

The English resident wrote a stirring description of the arrival of the English, addressed to a friend,[10] 'God be praised great matters have passed with us. On 6th Sir Francis Drake with twenty-six goodly ships sailed into the harbour in royal order, a goodly sight to see.' Drake had landed, and the Governor had sent refreshing food to his fleet, oil, apples, grapes and marmalade.

The English resident went four times between Drake and the Governor, and it was finally arranged that they should meet above Vigo where the English merchants and their goods would be handed over to Drake. 'Drake's company made all the country quake and run away', wrote the delighted resident, who no doubt had been much dismayed by the recent seizure of English ships and the imprisonment of the merchants.

But the inhabitants were less peaceful than their Governor; they made great fires and raised the country, and soldiers, drums and ensigns marched on the shore, ever watchful.

Carleill in his despatch wrote that when the storm had abated, Drake had sent four of his ships above Vigo, where some Spanish boats were lying with 'some good things for our relief'. Carleill was put in command of the little contingent, his own *Tiger*, the *Thomas*, the *Frances*, the *Galley* and some pinnaces. Lying up the river were many boats laden with household stuff belonging to those who had fled inland. In one was a chest full 'of the furniture of the high Church of Vigo, copes and plate, and one cross as much as a man might carry, being very fine silver of excellent workmanship, and all gilt over double'. Carleill and his men carried this loot back to the fleet.

The English resident described the treasure in greater detail, 'the great Cross of Vigo with two other crosses and all their chalices and their rich copes and all their plate that was belonging to the Church'.

There was pride and delight in Drake's fleet that night; the Church of Rome had been despoiled and God's will had been done.

The next morning, continued Carleill in his despatch, the
General with his fleet came into the harbour for shelter. Meanwhile an English ship, a stranger, the *George Bonaventure* of London,
had arrived and had landed her men, and one of them had been
killed by some peasants. Carleill sent Captain Sampson and eight
men ashore to intervene, but two hundred Spanish shot and pikes
attacked them; two Spaniards were slain and one Englishman
wounded.

The next day the Governor came marching from Bayona with a
force of two thousand foot and three hundred horse and assembled
in sight of the fleet. He carried a white flag and demanded to talk
to Drake. Two pledges on either side were exchanged, young men
to be held as hostages in case of trouble. So the Governor and
Drake met in a boat half-way between the English ships and the
shore, very private, with only Frobisher present. Peace was agreed
and restitution arranged for the English merchants, and they were
given leave to go. But after all this commotion the merchants did
not accept the Governor's offer, and chose rather to remain in
Bayona to collect the debts they were owed.

Then the rain fell, and the land became as wild and wet as the
Scottish islands. The Spaniards were growing restless, and there
was talk of some thousand soldiers assembling inland, and a bishop
with six hundred more expected that very night. So the English
thought it would be wise to leave. But first they would take a few
small ships lying in the harbour, for the two caravels captured on
the voyage had been damaged in the gale.

After this final act of piracy, the Spaniards were heard to say
that if the English remained another sixteen days they would wash
their hands in English blood. Indeed they had been very forbearing
with the invaders, but they were too weak to take action.

The wind 'waxed great' and the English put to sea. Carleill laid
aside his pen and became a mariner, making his 'nimble *Tiger*'
leap the waves. But when at last they reached the Canaries, three
hundred leagues away, the *Tiger* and the *Elizabeth Bonaventure* had
lost their pinnaces, while the *Primrose* did not rejoin them for six
days.

On November 3rd they put into the Island of Palma where the
inhabitants fired their great ordnance at the English Admiral. A
strong surf prevented a landing, the little fleet anchored near Hiero,
and a discussion arose as to whether they should attack the island.

But a fair wind arising, they decided to take their chance and put to sea again, making for the little group of islands off Cape Verde.

The storms that had blown at Bayona had brought good luck to the Spaniards. For the two Spanish treasure fleets had evaded Drake, one had slipped into San Lucar safely while he was leaving Bayona, the other had returned home while he was still at Plymouth, awaiting the Queen's pleasure.

Drake was now left with only two objectives to pursue, to follow the outgoing Spanish fleet which had no escort, hoping that he might intercept it on its return journey, and to harry the ports on the Spanish Main.

Meanwhile Philip II, fearing that the Atlantic islands or the Caribbean ports would be sacked by 'El Drago', was planning to despatch a great fleet to meet him on his way home.[11] As they were not to sail till April they would never prevent the destruction of the ports, all they could do was to take their revenge. An anxious winter lay before the King of Spain.

On November 16th Drake's fleet arrived at Santiago, one of the Cape Verde Islands. At first the town shot ordnance, then fell quiet. When night came, Carleill landed with a thousand men, prepared to 'direct the enterprise more like a wise commander'. They marched over very rough ground, calculated in that darkness to bewilder any leader, but at last they reached 'a fair plain', and Carleill assembled his troops and divided them into three parts. From the plateau where they were they could look into the town, and it appeared to be empty, no enemy to resist them. Carleill sent Captain Sampson and Captain Barton, with thirty shot each, to investigate. In they went, and soon the great ensign with St. George's cross on it was floating from the fort, and at the same moment Carleill's men shot fifty pieces of ordnance, for this was November 17th, Elizabeth's Accession Day, which was always celebrated in England. The guns from the ships thundered back, and the rocks echoed with the shouts of giants.

Then Carleill brought the troops into the town, which was quartered out for its lodging, every captain taking charge of his quarter. It was a beautiful town, about seven hundred well-built houses there and nine churches. A rivulet of fresh water flowed into the valley from the cliffs behind, and made a deep pool where Drake's ships lay to be watered. There were gardens and orchards full of oranges, sugar-cane, coconuts, potato-roots, onions and garlic—coconuts had already appeared in England, the hard shells set in silver and made into drinking cups. In the high cliffs surrounding the town were monkeys that raced and swung from rock to rock, while in the streets were multitudes of newts 'that it would amaze men to see them'; there were also bears, goats, deer and hens in the countryside. In the hospital, a fine building, lay some negro bond-slaves of the Spaniards and Portuguese 'sick of very foul and frightful diseases'.

There was treasure somewhere, but where? The English found an Italian and practised on him 'a certain kind of torment' to find out where it was hidden. He confessed that the inhabitants had fled into the mountains, carrying it with them. Another prisoner told them some ordnance had been dug into the ground in Praya, a town nearby.

Still in search of treasure they took a negro for guide, telling him that if they caught the Spaniard who had been his master, then that Spaniard should be slave to the negro. So the black man led them twelve miles into the country to Praya, but the inhabitants had fled from there too, taking their treasure with them. The thwarted English set fire to the place, and the people who were in hiding 'seeing the fire made a great cry among the bushes and weeds'.

It was here that an English boy went wandering from his companions and met some Spaniards. They cut off his head, ripped up his belly, carried away his heart, 'and straggled the bowels about the place in the most brutish manner'.

The English remained in the city for fourteen days, while Drake tried to arrange a ransom with the inhabitants, but unsuccessfully. For neither the Portuguese Governor, nor the Bishop, nor any of the townsmen would come to parley with them. Perhaps the knowledge that they had broken their promise to William Hawkins four years ago, and had murdered many of his men, made them fear English vengeance. And they had already experienced the burning of part of their town by the French: safer far to keep out of Drake's way. But where, oh where, was the famous Spanish pride? Sapped by the Caribbean sun, by the negro slaves, by those fine houses and nine churches . . . ?

Some disorders among the English troops began, but Drake and Carleill acted quickly, knowing that looting men were difficult to control. A gibbet was set up and a man hanged for committing buggery with two boys from the *Ark*.

Time was employed in administering the Oath of Allegiance to the Queen,[12] which the hurried departure of the fleet from Plymouth had prevented. It was a long ceremony but that too had its uses. Drake read the statutes and laws for the government of his soldiers to the colonels and captains, who in their turn explained them to their bands, 'suffering every man frankly with due reverences to speak, object and by writing, if they list, to offer unto any of the Council what they can against any of them, which objections considered, they shall resolve upon those laws and penalties'.

After this curiously democratic proceeding the oath was taken by officers and soldiers alike: 'I . . . do swear and promise to do all loyal true and faithful service unto the Queen of England, her most excellent Majesty. . . .' And then came the oath of discipline, 'to fulfil and keep all such lawful ordnance as His Excellency hath or shall set forth and establish for the better ordering of this army, as much as concerns me, so long as I shall serve in the same under him. So help me God by Jesus Christ.'

The time had come to go, and in Santiago the English left writings in various houses revealing their scorn of the people's cowardice, and as revenge for the brutal treatment of the English boy they burned Santiago too. Finally they set sail, carrying with them all the loot they could find.

But the loot was hardly bought. In the great heat of a November summer, while the sea was like golden oil and the sails hung limp, the first sickness fell, taking its toll of a hundred men. After this they went on dying, two or three a day, in great pain, with a burning ague and covered with a small rash like men who had the Plague. The negroes in hospital in Santiago suffering from 'very foul and frightful diseases' had reaped their revenge.

But eventually they arrived at Dominica, the first island of the West Indies. It was fertile, full of trees, potatoes, coconuts, plantains and cassavi, a kind of bread. The natives were painted a tawny red colour and were a handsome people, hostile to the Spaniards; they treated the English kindly, watering their ships and giving them cassavi. In return the English handed out beads and glass, and other loot they had taken in Santiago.

But it was felt that they were dangerous people, being great eaters of men and wearing their enemies' teeth strung into necklaces. Although they 'showed some sorrowful countenance at our departure', nevertheless as the English ships sailed down the coast, the natives ran along the seashore before them, shooting arrows and shouting and blowing their horns.

Then to an island lying to the westward, St. Christopher, where the ships were aired, the sick people refreshed and twenty men were buried. They remained there quietly for three days, seeing no natives. Fine trees there were, many pelicans and night birds, great snakes and huge land-crabs and other things 'like serpents, very strange'.

Here a council of war was held, and a decision made to sail to the great Island of Hispaniola, where was the famous city of San Domingo, the 'most ancient inhabited place in the West Indies'.

On the way there they fell in with two barks bound for San Domingo, laden with beef, bacon and other food. On board one of them was a Greek, who told them that the haven of San Domingo was barren and the land well fortified, boasting a castle armed with heavy ordnance, 'one of the strongest in Christendom'.[13] There was no landing place within ten miles of it. The Greek offered to act as their pilot, and his offer was accepted. Perhaps it was through this Greek's agency that the *cimarrones*, or escaped negroes, who were in possession of the country, came down from the hills and seized the watch-house by the shore, killing the Spaniards who came to them, to prevent the town from receiving news that the English were landing.

The English fleet lay near the island; a force of between eight hundred and fourteen hundred pikes and muskets was put into pinnaces and small boats, with Drake in the *Bark Francis* as Admiral. All night long they crept into the landing place, Boca da Hayna, and finally stood on the shore of a quiet haven early on New Year's Day. The Spaniards had always maintained that a landing was impossible here, and had no picket on the shore. In a letter written to Spain by an inhabitant are the words, 'To have landed there is to the natives of this land a thing more incredible than I can express.'[14]

Drake returned to his ships, leaving the soldiers to Carleill, who led them for four hours in the direction of the town. Then they formed into two columns, 'and with music playing and standards flying', began to march rapidly.[15] About a hundred and fifty brave horsemen 'of the better sort' advanced from the town to meet them, but soon retreated. From the chart of the attack[16] on San Domingo it appears that the Spaniards drove cattle towards the advancing English to scatter their ranks, and no doubt terrified animals advancing in a cloud of dust would prove very disturbing.[17] This incident is not, however, mentioned in the accounts of the eye-witnesses. Both gates were manned, and ordnance had been planted outside the walls. The two English columns attacked the gates at the same time, Carleill leading one force, Captain Powell the other. Carleill vowed that with God's good favour he would not rest till he and Powell should meet again in the market-place.

While Carleill 'advancing his voice of encouragement and pace of marching' set out with his men, the Spanish ordnance discharged on them, and the first man to be killed fell very close to Carleill. After that the English ran pell-mell into the town through the two gates, driving the Spaniards before them. Carleill and Powell met in the market-place as they had planned; this they proceeded to fortify with barricades, 'the city being far too spacious for so small and weary a troop to guard'. The Spaniards in the castle retreated, leaving the gate open,[18] some fleeing in boats up the river and thence into the country, carrying with them their treasure and a great image of silver from the church.

While the English were entering the city, Drake's fleet was battering it with guns on the other side, and this had gone on for two or three hours. 'Thus the Spaniards gave us the town for a New Year's gift', wrote the diarist of the *Primrose* Log.

Indeed, San Domingo was in a very sorry state of degeneracy; the acting warden of the fortress had written in 1582, 'Men there were, without weapons, living in an abandonment that could not be exaggerated';[19] they feared the French pirates, they feared the negro slaves lest they should revolt, they dared not go ten miles from the town for fear of the Indians. The inhabitants were mostly merchants, unused to war, living in great houses, the walls largely built like the walls of a church with doors greater than those of English churches, 'with such cost of iron work that it is wonderful'. There was a cathedral, three monasteries, two nunneries and an official residence for the Governor. A strange fatalism seemed to have overtaken them; they had nothing ready, no weapons, no ships. There were in all about eight hundred men capable of being mustered, but their training was bad, and their armour worse. All they seem to have done was to sink a galley and a boat or two across the harbour bar when they had first heard of the approaching English.

Drake's men set to work on the loot. They found a store of meat, and of cocks and hens, the hens alone valued at £1,000. There were spices, oil, cassavi and fruit, but no gold or silver, for the inhabitants had fled, taking their treasure with them. Even the President had gone.

The houses were full of luxuries, drinking glasses made on the island, linen, woollens, and silks from China, and so much sugar 'that we esteemed it not'. There was a great store of copper money to be shared out; eighty slaves were taken from ships in the harbour, Frenchmen, Greeks and negroes. The English set fire to the castle, burnt the images of wood in the churches and destroyed 'all their fairest work there', the choir screen, organ and bells. They seized the royal books and register in order to exact ransom from them. A grim story was revealed by the chaplains, the dean and chapter in a letter to Philip II; the English, they wrote, had turned the church into their business centre, their warehouse and dispensary; they had used the two chapels as a gaol, and had put their hostages there, and 'those people used the chapel as prisoners must any place in which they are long detained'.[20]

The desecration of the church was, of course, deliberate; it was a Catholic place of worship, as outlandish as any pagan shrine; fine architecture and images should not be spared, for their beauty glorified a faith that was evil and to destroy both together was a duty. So thought Drake with all the zeal of his fierce little mind; and so thought Carleill and his men.

We have grown so far away from them that we resent the destruction of art more than the iconoclasm; our own view would have shocked them profoundly, and our priorities have seemed frivolous. So we signal to each other from distant peaks, unable to understand.

But despite the havoc, it must be conceded that the English behaved moderately for the age in which they lived. The town had been taken by assault and had not surrendered, and the destruction was an act of war. Few of the inhabitants suffered death.

For the space of a month Drake held San Domingo, with its green woods and orchards of oranges, lemons and pomegranates. It was the first island taken by the Spaniards in the West Indies, an important place, keeping its own Parliament. On entering the Governor's splendid house, a strange sight was to be seen, a 'fair

staircase' and a long gallery to walk in, and there, 'very handsome
and straight ahead, so as you cannot escape the sight of it', a large
painted escutcheon bearing the arms of the King of Spain, and in
the lowest part of the escutcheon a globe, showing the whole earth
and sea. On it was a horse 'lifted as about to leap', with a scroll in
his mouth whereon were the words *Non sufficit orbis*, which is as
much as to say 'the world sufficeth not'. The Spaniards who had
come to treat about the ransom of the town, 'some of the better
sort', when asked the meaning of the painting 'would shake their
heads and turn aside their countenances in some smiling sort,
without answering anything, as though greatly ashamed thereof'.
So the English told them, in no uncertain terms, that if the Queen
of England should fight the King of Spain 'he should be forced to
lay aside that proud and unreasonable vein of his'.

Drake demanded a million ducats to ransom the town, and the
Inspector of the Royal Treasury had several meetings with him
before a solution was reached. In a letter to Philip II the Inspector
gave a fascinating picture of his meeting with the General and ten
English officers[21]—Carleill must certainly have been at this parley.
The Spaniard said that they could only afford 12,000 ducats, and
Drake thereupon reduced his demand from 1 million to 100,000
ducats and later to 40,000. At a certain stage a dangerous theological
discussion arose, resulting from a recent broil on the same subject,
and Drake opened a Bible and 'an accursed preacher of his' began
to discourse on it. This was too much for the Spaniard, who interrupted sharply, saying that his profession was not theology, nor
had he come for a disputation, 'whereupon Francis Drake ordered
the argument to be closed, and closed it was'.

Drake spoke through his interpreter, who used French, Latin and
Italian. He had an Englishman with him who spoke a little Spanish—
this may well have been Carleill, with his five years' experience
in the Low Countries behind him. Then comes a fascinating picture
of the 'corsair', as the Spaniards often described him, 'blonde,
rather heavy than slender, merry, careful. He commands and
governs imperiously. He is feared and obeyed by his men. He
punishes resolutely. Sharp, restless, well spoken, inclined to
liberality and to ambition, vainglorious, boastful, not very cruel.'
How clearly one sees him, the loud, pleasant voice, the bright eyes,
the bounce; how wrong to underestimate him as a mere braggart,
which some of his enemies in England had done.

The inhabitants brought him their jewellery and treasure, hoping to stop their conquerors from burning the town.[22] Every morning the English fired the houses on the outskirts, but they were magnificently built of stone and burned with difficulty. From daybreak till nine o'clock when the sun stood high overhead, a scorching ball, the mariners worked, but not one-third of the town was destroyed. In the end Drake had to accept the offer of 25,000 ducats, but not before the Cathedral had become an empty shell.

A few violent incidents there were, but not many, so cowed were the Spanish. On Drake's first entry into the town he had sent a messenger with a white flag to parley with some of the townsmen hidden in the hills. The messenger had fallen in with some Spanish officers from the captured galley, who had furiously struck him through the body with a stave. The negro boy had staggered back to Drake, told him his story and then had fallen dead at his feet. The General, 'greatly passioned', for the English had used the Spanish messengers well, caused two imprisoned friars to be hanged at the place where the boy had been struck. He told the Spaniards that he would hang two prisoners a day till he received the murderer into his hands. At that the captain of the King's Guard acquiesced, and the offender was handed over. But Drake was not content; he must bring the Spaniards to their knees. It was thought to be 'a more honourable revenge to cause them to perform the execution themselves, which was done'.

In the English ranks discipline was also enforced, and an Irishman hanged for murdering his corporal.

Looting is not good for discipline, it carries its own seeds of destruction; Drake saw that he must be away, so that his men could taste a harder life. From San Domingo they put over to the Main, and sailing along the coast came at last to Cartagena.

The harbour lay some three miles from the town which they had to pass on their way. The Governor was ready for them; they saw him parading four hundred and fifty Spaniards in martial array, with some Indians and the crews of the galleys lying in the harbour.[23] They made a brave show, but the Governor was well aware that there were no real soldiers among them. For these men were 'merchants and artisans unaccustomed to war'.

Drake's ships entered Boca Grande without meeting resistance; six hundred men landed under the command of Carleill, with

Captain Powell and Captain Morgan leading the companies in the rear. In the vanguard was Captain Sampson with the pikes; here also marched Captain Carleill, the Lieutenant-General. 'Every man came so willingly on the service as the enemy was not able to endure the fury of such hot assault.'

At first, because of bad guides, they lost their way; then Carleill ordered them to march along the shore close to 'the sea-wash'. About two miles from the town, 'in a rough and bushy place', they encountered a hundred Spanish horsemen, but the English shot sent them flying.

At that moment they heard firing, and knew that according to plan, Drake with the Vice-Admiral and the sea-captains in pinnaces and boats was attempting the fort at the mouth of the harbour. The opening was narrow, like a gutter running between high rocks, and protected by a chain slung from side to side. As the English tried to force an entry, the rudder of one of the pinnaces was torn off by the chain, the men's hats beaten from their heads and the oars out of their hands, while the top of a main-mast was smashed. To oppose them were two Spanish galleys and a galleass full of armed men, determined, as they said later, 'to kill all the English except twenty of the best who were to be turned into galley-slaves'.

Meanwhile the troops under Carleill had left the sea-shore and were marching along a spit of land between sea and harbour called the Caleta; it was flanked by a stone wall and a ditch. Here the Spanish Governor had caused Indian poisoned arrows to be stuck upright in the ground; if the point of one of these pierced a man's skin, death resulted rapidly. Fortunately, by marching along the beach, the English had avoided most of them.

There was a gap in the fortification of the Caleta, and this gap was a back door left open into the town. The Governor had tried to make it into a 'place of strength', erecting a barricade of wine-butts filled with earth, standing one on the other.

Alas for the Spaniards, it was in no sense a place of strength. The Governor had been advised to dig a trench across the Caleta from sea to sea, but this he had not done,[24] even though general preparations had been going on since Epiphany. Barricades and earthworks, some very efficiently made, had been erected in various places, but the defences should have been concentrated on the Caleta, and they were not. A feeble optimism seemed to have sustained those easygoing Spaniards in this land where no winter came to strengthen them, and the sun shone too steadily on the many-coloured sea.

They had put six great pieces, demi-culverins and sakers in the gap, and these opened fire on the English as they approached. The Spanish galleys beat on them too, while three hundred Spanish shot and pikes stood firm, awaiting the enemy's arrival.

Carleill forbade his men to shoot till they came to the wall side of the gap and then with pikes roundly together they rushed in; 'down went the butts of earth, and pell-mell came our swords and pikes together'. The English pikes were longer than the Spanish, and few of the Spaniards wore armour. In this furious entry the Lieutenant-General slew the chief ensign-bearer with his own hand 'who fought very manfully to his life's end'. Captain Alonzo Bravo Monteimayor, the Spanish captain, was wounded in six places and taken prisoner.[25]

A Spaniard writing of the attack described how a voice had been heard crying out in perfect Spanish, 'Retire, gentlemen, for we are lost.'[26] This voice, he thought, had proceeded from the enemy line. The Governor of the town kept calling out 'Do not retreat, brothers, but fight', and when his men ran he beat them with the flat of his sword. But they continued to run, and were joined in their flight by the negroes. They fell into a trench dug across a street and tried to hold it, but they found that the English Sergeant-Major and some of his men had gone in at the far end; the English lay low, then when the Spanish Governor rode up with his soldiers, they suddenly rose and attacked them and the Spaniards fled.

Carleill's men fought their way to the market-place, but there were Indians 'lurking in corners of advantage', armed with poisoned arrows. Now the Spanish retreat was becoming a rout; people were pouring over the San Francisco bridge to reach the open country, where the women and children were already in hiding.[27]

The Spanish tried to move the galleys out of the harbour, but the tide was low and there was not enough water. They dared not risk waiting for the tide to turn, so they ran the ships aground, unchained the galley-slaves and burned the galleys.[28] Many of the slaves were killed, but many swam and joined the English.

And so the town fell. The Governor wrote to Panama, 'I can only say that it must be God's chastisement for my sins, and for those of others.'

Three days later the English began to burn the houses, hoping that the inhabitants would return to ransom their town, and true enough, in they came with their flags of truce.

At the time they had been building a new church, and because the English shot off a great piece of ordnance nearby, part of it was shaken down. The Spaniards then refused to ransom the town, saying that they prized their church more and that now it was damaged. So then the English began to burn more of the town and at last the Spaniards came in with their offer of one hundred and ten thousand ducats, valued at five shillings and sixpence sterling. Their ransom was larger than that offered at San Domingo, for Cartagena was a place of greater importance, having a fine harbour and inhabited by rich merchants, whereas 'San Domingo was full of lawyers and brave gentlemen'.

Drake held a council of war to settle the question of the ransom and to ask his captains their views on the course of action that should now be taken;[29] were they to continue raiding the coast or were they to return home, 'foregoing the bountiful mass of treasure' they had expected to find? The answer was given that the expedition should return home with the honour it had already earned, and then the adventurers would be ready should the Queen need them again. The taking of the Spanish cities had produced less than had been expected and now men were sick or wounded and those that remained 'were of slack disposition'.

The captains were questioned about the ransom; should the Spanish offer be accepted? One hundred thousand pounds had been demanded, came the answer, 'which seems a matter impossible to perform', and so the first offer should be accepted, especially as the English had taken 'their full pleasure, both in the uttermost sacking and spoiling' of the town. As for the poor men in the force who had spent their all on provisions and apparel for the expedition, they should be compensated. And the captains declared that whatever profit they should themselves draw from the venture, they would bestow on the soldier and the sailor, 'wishing with all our hearts it were such or so much as might seem sufficient reward for their perfect endeavour'. This act, said the captains, was 'to encourage them and to nourish this ready and willing disposition of theirs, both in them and in others'.

Then came the signatures, Christopher Carleill, Captain Goring, Captain Powell, Captain Sampson, and so on till all the captains had signed.

In an age when Army captains had a reputation for dishonest dealings with their men, it is refreshing to hear these words of generosity tempered by reason spoken in the Caribbean, where disappointment might have given way to greed. Carleill was 'careful of his military honour', and when he put his signature to this document, he suspected that he would have to be content with little else.

After receiving the ransom the English moved into the Priory which lay outside the town. They maintained that this building had not been brought into the Spaniards' composition, so realizing the defect in the agreement, the prior offered a thousand crowns for it, 'leaving us to take our pleasure of his block-house'—ominous phrase—which the Spaniards could not afford to pay for as well. And considering the inefficiency of the Spanish resistance it was probably better for them to lose their block-house, and to save their money. But where was the famous Spanish pride?

With a human inconsistency, Drake spared the Franciscan monastery, for the wife of his prisoner Captain Alonzo Bravo Monteimayor had recently been buried there. Drake had caused her to have a solemn funeral with flags reversed and drums muffled, while he himself had been present. Nevertheless, while lodging in this prisoner's house he had taken a great ransom of jewels from him.

For six weeks the English stayed at Cartagena and the sickness among the men continued. Those who escaped death could not recover their strength, and many remained 'much degraded in memory', so much so that it became a common saying when a man made a foolish remark, that he had suffered from the 'Calentura', the name given by the Spaniards to this ague. The cause of the disease was thought to be the evening or first night air, termed 'La Serena', and since the English kept watch continuously, they were exposed to this danger, which was exceptionally bad at San Domingo.

The English ships fell down to the harbour mouth and began to water themselves for the homeward voyage. Here was a great well, set among orchards which covered the island for two or three miles. Many fruits and herbs grew here, lemons, pomegranates, citrons, olives and peppers.

A small skirmish took place about this time. A couple of Spanish barks, unconscious of the presence of strangers on the island, came into harbour; then seeing the English pinnaces making for them, they ran themselves ashore and their crews fled into the bushes. Presently the English, in a foolhardy manner, boarded the empty barks, but while they stood there unprotected, they were shot at by the hidden Spaniards; Captain Varney was killed, and Captain Moore was wounded and died later. Tom Moore was an old friend of Drake's, and one of his earliest followers. This event sobered the English, who were becoming too contemptuous of the Spaniards.

Despite the haggling over the ransom, conquerors and conquered seemed to have been on easy terms, and even to have feasted together. Men living in exile thirst for news, and the English and Spaniards were both Europeans, a fact which drew them together in that remote land. So the Spaniards put up a civilized performance—or a shameful one—whichever way you care to look at it.

At these feasts Drake, loquacious and boastful as usual, told them he wanted to take Panama on his way home, and a rumour went round that he was carrying pinnaces of light draught to go up the river, constructed so that they could be taken to pieces and carried.[30] Later another story was told that he was at odds with his captains and gentlemen, that both sides were drawing up documents,[31] and that the raid on Panama was called off for fear that they should meet the Armada on its way home. If there had indeed been friction, Drake had solved it wisely by calling a council of war.

The time of departure came; incredibly we read that there were some signs of sorrow on the part of the Spaniards. But in war nothing is impossible, the rules of life are turned upside down, and astonishment is a forgotten emotion.

After two or three days at sea, a great ship which the English had taken at San Domingo, called the *New Year's Gift*, sprung a leak, being heavily laden with ordnance, hides and other spoils. During the night she lost the rest of the fleet, and it was not till the following day that the General found her, the men all tired out with pumping. So Drake decided to return to Cartagena.

At the sight of the English returning, the townsmen fled into the country. But the General explained to them what had happened, asking the Governor if he could send some bakers ashore to bake bread, and the Governor, 'for fear', granted them all the ovens in the town, issuing a proclamation that every man was to help with wood and water. Meanwhile the cargo was being moved from the *New Year's Gift* and distributed among the other ships.

The *Tiger*, 1588.
Engraving by Visscher.
Typical of the 'reformed'
ships of Elizabeth's reign

Visscher excudit

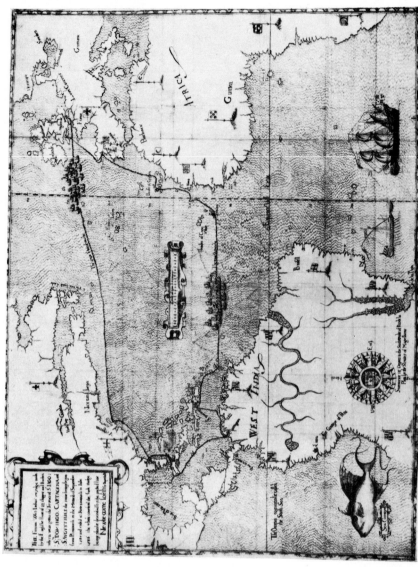

Boazio's chart
of *The Famous West Indies*
Voyage

Carrickfergus Castle

DRAVN AFTER ◦ THE ◦ QVICKE

Irish Kerns

On April 18th they were ready to leave for the second time, and a few days later dropped anchor at an island called the Grand Cayman. It was uninhabited, only strange kinds of beasts living there, alligators and crocodiles. The English killed some, and they made good meat. Other little beasts there were too, cats and little serpents about two feet long called 'guanos', with 'a number of turtles of huge bigness', good to eat.

A week later they came to Cape San Antonio in Cuba, but found no water there. They sailed on for about fourteen days, but through lack of a favourable wind were forced back to Cape San Antonio again. Because of the scarcity of their water supply they devised a new method of procuring it, making pits on a piece of 'moorish ground' and diverting the rain water which had recently fallen. The General himself worked with his hands, digging with the meanest, encouraging the men by his example and boundless enthusiasm. His red face and bright eyes, his stocky body, were to be seen here, there and everywhere, as he commanded, threatened and praised. Even the pictures we have of him breathe a certain vitality, as though something of the man had passed into the canvas. Beside him, Carleill, working too with his spade, was something of a dreamer, with his broad head and tapering face. For Carleill was a scholar as well as a military man, a type that was as much part of the Elizabethan Renaissance as Drake himself—who was all man of action.

On May 13th they left Cape San Antonio for the second time, rounded the Cape of Florida and made for St. Augustine. Their strength was low, and all desired to return to England. But the defence of Sir Walter Raleigh's colony at Roanoke in Virginia was an important consideration, for if St. Augustine was destroyed it would be unable to threaten the colony.

Coasting along the shore, they saw an object resembling a beacon, which turned out to be a scaffold standing upon four long masts, used as a watch-tower. Here the General himself landed and marched with the companies, Carleill leading the vanguard. They drew up in formation behind the sand-dunes, flags flying and drums beating, then marched to the music of cornets, sackbuts and flageolets.[32] About a mile up river they saw a newly built fort, and beyond it a little village of wooden houses, all of Spanish workmanship.

Ordnance was prepared and Carleill himself shot at the flag on the fort and struck it through; one more shot hit the wall which was made of massive trunks of trees packed close together, looking like the masts of ships.

That night Carleill took a little rowing skiff and with the two Captains, Morgan and Sampson, and half a dozen armed men, went to see what guard the enemy kept. But after firing in a half-hearted way the Spaniards fled, leaving the fort empty. Carleill did not realize they had gone, and returned to his men.

Later there came towards them, rowing across the river in a little boat, a Frenchman, a prisoner of the Spaniards, playing on his pipe as he came. The tune he played was his password, and to Carleill it was music from a distant world, for it was none other than 'the tune of the Prince of Orange his song'.

Laughter and delight greeted the Huguenot, and men who had fought in the Low Countries remembered the old heroic days. The newcomer offered to escort the English to the fort, which he swore was empty. So Drake and Carleill in two pinnaces full of soldiers, put out across the river again.

Meanwhile the English left behind in the woods heard 'a very strange cry', and savages suddenly appeared from amongst the trees and assaulted them. But they were soon driven away.

Next morning those in the fort examined it, and found fourteen great pieces of brass ordnance, and a chest having in it about two thousand pounds sterling of the King's treasure to pay the garrison. For there were about a hundred and fifty soldiers kept there.

Then the English embarked in their pinnaces and went up the river to the town called St. Augustine. They advanced on it with red flags flying, a signal that no quarter would be given.[33] There was a light skirmish and Captain Powell, the Sergeant-Major, was shot through the head. He fell from his horse and was stabbed by two or three Spaniards. His death was greatly lamented by his men, for he was honest, wise and brave.

In St. Augustine the English found forty pipes of meal, but neither wine nor oil nor other victuals, for during the attack on the fort the Indians had returned and pillaged the town.[34] Natives clad in skins came in to greet the invaders, but soon afterwards they started to die, and it was thought that the English god had set his mark on them and caused their death. Each native tribe had its own king, and each king had many wives, one having as many as a hundred and forty. Many strange tales the English heard about the natives, one of the strangest being that they spoke once a year with the devil in the high mountain.

Mutual fear began to take hold of both sides; an Indian betrayed a plot to the English that one night they were to be murdered in their sleep. So in revenge the English killed the king who had plotted their death, and burned the houses, two hundred and fifty of them, leaving none standing.

They were told that the Spaniards kept another garrison at St. Helena, an island lying northward. So it was resolved, in a full assembly of captains, to undertake the enterprise of St. Helena and then to seek out the English colony at Roanoke in Virginia.

So the flat land of Florida was left behind, like a white ribbon stretched beneath an enormous sky; the sweet woods and grass plains, the great stores of fish and oysters, the flocks of white cranes were things of yesterday. Now the ships sailed between little islands while heavy-winged pelicans flapped beside them.

Near St. Helena the shoals were dangerous, and as they had no pilot it was thought wise to give up the enterprise. For the night before, the Admiral had been in four and a half fathoms of water as far away as three leagues from the shore. Yet they knew well enough by hearsay that there was a way in, for ships of a greater draught than their own had entered.

In June, seeing a great fire on the coast, the General sent his skiff to the shore, and there was found some of the English colony that Sir Walter Raleigh had left a year before. These men were brought aboard and they piloted Drake's ships into their harbour. The General wrote letters to Ralph Lane, the leader of the colony at Roanoke, some six leagues away, and these were carried there by a messenger.

The next day that intrepid man and great speculator, Ralph Lane, arrived himself, with much jubilation. With the captains' consent Drake made him an offer—either that Drake would leave a ship, a pinnace and some boats and a month's victuals so that he could explore the coast, and then all of them would return to England, or else that Drake should carry them back to England straight away.

The brave colonists accepted the first offer, but when the ship had been handed over and some of the men were already aboard her, there arose a terrible storm that lasted for three days, with thunder, lightning and hailstones as big as hens' eggs. The fleet was in great danger, and many cables were broken and anchors lost. Some of the ships, including the one given to Ralph Lane, were forced to put to sea and were not sighted again till they all met in England. The storm, said the colonists, was extraordinary and very strange.

Notwithstanding, Drake made the same offer again, but this time the second course was adopted. No doubt 'the strange and extraordinary storm' was taken for a portent. For on June 18th the rest of the colony boarded Drake's ships and set sail for England. Later an expedition organized by Raleigh came to relieve the Roanoke colony with food, and found it had gone.

The voyage home was long and hard, but at last, on July 28th, 1586, the ships arrived in Portsmouth to be met by a great crowd of 'worshipful from city and town'.[35] Drake and his captains were escorted to London, and were entertained and feasted at Court, and there was the Queen graciously smiling and extending those elegant hands to be kissed, and with the flash of genius which rose in her on those occasions, winning each man's passionate devotion to herself.

Soon the gains and losses of the voyage were being assessed. Some seven hundred and fifty men and twelve officers had died, about three-quarters of them through sickness; Captain Powell, the Sergeant-Major, also Captain Moore, had been killed. In a list of names of those who did not return is that of Alexander Carleill, a relation of Christopher's, but who he was we do not know.

The total value of treasure was estimated at three score thousand pounds, whereof the companies that had travelled were to have twenty thousand pounds, the adventurers or speculators the other forty. About £6 to the single share was at first suggested.

Drake and a Commission signed a statement in March 1586/7,[36] and this statement had already been examined by Frobisher and Carleill with the same members of the Commission in December. It was noted that Drake himself would bear the expenses of the delay at Plymouth before the expedition left, while Elizabeth was undergoing her period of indecision about their departure, 'which could not be but a great matter, the thing hanging so long'. Even so, the charge was big to the adventurers, and the bullion they brought back was not able 'to countervail the charge outward'. 'Drake', the statement ends, 'dealeth very liberally and truly with the adventurers and beareth himself a very great loss therein. . . . And considering the worthiness of the enterprise . . . so well performed to the honour of Her Majesty and good of our country we can do no less than humbly pray your Honour to be a means to Her Majesty that consideration might be had of the painful and dangerous attempt achieved by him and the captains and gentlemen that served with him in action.'

In the end the adventurers were paid 15s. in the pound.

In May 1587 Carleill was asking the Privy Council for £400, the charges of his preparations for the West Indies voyage.[37] The Privy Council acknowledged that he should receive more, but since the voyage had not proved as successful as they had hoped, Carleill was allotted £280.

The success of the expedition was not financial, it was a moral victory which had far-reaching results. The King of Spain had been attacked in the New World and the Spanish possessions there shown to be very poorly defended. They were a prey to any pirate who chose to descend on them, especially 'the corsair, El Drago'. This great empire of Spain was proving to be a liability; its reputation was badly cracked. Drake himself had written modestly to Burghley on the way home from Roanoke, 'There is now a very great gap opened very little to the liking of the King of Spain. God work it all to His glory.'[38]

Although Panama had not been taken according to the original plan, nor a permanent post established on the Spanish Main, Drake hoped to remedy this by returning to the West Indies on a second voyage. But events were moving fast; barely a month after the expedition had returned to England the Babington Plot exploded, with Walsingham as chief puppet-master manipulating the strings, and as a direct result came the execution of Mary Queen of Scots. Relations between England and Spain were too strained for Elizabeth to let Drake go to the West Indies, for England was now officially at war with Spain and the arrival of the Armada a very present danger.

So in March 1586/7 he was again in Plymouth, preparing a squadron 'to prevent or withstand any enterprise as might be attempted against Her Highness'. He was to stop Spanish ships from going to Lisbon to join the Armada that was forming there, to blockade the Spanish and Portuguese coasts so that no supplies could reach Lisbon, to set upon any Spanish ships approaching England or Ireland, and to distress ships lying in Spanish and Portuguese harbours.[39]

And so began the famous Cadiz voyage. But Christopher Carleill did not sail with Drake. His future lay once more in Ireland.

7

IRELAND AND THE ARMADA

CARLEILL RETURNED to Ireland as Governor of the Palace of Carrickfergus, Seneschal of Clandeboye, the Dufferin and Killaltaghe,[1] taking over these duties from Nicholas Dawtry. He was also to become Governor of Ulster, following Francis Stafford.[2]

The Privy Council wrote to the Lord Deputy Perrot and the Council in Dublin earnestly recommending him to their good deserts. And kind words were said about his many services to Her Majesty in divers places, particularly in Ireland; he should be encouraged in all his reasonable causes that he might the better be able to serve Her Majesty; his Lordship should establish him at Carrickfergus in as large and ample a manner as any ward in these parts of like numbers of men.[3] There was a curious addition that he should be put in effectual possession of the Seneschalship, with some extraordinary care and regard that he should not be interrupted in the exercise of his office by any other before the Privy Council had given its consent. The office was too mean for Carleill, the Council continued, and when some other office became vacant he should have preference.

Clearly Sir John Perrot was not to be trusted.

Consulting the records it is with some surprise that we find Carleill being established at Carrickfergus, not in 1587 by Sir John Perrot, but in 1588 by Sir William Fitzwilliam, the next Deputy. He did, however, draw pay for the third quarter of 1587, at least as Constable of Carrickfergus,[4] though he did not go there.

Incredible as it may seem, he met again with ill-treatment at the Lord Deputy's hands. Not all the words of the Privy Council in England could save him. In January 1589/90 a certain Francis Wells was to write from Ireland to Walsingham about his own sufferings under Perrot, despite the letter of recommendation he had brought from the Secretary. 'It is no marvel', he concluded, 'seeing he has used your son Carleill so thwartly *again*'.[5] (Author's italics.)

A personal recommendation to the Lord Deputy, it seems, acted as a malediction to anyone arriving in Dublin. Had not Walsingham noted in the margin of his book, 'Straight dealing especially such as I favour'? So Perrot blundered on towards his doom.

Walsingham had no intention of subjecting his stepson to more ignominy. In the summer of 1588 and in the following spring he was using him on diplomatic and military missions, and one may suppose these started as soon as it became evident that Perrot would not cut the local 'practising' that surrounded the appointment of the Governor of Carrickfergus. The situation between England and Spain was tense, and a good man would be invaluable in other fields. Not so long ago Walsingham had jotted down during the crisis succeeding the Babington plot, 'To send for Carleill and the captains'—a significant phrase.

In July 1588 Carleill had been in Dublin long enough to have made a friend of Richard Meredith, Dean of St. Patrick's and Perrot's chaplain, for he wrote recommending him to his stepfather in London.[6]

Meanwhile the Palace of Carrickfergus and the Seneschalship of Clandeboye had been put into the hands of a deputy, Captain Henshawe.[7] Carleill was to write of him that he 'had far better stuff of a soldier-like carriage in him than is in a great number of the captains and other officers here', and that there was no one better to whom he could commit the handling of government if he had to be absent.[8]

During the summer of 1588 we come upon Carleill in Scotland, shortly before the arrival of the Armada in England. The position in Scotland was 'tickle',[9] for Elizabeth feared that James might join the Spaniards. William Ashley was sent to Scotland in July to deal with this alarming situation, and in August he made offers to James because of the danger of revolt in the country when the Spaniards should arrive 'in the narrow seas'. An English duchy was spoken of, a yearly pension of £5,000 and the maintenance of a bodyguard of fifty gentlemen about him. This was more than Ashley had been instructed to do, but he felt that the danger was great. James was delighted, but he was to feel less delighted when, as soon as the Armada had been defeated, the offer was withdrawn.

Carleill was involved in these negotiations, for we possess a very damaged document dated October 13th, 1588,[10] a letter from William Ashley to Walsingham mentioning some letters he had received from him, which had been thankfully taken by the King. These letters had been carried to Scotland by Christopher Carleill.

From Scotland he could cross easily to Ulster—he still had his own ships—and that was what he did when the negotiations were over.

The men who held the office of Seneschal of Clandeboye were regularly used to watch the situation in Scotland. As late as 1593, after Carleill's death, Captain Dawtry was to write that the 'continuance of that office and officer is of no small importance for the hinderance of the invasion of the Scots and to keep spyalls [*sic*] both in Scotland and Ulster, to learn their secret combinations to cross their purposes before their perfection . . .'.[11] These 'spyalls', he was to write later, were paid at his own expense and he had never charged the Queen a penny during the time he had been Seneschal.

Dawtry had resigned in 1587 in favour of Carleill. Perrot had sent Dawtry to Scotland in 1584 to find out what part James had played in the Scottish invasion of Ulster, and while there he had nearly been assassinated.

Now these hazards had been passed to Carleill.

The Irish scene was quieter since Carleill had fought in Ulster in 1584. True, there was endless bickering between the seven sons of Shane O'Neill and Turloch Lynneach. Turloch also had a blood feud with Hugh O'Neill, Earl of Tyrone. It was not possible that these two men should live in peace together, the Earl reared in the Court of Elizabeth, sophisticated, politic, ostensibly a friend of England, but in reality full of hatred cunningly hid, and Turloch Lynneach, brutal, drunk, aggressive and growing old. His sight was failing him; he had had incisions made in his head to help his sight and these had increased his violence.

Perrot had divided Ulster into three counties and four seigneuries. Some governors of forts and castles had authority to compose differences between inferior subjects; cities and towns had subordinate magistrates. But the partitioning of the whole of Ireland into counties, which he had wished, was not to take place for the next twenty years.

The Scots were well established in the north, ostensibly as loyal subjects of the Queen, holding their own land from her. Sorley Boy was Constable of Dunluce Castle, keeping it with the help of one of the Queen's officers. In return he was to send fifty beeves yearly to Carrickfergus Castle, and it would be Carleill's duty to receive them for the Queen. Sorley Boy now held the MacQuillan territory extending from Boyne to Bann, his nephew holding the coast between Larne and Ballycastle. The English declared that Ulster, left alone by marauding Scots, showed a better disposition than the lands in the south towards peace, civil government and the reformation of religion. They did not as yet realize that in the Earl of Tyrone they had as dangerous an enemy as anyone they had yet known; that rebellion lay, as yet, round the corner.

In Dublin the opposition against Perrot was, if possible, stronger than it had been in 1585. He had handled the Council too roughly. Adam Loftus, Archbishop of St. Patrick's in Dublin, was the archenemy. He resented Perrot's schemes to transform his Cathedral into a University, and this cause grew larger and larger, while plots began to flourish, forgeries of letters were made, and vicious men exploited the explosive situation. Loftus's son was married to Sir Nicholas Bagenal's daughter, Bagenal the old man whom Perrot had knocked down in one of his rages and who now asked the Queen to draw him out of Perrot's hands because of his years.[12] Sir Richard Bingham, Governor of Connaught, quarrelled with Perrot too, over the rebellion of the Burkes in Connaught. The letters from the Council to the Queen in England grew more and more extreme.

So when Carleill arrived in Ireland in 1587 he found the Irish and the Scots in Ulster easier to live with than the English in Dublin. He must gladly have accepted the missions which his stepfather provided for him, returning only sometimes to this quarrelsome Dublin society.

Perrot's days in Ireland were numbered. A year after Carleill's appointment as Seneschal of Clandeboye the Queen received a letter written reputedly by Turloch Lynneach condemning the Deputy. Turloch angrily denied it. But Perrot could bear no more; in April 1588 he wrote to the Queen begging for his recall because he could please and pacify Her Majesty's Irish subjects better than her English ones.[13]

At last the Queen gave him leave to go. He would return to his

Castle of Carew in Pembrokeshire and perhaps cure himself of the stone and of the gout. But before he left he called together all the chiefs whom he feared might deal with Spain and demanded that they give pledges for their fidelity. As he went to his ship on the quay the Irish accompanied him, weeping, and old Turloch Lynneach watched him embark while tears rolled down his cheeks.[14] Perrot from the deck of his ship must have seen the unwieldy shape slowly growing smaller till it faded away altogether.

In June 1588 Sir William Fitzwilliam arrived in Dublin and received the sword as the new Lord Deputy. No one could love him, for he was a man of steely character, cold and careful, lacking Perrot's rages and his charms. Perrot's mercurial nature, his violence even, appealed to the Irish; sometimes too he loved them. The choice of Fitzwilliam as Deputy showed how little the Queen understood her Irish subjects. She had thought Fitzwilliam to be a safe choice. Alas, both the English and the Irish were to dislike him, and like Perrot he was to lose his reputation in that terrible country.

As soon as he arrived he wrote to Walsingham that he was now settling Captain Carleill at Carrickfergus,[15] and indeed Carleill wrote to Walsingham on his pinnace on the way there, thanking him for having spoken to the Deputy and asking him to acknowledge the kindness done to him.[16]

And now his life at Carrickfergus was regularized, for at the end of August he was writing again to his stepfather, 'As soon as I can get a little money to bear my charges, I mean, God willing, to fetch my wife.'

This was the first time he had mentioned a wife to Walsingham, indeed the first time his existence had provided enough stability for marriage. She was called Mary, and she had neither money nor position; she had no coat-of-arms to quarter with her husband's when he applied to the College of Heralds in 1593, and he was as poor after his marriage to her as he had been before. But she could write a good letter, and a few years later she was to write to the great Lord Burghley himself, begging for help for her little family.* She must have been a woman of character.

Carleill, had he wished, could have made a strategic marriage. A prosperous widow would not have scorned the stepson of the

* See page 174.

Secretary of State and the cousin of George Barne, Lord Mayor of London. Carleill could have regained some of the money he had lost in the service of the Prince of Orange, and would not have forfeited the respect of his contemporaries by such an action. But he preferred to marry for love. And this is not surprising when one remembers his entanglement with the beautiful Antwerp seamstress five years before.

In Carleill's letter to his stepfather from Carrickfergus, he wrote, 'The people are glad to see me because of the acquaintance they had of me'; after he had been one year among them, he continued, he hoped to bring them to a better pass; there had been sinister practices over the conveyance of the governorship to him, and some there were who would not willingly give up those practices.

Carleill's ship slipped quietly into the curved harbour of Carrickfergus and lay against the wall with its flight of stone steps leading up from the sea. In the evening light the Norman Castle with its great square keep was soft and brown, the colour of a moth, and on the quay the cobble-stones were laid in a precise pattern, like an Oriental carpet. At one end was the ducking stool, for the use of common scolds. Carleill knew the Governor of the Castle, Egerton, a lawless fellow but a good soldier, who guarded it with twenty men. Going into the Castle with him he climbed to the Great Chamber in the Keep, an enormous whitewashed room with walls a yard deep and spanned by a huge masonry arch. Through windows cut in those white walls, he could look out on the grey sea and the hills beyond.

Winding downwards again he went out and so through the Old Gatehouse to his own Palace. In it were 'the fairest and largest rooms for sewage and brewing as in this land, beside sundry good lodgings'.[17] There were artificers installed here, brewers, bakers and labourers, and a ward of twenty soldiers. There were also a strong-house and mill to grind corn. The Palace was set at one corner of the town wall, where the water gently lapped the old stones. The Scots 'desired its downfall more than that of any other town or castle in Ulster'.

Thus had written the Lord Deputy of 1580, adding that because the country people were armed, no officer in Ireland was called out more often or more dangerously into the field than the Governor of Knockfergus.

The Palace or Storehouse where Carleill lived had been a Franciscan friary, suppressed during the Reformation.[18] When the Grey Friars had left they had put a curse on the building, condemning it always to be an abode of thieves. And so the country people, deeply superstitious, must have shifted the monks' curse on to the occupying English.

They were offended, too, to see the English stores lying in the church upon the tombs of O'Neill and de Lacy—de Lacys had been the first Norman governors of the Castle. Some miles away on Lough Neagh stood the castle that Shane O'Neill had built himself, and it was called 'Hatred of Englishmen'. The country people were armed; despite Carleill's confidence he had a stiff task before him.

The English were doing their best to plant and to trade. There were 'rotten and ruinous houses and cottages' in the town, but later during Carleill's time, stone and lime houses were to be built, some with mighty walls like those of the Castle. They were occupied by the merchants, by the Mayor and the Town Council. The merchants had flourishing guilds, and in 1593 the numbers were to be restricted to seven. Gascony wine came from France in sailing ships and was sold in Knockfergus for a few skins the hogshead. Markets were apt to be lawless assemblies, and the country people visited the town with reluctance. Carleill was to issue a Proclamation about the holding of markets, designed to strengthen confidence in his rule.

'Whereas by reason of the great wars in the north-east parts of Ulster',[19] it ran, 'the commonweal of Carrickfergus, as of the country near about, hath in a manner been quite defaced and overthrown, this country being so despoiled. . . .' The people were now replanting, the Proclamation continued, but they had been so long without civil government that they were ignorant of established markets; the poor husbandmen and followers and undertenants of the lords and chiefs of the country had been molested and crushed for the debts of their lords, and were in great fear that they would be badly treated if they went to market; anyone coming there between Friday noon and Saturday night should be protected and defended from any kind of debt owing to them or the lords under whom they were living.

This was a bold declaration to make; Carleill and Egerton between them commanded only forty men. That big-mouthed Dawtry had sworn that during his tenancy of the Castle he had kept off a thousand Scots with eight men alone.[20] That may well have been true, but he was defending the fortress only, and Carleill had to defend the country people of Ulster from each other.

He was well qualified to handle the Irish peasant, for he had handled Sorley Boy and Donald Gorme with tact in 1584.*

The peasants would come into the little town clad in their filthy saffron shirts, hair tousled over their eyes, always ready to sing, dance, clown, play cards or dice.[21] They lived very poorly, eating butter mixed with oatmeal, while oatmeal was also used mixed with cow's blood to make a jelly-like substance. They drank much milk and made bonnaclabbe, a form of sour milk. Wild flesh they enjoyed when they had conquered their laziness enough to go hunting; they ate wild herbs, watercress and shamrock. Usquebaugh was their great delight, an Irish whiskey containing raisins and fennel seed, very hot, which was much appreciated by the garrison at Knockfergus. It was drunk too in the great halls of the chieftains, the company sinking into a delicious stupor over the fire while the bards poured forth songs telling of the great deeds of their ancestors, mixed with imprecations against the English.

With all their rough ways went a certain formality of behaviour, a set of rules inherited from a civilization which had disappeared. These Irishmen were its descendants in time, carrying with them still a little of its glory. The illuminated manuscripts of dead monks were yet to be seen, the ruined monasteries now open to the winds, the Runic crosses delicately carved, the round towers, the scarred churches where jackdaws cawed and dropped their sticks, moss and creeping ivy the green enemy. These were the legacy of a highly organized society, now gone.

The sixteenth-century bards or poets were still held in honour, because they were a link with this glorious past. They were patronized by the great lords of Ulster, who enjoyed their flattery and their tributes to dead heroes. But now their music and poetry had become stereotyped, held rigidly in a style that had once served its purpose as a cup to contain a living literature. Now only the form remained, rigid, metrical, heavy with archaic language, an impediment rather than a support. For there was small inspiration to uphold.

* See pages 96–7, 102.

The profession of 'brehon', or lawyer, had also descended from this past. But now the legal profession formed part of a caste system which was unbreakable. Legal knowledge was handed from father to son, by word of mouth, unchanged and unchangeable. There on the open hillside, at the assemblies or 'tuaths', the 'brehon' laid down the law, while his audience listened reverently and paid the tribute demanded of it.

Medicine, too, was held in the grasp of certain families, the recipes passing from father to son; prayers and incantations based on twelfth-century texts were used, herbs too. Nothing written down, nothing new attempted. Their reverence for the past kept the Irish of the sixteenth century in strait-jackets.

The system of 'fostering' was peculiar to them. A rich woman would not nurse her own children, though it appears that Nature had endowed her all too lavishly for that purpose. No, she would farm out her own children to a neighbouring sept and herself nurse the children of that sept. The O'Cahans were the 'fosterers' of the O'Neills, and between foster-brothers there was greater love than between blood brothers.

The weakening of the family tie is understandable when one realizes how weak was marriage itself. It was no shame to beget a bastard, and the father gave the christening feast for his illegitimate son. Some women had a different father for each child. The custom of 'tanistry'* finds a natural part in this way of life, since the tie between father and son was shifting and ill-defined.

The English could not approve of these ways, nor of the embarrassing habit of Irish men and women of discarding their mantles in the house and of walking naked. The English clung to their great ruffs and doublets and felt that they came from a superior race.

There was a strict caste system among the fighting men who surrounded a chieftain; first in order came the gallowglass, either hereditary or the more recent hirelings from Scotland, then the kerns, and lowest of all the foot soldiers or 'daltins' who served the horsemen. The poet Spenser wrote of them, 'they steal, they are cruel and bloody, full of revenge, delighting in deadly executions, licentious, swearers and blasphemers, common ravishers of women and murderers of children, very valiant and hardy, great endurers of cold, labour, hunger and all hardness . . . very present in perils,

* See page 91.

great scorners of death'. Spenser handed out praise and blame with a certain generosity; the result is a picture of living men and women so extraordinary that it could hardly have been invented.

These lazy, dirty people who lay on the hillsides delousing themselves could fight terribly in battle, darting in on their little horses like a company of elves, then away, only to attack once more with greater fury.

To govern them, one must know them. Perhaps Carleill's affability helped, a trait always appreciated by the Irish. With a garrison of twenty men behind him he was to rule over miles and miles of land in Ulster. He could govern by diplomacy, and in no other way.

'God breathed and they were scattered', was inscribed on a medal made in England to commemorate the victory over the Armada. The Spaniards had been so sure of God. He would give them victory over the heretics. He had not done so. With peculiar relish the English now claimed Him for their side; on September 15th the Lord Deputy Fitzwilliam was to write to Burghley that God had fought by shipwrecks, savages and famine for Her Majesty against those proud Spaniards.[22]

The storms of God rolled up from the south and the south-west and mighty waves lashed the Irish coast. Not only were there tempests for the Spaniards to endure, but strange periods of fog and rain, ghostly interludes between outbursts of violence. On September 5th, wrote Sir Richard Bingham in Connaught, 'there blew a most cruel storm the like whereof hath not been had a long time'.[23] The Spanish purser, Pedro Coco Caldaron, on his return to Spain, said that from August 24th to September 4th he had sailed, without knowing whither, through constant storms, fogs and squalls;[24] his ship must have been somewhere between Scotland and Cape Clear in Ireland.

The men of the Armada were very sick with typhus, they were weak with starvation and lack of water, there was quarrelling and dissension among the officers, the maps of Ireland they used were ridiculously incorrect. The ships' masts were the longest the English had ever seen—the Deputy Fitzwilliam was himself to record the fact—and this made the vessels top-heavy. Everything worked against the Armada; the Spaniards had nothing but their courage to sustain them.

Ship after ship drove to leeward and fell on the reefs, or rolled helplessly in the enormous swell. The Irish were on shore waiting for the survivors. There was treasure aboard, men said, to pay the troops which should have landed in England, and Spaniards swimming ashore with golden chains round their necks and gold coins sewn into their doublets, while many wore jewels. The drowning men hoped that a common faith would bind them to the Irish, and struggled ashore expecting to find friends. Instead they met enemies; they were battered with axes, cut with knives, stripped of their clothes, robbed and left naked on the beaches to die of cold and loss of blood. Fenton was to write: 'God be thanked the people of these remote parts stirred not, but made to the sea coast being, as it seemed, more greedy of spoil than apt to hearken to other things.'*[25]

Then the English garrisons arrived and the destruction became more orderly, though none the less terrible. Some survivors who had offered resistance were induced to give up their arms, and were marched towards Dublin as prisoners of war. Then without warning, three hundred were driven together in one place and massacred; one hundred and fifty escaped, and with them, de Nova, whose narrative we have.[26] Slaughter on a bigger scale took place later in Connaught. On September 17th the Governor and Council issued a Proclamation that all persons keeping Spaniards should bring them to the Justices and Sheriffs within four hours, upon pain of death.[27] Prisoners were taken to Galway town and were put to the sword, nobles excepted. Then their captors went into O'Flaherty's country to execute more; in Sligo the same Proclamation was published and more prisoners slaughtered and ordnance reported. All this Sir Richard Bingham recorded with precision. He had indeed acted rapidly and with strength, and who can gainsay the need? For he wrote that fifteen or sixteen ships had been cast away on the coast of Connaught and that six or seven thousand Spaniards must have perished.[28]

The Irish chieftains behaved on the whole with chivalry and kindness. The Spaniards were no enemies of theirs, they shared one faith, and both nations hated the English. For weeks, for months, they hid the survivors in their castles, clothed them and let them hear mass. Sir Brian O'Rourke, a great enemy of England, living in

* See note 25 in References for Chapter 7, page 191.

Breffni, in the north-east of Connaught, passed them on to O'Cahan, near Coleraine, and thence to Sorley Boy in Dunluce Castle. An escape route to Scotland was set up, using Scottish boatmen for the task.

In de Nova's story we have a brilliant picture of Sorley Boy, receiving orders from the Lord Deputy not to ship any more Spaniards on pain of death, and to surrender those he had. With tears in his eyes he returned from speaking with the messenger and told the Spaniards in his castle of the reply he had made, that he would rather lose his life and goods and those of his wife and children than barter Christian blood.

Not all the chiefs were as staunch as Sorley Boy. The Earl of Tyrone was purported to have reproved O'Donnell with great bitterness for his unkindness to the Spaniard, saying that 'he and his posterity may go seek them a dwelling in another country for they have betrayed the Spaniard who were their best friends and their only refuge in all extremity';[29] O'Cahan, too, who at first had helped them, later obeyed the Deputy and turned them away.

De Nova recorded the extremes of kindness and of brutality he had received from the 'savage people'. And it was certainly true that once a man had been stripped of all his possessions, the countrymen—but more especially the women—could afford to do him a kindness. The Lord Deputy wrote that 'the country people, having stripped the Spaniards of their rich apparel and robbed them of a great store of money, chains and jewels, turned them loose and permitted them to range up and down the country, so now they have linked themselves with those who have lately landed'.[30]

The confusion and terror that overwhelmed the English in Ireland was very great in those early days of the wrecks, when horsemen were sent flying from sheriffs and governors of provinces to the Lord Deputy in Dublin. No one knew if these ships were the spearhead of an invasion to be followed by help from Spain, or if they were the remnants of the Armada that the 'Queen's Majesty had broken';[31] so wrote the Lord Deputy on September 28th. For the defeat of the Armada was not yet an acknowledged fact; in Europe it was not to be accepted for weeks, so incomprehensible, so impossible was the news.

Both the Deputy in Ireland and the Privy Council in England received alarming letters from the men on the spot. On September

10th Sir John Popham wrote from Cork[32] that twenty-three ships
had been sighted or wrecked on the south coast; on September 18th
Sir George Carew wrote to Walsingham from Dublin[33] that
sixteen sail, many of them great ships, had been wrecked between
Lough Foyle in Ulster and the Dingle in Kerry, and three thousand
Spaniards killed and two thousand drowned. Fenton, on October
7th, went into alarming details;[34] two thousand Spaniards were
holding a castle in MacSwyne Doe's country; it was crammed full
of treasure and ammunition, and O'Neill was helping them; off the
coast lay a Spanish ship containing four hundred men and the
Duke of Medina Sidonia himself, commander of the Armada;
Sligo was surrounded by 'unsound and hollow Irish', and was only
twenty miles from the Spanish fort. He ended with these words,
'Your Honour should write to England for some ships to be sent
to lie upon the coast and also some good strength of soldiers, for it
is not unlike but Spain will nourish the action and contravene it
with new supplies of force.'

The Deputy had already approached Elizabeth for men, money
and munitions, writing on September 12th, 'we look rather to be
over-run by the Spaniards than otherwise'.[35] And on September
16th he was begging Walsingham to hasten five or six ships from
Bristol to their help,[36] while Bingham was pleading for footbands
to take action against O'Rourke, his deadly enemy, and for lasts of
powder.

The news flew from one place to the next, sometimes, of course,
distorted. A messenger would take four days to reach Dublin from
the north. Before the Deputy had sent his report to England, an
order, quite impossible to fulfil, might arrive from the Privy
Council. On September 18th it instructed the harassed Lord
Deputy to recover the ordnance from the wrecked ships and to
keep the prisoners in a convenient place 'that they may be forth-
coming when their Lordships require them'. Meanwhile they were
to be examined and their names sent up.[37]

The Lord Deputy, with the letters of his governors in his hand
telling of the slaughter already done and of the numbers of
Spaniards still at large, must have wondered how he could enforce
the Privy Council's instructions. On September 22nd he tried to
rectify the situation by giving a commission to Sir Thomas Norris,
Sir George Boucher and Sir George Carew, to take all hulks, stores
and treasure, and to apprehend and execute all Spaniards found

there, of whatever quality soever; torture might be used in prose-cuting the enquiry.[38] A Proclamation was issued that every man, within four days, should bring in any Spaniard he held, on pain of death.[39]

Torture was an established practice of the time in questioning civil prisoners, but official permission had to be given before it was used. On the same day Sir George Carew wrote to Walsingham, 'There is no rebellion in the whole realm, so much terror prevails.'[40]

The seriousness of the situation was understood in England, for on September 14th the Queen told Sir Richard Grenville to make stay of shipping to transport soldiers to Waterford, seven hundred men in all.[41] Sir Walter Raleigh was also alerted,[42] while the Lord Lieutenants of certain counties were told to put men in readiness to leave for Ireland within an hour's warning.[43]

Though Fitzwilliam shortly afterwards stated that he could do the work alone without any help from England,[44] nevertheless as late as October 29th the Privy Council told him they were sending two thousand men to Ireland,[45] and that five hundred must be added to them by the Irish chieftains in the north. Fitzwilliam was told not to move against the Spaniards till this help should arrives.

But meanwhile on November 4th he had set out on his journey into the north, ostensibly to attack O'Rourke and MacQuillan. To go there at such a moment was a wise move, but the vipers at Dublin twisted his journey into a practical expedition to seize treasure for himself from the wrecks. The Queen, this time, stood by her Lord Deputy and applauded his action.

The journey lasted for seven weeks. In his letter he described how he had ridden along Streedagh Strand where one thousand two hundred corpses had recently lain,[46] and he had seen the timber of the wrecks strewn everywhere, 'more than would have built five of the greatest ships that ever I saw . . .'. All the countrymen with their cattle had fled into the mountains, O'Rourke among them.

He brought home with him twenty sick prisoners of war, for the rest were dispersed over Ulster, about four or five hundred, he was to write, in poor estate and succoured by the country people. He reported that he had sent orders that the Provost-Marshal with six horsemen was to ride up and down continually through the English Pale to execute as many Spaniards as they should meet. The Chancellor and Council in Dublin were to issue a Proclamation that no man should relieve or keep any of them on pain of death.

But before this Proclamation, wrote the Deputy, 'divers had been executed in this province'.

He referred to messages which de Levya, while leader of the survivors holding the castle, was said to have written to Spain begging for reinforcements. The Deputy ended his letter, 'If there had been but a thousand men with victuals and powder, of both of which he was unfurnished, sent him out of Spain, to have assisted him and his two thousand six hundred men which now are all rid hence, I see not how but that before I could have given your Lordships advertisement, Her Majesty might have been dispossessed of Ireland.'

The Privy Council congratulated the Lord Deputy on his journey, and he was told to find out the quality of his Spanish prisoners and where they had served in the fleet. Then he would be told what to do with them.[47]

The *Gerona*, packed with survivors from other wrecked ships, set out from the north coast of Ireland in October.[48] She left Dunluce Castle, Sorley Boy's stronghold, the gales now blowing hard, and she came in sight of the Giant's Causeway, a devil's place, fit setting for a tragedy. Its gigantic stepping-stones, its cliffs striped with organ pipes where the wind shrieked, loomed through the flying spray. The *Gerona* struck the Rock of Dunboyes and sank; most of the Spaniards were drowned.

Another ship was sunk off the north coast of Ulster and this happened on September 6th, and her name was the *Balenzana*. Thus wrote Ashley from Scotland to Walsingham,[49] adding that fifty survivors had arrived there. In the Spanish list of Armada ships, there is one called the *Balzana*,[50] a Portuguese galley carrying seventy-two sailors.

These two wrecks were the nearest ones to Carrickfergus, and it is unlikely that many stragglers reached that part of Ulster. There were no reports sent to the Lord Deputy, as far as we know, either from Carleill, Egerton or Henshawe.

But we know that somewhere in Ulster, Carleill came upon the problem of wandering Spanish prisoners. For a curious clash of wills over their treatment blew up between him and the Lord Deputy. We do not learn about it in the State Papers, nor did Carleill write about it to his stepfather. But Petruccio Ubaldino, an Italian historian, in the year 1589, wrote an account of the defeat of the Spanish Armada to give to Sir Francis Drake as a New Year's gift for Sir Christopher Hatton.[51] And he had a great deal to say about Carleill, and some rather unpleasant aspersions to make about Fitzwilliam. Reading them we are amazed at his outspokenness, so soon after the event.

He wrote that Carleill *was an old soldier well known in the Low Countries and Governor of a part of the Irish coast, Ulster, with his companies, and into the hands of this man there fell fourteen Spaniards who had saved themselves from their wrecked ship, and who gave themselves up to him begging that as a soldier he should spare their lives. It seemed to him that he should use military pity, and therefore he received them chivalrously without cruelty or grudging. But having some commission to carry out, he sent them to Sir William Fitzwilliam, the Lord Deputy, writing about their case, paying out money for their expenses and recommending to him that he should honour the promises made to them. But this did not help these poor wretches in the least, for the Lord Deputy was sour of soul and severe—believing it perhaps to the benefit of the Crown and his own honour to act thus—and sent them back to Captain Carleill with orders that he should put them to death in any manner—meaning on the gallows, as was done to other similar survivors by other persons. Nevertheless, Captain Carleill, being a gentleman by nature and an experienced soldier, careful of his honour and not wanting to sully his hands with the blood of those poor people, put everything to the decision of the elements (it not being possible for him to do any more) and relying on the promises of a few Scottish boatmen, he embarked them on a small ship of theirs, which by chance was in those parts, gave them money to get rid of them, sending them to Scotland, for he was a man desirous of diminishing the blame (one must believe) put on his nation in those days on account of some particular person who practised rash and ill-considered cruelty—a thing which he hated, as also did Sir Richard Bingham, he too a soldier and an amiable gentleman who was then Governor of Connaught, another part of that coast.*

It is interesting to hear this mild description of Sir Richard Bingham, he who has left a name for cruelty behind him, of whom it was said in 1596 that no peace could ever be in a land over which he ruled. Fitzwilliam, however, who certainly behaved with no greater ferocity than Bingham during the Armada crisis and with much justification, was chosen for Ubaldino's attack. So lightly does history make or mar reputations.

Carleill had been obeying Fitzwilliam's Proclamation when he sent his prisoners to Dublin. But his recommendation of mercy was not one that a Governor of a province should have made to a Lord Deputy; it smacked of insubordination, even of impudence. Fitzwilliam angrily returned the prisoners, instead of disposing of them himself; Carleill burst into flames—the quick temper was never far away—and flouted the Deputy's orders. He sent the prisoners to Scotland, and we learn that on October 30th ten marks were given by the town of Edinburgh to the support of fourteen newly arrived Spaniards 'with the other two that remained of the rest behind'.[52] Perhaps these were the men whom Carleill had saved.

It is unlikely that Carleill was any more squeamish about the shedding of blood than any contemporary soldier. But he was, as Ubaldino wrote, very correct in his behaviour and careful of his military honour, and he had given his word. Two years later, Fitzwilliam, now reconciled to Carleill, was to describe him as a 'religious gentleman'.[53]

During this crisis, while his decision was being made, memories of the Prince of Orange must have come to him, and of the garrison of Middelburg being escorted to their boats after the town had fallen. And there his mind must have rested awhile . . . for the Prince was dead now, shot by an assassin's bullet, four years ago.

Three small pieces of ordnance from the *Gerona* lay beneath the sea near Dunluce Castle.

During the summer of 1589 the Lord Deputy instructed Sir George Carew to obtain great boats and casks at Carrickfergus,[54] and then with the two and a half bands from the Castle and Mr. Warren's twenty horsemen from the Ards, together with cables from his own office, he was to go north to redeem the sunk ordnance.

There had been a rumour that two Spaniards and a Scottish captain had been sent by the King of Scotland with letters to Angus Macdonnell and Sorley Boy;[55] they had weighed the ordnance and had reported a great store of gold and silver there. Another rumour had it that the treasure had already been recovered. But it was a foolish rumour, for Sir George Carew with all his great boats and casks could not perform the feat.

8

A SIXTEENTH-CENTURY
SYMPOSIUM

PROBABLY DURING the spring of 1587, when Carleill first
arrived in Ireland to take up his appointment, an event took
place which sheds a different light on the men who lived within
the Pale. Their lives were not only occupied with violence and
corruption, the clash of arms is not all that we hear. A small
gathering of earnest philosophers took place on three successive
days near Dublin, men who accepted the need to seek by reason
for a better life which would lead to the ultimate good. A curtain
has been drawn aside, showing us a scene, very different from the
sordid world conjured up by the State Papers, in which Carleill
seemed totally engulfed. Without this curious quirk of history he
would have remained, for us, a man of action only, and our knowledge of him would have been quite limited.

Ludovick Bryskett was an Italian by birth who had been brought
up in England and as a young man had entered the household of
Sir Henry Sydney at Penshurst. He had been one of two friends who
had accompanied the young Sir Philip Sydney when he travelled on
the Continent in 1572. When Sir Henry Sydney had been sent to
Ireland as Lord Deputy, Bryskett had gone with him as Clerk to the
Privy Council in Dublin. He had been made General Controller of
the Customs on wines in Irish ports, finally Clerk to the Council in
Munster. While in Munster he made a friend of the poet Edmund
Spenser, who seems to have taught him Greek; again a sign that the
lives of these public servants had time to contain certain civilities.

Bryskett had the makings of a scholar in him and he succumbed
to the temptation of leaving Dublin and of retiring into the country
with his books, where he could practise the arts of husbandry. He
built himself a cottage near Dublin, but not too far from the town
for his friends to visit him. And from time to time he broke the

luxury of his solitude and replenished his purse by taking some temporary service under the Queen in Dublin.

In his cottage, in the quiet of the countryside when the valleys were blue in the morning and the sea sometimes like glass, sometimes broken with ripples like the scales of a trout, he would fall into a pleasing melancholy, while he reflected on the teachings of Plato and Aristotle. And when the fine rain came and the hills were blurred with clouds, and his pastures were as green as emeralds, he would sit at his table reading and writing, while his retainers served his frugal meals.

His physician had just prescribed for him a course of light physic, after chiding him as usual for the hermit's life he was leading. It was a lovely spring morning, and a group of his friends, hearing that he was resting, decided to walk from the city to visit him. There was Dr. Long, the Primate of Armagh, Sir Robert Dillon, Mr. Dormer, the Queen's Solicitor, Captain Thomas Norris, Captain Newnham St. Leger, Captain Nicholas Dawtry and Captain Christopher Carleill. Not a group of men possessed of outstanding intellect, but with them went the poet Edmund Spenser, and because of him the words spoken those three days have been recorded.

Spenser had come to Ireland in 1580 as Secretary to Lord Grey of Wilton, the Lord Deputy, and in 1581 had been appointed Clerk to the Irish Court of Chancery, a post that he was to hold for seven years. He had already written his *Faerie Queene*, which had impressed Sir Walter Raleigh so much that he had brought the writer to England to present him to Elizabeth. Now men in Dublin were talking of it and asking for it to be read to them.

Of the small company of friends who visited Bryskett, Sir Thomas Norris was the younger brother of Sir John Norris, the General, and he had come to Ireland in 1582 as Captain of a troop of horse in Munster. His military companion, Nicholas Dawtry, was an eccentric figure, very fat, boastful and foul-mouthed, but no mean performer either with sword or with pen. He is said to have been the original of Shakespeare's Sir John Falstaff in *Henry V*, the dishonest captain who filled his company with scarecrow soldiers, replacing the good recruits who had bought their way out of the service by bribing him; the muster-rolls remained the same nevertheless, showing a list of names of men not there.[*1]

* See page 50.

This spring morning the friends found their host in melancholy humour. He explained to them that he had retired from the world in order to read books that would increase his knowledge of the duties of a Christian, and so had turned to history and moral philosophy, hoping to understand the character and behaviour of man.

The Primate intervened here, wishing that moral philosophy be taught to the young, so that men's passions should be brought under the rule of reason, and their journey to Heaven be eased. He asked Spenser to discourse on the subject.

Spenser excused himself; he had already written the *Faerie Queene*, he said, 'to represent the moral virtues, assigning to every virtue a knight to be the patron and defender of the same'. Adroitly he shifted the exposition on to his host; would Bryskett not expound Giraldi's *Dialogue of Civil Life*, a work which he had been translating, and thus provide them with the matter for discussion they needed?

The company not unnaturally showed 'an extreme longing after the Faerie Queen, whereof some parcels had been by some of them seen'. Where better than in this green and gentle pasture to listen to the flow of Spenser's verse, like a stream gliding from sunshine into shadow and into sunshine again?

But Spenser persisted in handing over to Bryskett, and it was finally decided that the company should meet on three successive days at his cottage, setting aside one day to each of Giraldi's dialogues. The discussion would turn on the manner of life to be undertaken by those wishing to attain the best end in life. What was accounted to be the best end would also be resolved. The conversation would not follow Plato nor Aristotle absolutely, but gather from both and from others too.

The company spoke of the upbringing of children, for this was the first phase to be discussed. The talk wandered, as talk will, Bryskett finally contending that the end of man in this life was happiness or felicity, this felicity being divided into civil felicity and contemplative felicity.

Civil felicity, said he, was to be practised by men in the world and was an inward reward for moral virtues, where fortune could challenge no part or interest at all. But this felicity could not be experienced by a child, for he was unable to practise reason; there were also men devoid of reason, and these two groups could not be described properly as being happy.

Contemplative felicity was likewise an operation of the mind but of that part called intellective; the parts of the mind devoid of reason had no intermeddling with its processes. 'There follows', said Bryskett, 'that a man seeking felicity should abandon earthly cares and bend his studies to heavenly things.'

He continued to make these somewhat limited definitions of mental states, so beloved of sixteenth-century conversationalists, till Carleill summed up in a practical manner. He asked to hear Bryskett's prescription for the direction of man's studies throughout his life, so that he might attain to the civil and contemplative felicities.

Bryskett replied by speaking of a child's education where the foundation of the felicities was laid. Plato had said that magistrates should bring up children.

The Primate's recipe was that children should not be indulged. At that Carleill launched into a long oration on the education of young children, and how parents should be urged to pay more attention to this phase of life.

The conversation wandered—and we will not follow it—and at last the friends found themselves discussing the fighting of duels; Bryskett denounced it as a barbarous habit, worse now than it had been of old.

Carleill, the soldier, replied somewhat dryly that if combat was lawful in case of injury to the Prince, meaning war, the same reason should make it lawful also for other causes. But he was reproved and told that the injuries of private men could never be as bad as those against the Prince, which offended the Public State.

On this note the debate closed and the friends returned to the city.

The following day they came again, eager for debate. As soon as they arrived, Bryskett led them up the hill, along a pleasant green way planted with young ashes from whence they could enjoy the view of city and sea. They stood admiring their host's little world till one of the servants came to tell them that dinner was served.

Bryskett apologized for his frugal philosopher's meal, but Sir Robert Dillon urged that they should eat a short dinner and feed their bodies temperately so that their minds might remain sharp for other dainties.

Captain Dawtry was not one to go all the way with this, and cried sharply, 'I hope a philosophic dinner may be furnished with wine, otherwise I will tell you plainly I had rather be at a camping dinner than at yours.'

With some laughter a glass of wine was put into his fat hand. He held it reflectively to the window, admiring its colour, then raised it to his nose, and 'seemed to take comfort in the odour of the same'.

And so at the meal they spoke not of civil felicity, but of the felicity derived from drinking wine. Finally, fruit was brought and set on the table.

Ludovick opened the discussion by referring to yesterday's talk; childhood, then, had been likened to that part of the soul which gave life and was called vegetative. So must youth now be likened to that part which gave sense and feeling and was called sensitive. He spoke of the Tonbridge School where he had been educated, saying that by the age of fourteen years a child should have learned grammar, logic, rhetoric, music, poetry, drawing and perspective, be skilled with weapons and ready to run, to leap and to wrestle.

After a long discussion they agreed that moral philosophy was a valuable study, for it curbed the rebellious nature and was a great support and 'corrective for young men who were full of passion', and 'doing everything too much'.

Carleill said that if virtue and the sciences were to be learned— sciences and had not mentioned the speculative sciences in which young men should also be instructed.

He was told that the Virtues were divided into Speculative and Practic, or into Intellective and Active. There were five speculative habits, Understanding, Science, Wisdom, Art and Prudence.

Carleill said that if Virtue and the Sciences were to be learned— and he had heard doubt made of the manner of learning them—did Giraldi say anything on the subject, and especially 'if our learning be but a rememorating of things which we knew formerly, or else a new learning'?

Bryskett replied in a long discourse, pointing out that Aristotle thought the soul was void of knowledge and of science and could be likened to a piece of fine white paper, and that it had need of sense, vegetative and sensitive. Souls died with the body because they were connected with it, but the intellective soul survived. Plato, however, believed that the soul had knowledge of all things, that by rememorating she attained the knowledge of sciences, and this he had shown in the teachings of Socrates.

Captain Norris asked why Plato said the soul had knowledge of things before it came into the body. 'Because', answered Bryskett, 'before a soul comes into the womb it was with God', and he continued to dispute about the philosophies of Aristotle and Plato.

He had much to say about the music of the ancients in education. The ancient wise men, he said, recommended gymnastics and music to curb the violences of youth. Gymnastics by itself would produce 'fierce and hardy men', music alone, 'too soft minded and effeminate men'; a balance was necessary. He also extolled the study of poetry.

Here Carleill spoke: 'Plato being so learned a man, did not only make small estimate thereof, but banished it expressly from his Commonwealth.'

Bryskett reproved him, saying that Plato had only accused poets who tried to express high concepts that they did not understand, but he had not blamed poets who wrote to the honour of God. He had also condemned poets who ascribed the lowest human vices to the gods.

Spenser, the only poet among them, seems to have contributed nothing to this conversation.

Then Carleill returned to the subject of music, agreeing that the music of their own time 'effeminateth the mind and rather diverteth it from the way of bliss and felicity'. But were there not other disciplines, he asked, in which young men could be instructed so that thereby they might gain felicity?

Bryskett recommended geometry and arithmetic, after the practice of music and gymnastics. The talk then turned to logic and rhetoric. Here they floundered happily while the sun sank slowly behind the hill. Soon the friends rose to go, saying they must reach the city by sunset; next day they meant to discuss their author's third dialogue, on the ethic part of moral philosophy, examining every way a man might travel to attain felicity.

The next morning Bryskett, still a little weak from his physic and not yet dressed, looked out of his window towards the city and saw the company all in a troop coming together 'not as men walking softly to sport, or desirous to refresh themselves with the morning dew and the sweet pleasant air that invited all persons to leave their sluggish nests, but as men earnestly bent to their journey and that they had their heads buried about some matter of greater importance than recreation'. Quickly he rose, pulled his clothes on lest they tax him with drowsiness, and hastened out of doors to meet them.

The Primate said laughingly that they came to this poor farmer 'not to lay a cess upon him, but to coin upon him and eat him out of house and home'. So laughing together they strolled up the hill, praising the quiet state of Ireland now 'with the rebels rooted out'.

Today they spoke of the age succeeding childhood and youth, and how Roman consuls had held high office at the age of twenty-three years. The company decided that the age of twenty-five years was the best time for a man to enter public life and to control his estates, having left the follies of youth behind him. Dawtry, always ready for an argument, said that he had known men of some judgement at eighteen years old. They mused on that paragon, Sir Philip Sydney, who at the age of twenty-two had been employed by the Queen on an embassy to the Emperor. Both Spenser and Bryskett spoke of him warmly.

Bryskett said that the study of philosophy enabled a man to know himself, but he should make a trial of himself before he began the discipline, for learning put into a vicious mind could be dangerous. The philosopher gazed on God, and as he gazed, a desire for the good, beautiful and honest rose in him.

Carleill broke in then with his accustomed realism; 'You have shown the importance of knowing yourself,' he said, 'but I make a doubt whether all this you have laid before us be in our power or no', and then he went on to say that he had often wondered if it was really in a man's power to give himself to a commendable life, for were there not so many perverse men who preferred vice to virtue? 'And this maketh me often time to think that the doing of good or evil is not in our power, but that either destiny rules and masters all things or the stars with their influence doth draw us to be what we are.'

It appeared now that the matter was 'turning somewhat on religion', and a safe conduct was asked of the Lord Primate and given with a good will, for as they were discussing moral philosophy, 'we will', said he, 'put divinity to silence, so long as Giraldi wrote nothing repugnant to truth'.

Bryskett then expounded Giraldi's views on destiny; he believed in free will, not in an absolute destiny, for if destiny was all-powerful what need was there of the reasoning powers and powers of choice that had been given to man? The stars had power over his body, but not over his mind, for minds were made of a simple and spiritual substance; man must oppose himself against his destiny and fight with golden weapons, the Virtues. He concluded that man's will and election were free and it was in his power to follow vice or virtue, for neither destiny nor the Divine Providence of God imposed any necessity on him.

The Primate said that he disliked nothing in the discourse according to moral reason, but as a Christian he wished to know Giraldi's view on God's predestination; was it necessary that what God had determined about us should come to pass?

Bryskett explained Giraldi's view; predestination was an ordinance or disposition of things in the mind of God from the beginning, of what should be done by us in this life through Grace. But predestination did not tie man's free will, both went together; man's good deeds were pleasing in the eyes of God and his evil deeds offensive to Him, and both brought their reward or punishment.

Then the Primate began to interpose himself, as a Christian, in this talk on moral philosophy, and the conversation began to turn to some practical questions; for instance, what were the moral values of suicide?

Finally, Carleill said, 'Concerning my demands I am resolved. But since I see our doings proceed from election I would gladly know of you what manner of thing it is, for I cannot perceive whether it be a desire or an anger or an opinion, or what I should call it?'

'None of these,' answered Bryskett, 'but rather a voluntary deliberation following a mature and advised counsel, which counsel by Plato was termed a divine thing.'

After some talk it was agreed by most of them that they who followed profit only were the basest of men. 'Not so,' cried Dawtry, the materialist, 'only the rich are honoured and esteemed.'

Mr. Dormer, more objective, protested that as Bryskett had reckoned riches to be of small account among wise men, it would seem that Nature had in vain produced them.

'Exterior goods are useful to those who would lead a contemplative life,' answered Bryskett, 'but they are not the true end or good of man.' He went on to explain that vice made the mind subject to the body, and 'all wicked affections then take their hold, anger, furies, fond loves, and hated ambitions'. Aristotle had written that the judgement of pleasures was to be made at their going, and not at their coming, for they left behind them enormous sadness and repentance; through their sweetness they corrupted the senses and the mind.

Pleasure, continued Bryskett, was not virtue, nor yet man's true good, but it followed virtue even as the shadow followed the body; some people even held that only pleasures arising from virtue were delightful.

Norris asked that if virtue consisted in the mean between two extremes, how was that mean to be found?

'When a man does what he ought to do', replied Bryskett rather illogically, and as no one asked him to define this duty, the talk drifted away to geometry and arithmetic.

Then Bryskett said, 'Man's felicity is attained by virtue, but that virtue is his felicity that saith not mine author.'

Carleill, practical as always, asked, 'Since we are resolved that virtues are but the means to purchase felicity and not felicity itself, we would be glad to hear you declare how many there are, and of what quality.'

There were four principal Virtues appertaining to civil life, replied Bryskett, Fortitude, Temperance, Justice and Prudence, and from these ensued Liberality, Magnificence, Magnanimity, Mansuetude, Desire of Honour, Verity, Affability and Urbanity. And he spoke of each at length, following his author.

'The reward of virtue is friendship', he then said, and went on to extol friendship, saying that concerning civil felicity man should not be alone, especially young men who lacked experience and needed the instruction of others.

'It is a marvel', said Carleill, 'that friends should so easily break the bond of friendship if they were so fast knit as you have said, the cause whereof is worth the knowing.'

He was told that often friendships were false and of appearance only, but men should not turn from seeking true friendship and embrace solitude, for it could not serve the turn of happiness. All the virtues given above, continued Bryskett, could help a man to civil felicity, while vice could induce misery in him.

Heavenly felicity was reached through the contemplation of the most High and Gracious God, and should be the final end of all men's operations; thus said Aristotle. Sayes had found that actions and sciences could not bring a man to fullest perfect happiness, and he therefore applied his mind and understanding to the Divine Essence. Aristotle held that the proper office of the mind, being divine, was to seek to unite itself with its first principle, which was God.

Soon Carleill was asking for a statement on the immortality of the soul, for the knowledge helped the better understanding of contemplative felicity. Did Giraldi give any further light on the subject 'since such good fellows seek to cast so dark a mist before our eyes under the cloak of Aristotle's opinion'? Could Bryskett repeat what he had said yesterday on the subject?

Bryskett replied that he would close up the feast with this last dish, and thereupon plunged into a discussion as to whether the intellective soul was mortal or immortal, and quoting Aristotle, he told them that the intellective soul could understand, which was a spiritual operation, and it followed of her own nature that she was all spirit and therefore immortal.

A distinction was then drawn between the passable and the possible soul, and after much talk, the first was deemed as immortal and the second as mortal. From thence the conversation wandered into intricacies, till Spenser introduced multiplication into the argument, and Bryskett replied by plunging into Aristotle's metaphysics, and Giraldi was swallowed up in a greater name.

Then Spenser asked, 'What does your author mean . . . that there are in us two several souls, the one sensitive and mortal, and the other intellective and divine?'

Bryskett explained that, according to Aristotle, both the passable and the possible understanding were virtues of the intellective soul, which was a human soul and everlasting, not mingled with the body, but severed from it, not drawn from any power of matter, but infused into us from abroad. Once freed from the body she was a pure understanding not needing the body either as an object or a subject. Therefore through contemplation man became divine.

By now the long and languid twilight of the north was stealing into the valley, and shadows lay in the room. Bryskett's talk rose to that happy state of mysticism induced by a study of Plato.

'He that has reached a degree of felicity through contemplation', he said, 'desires to forsake his mortal body. This is the contemplation of death which the philosopher Plato called us to. God then becomes the centre of all perfection, and they wish to return to this heavenly country where they may, among the blessed spirits, enjoy their Maker.'

Then, after a pause, he neatly wound up his Discourse of Civil Felicity. The company rose, and 'giving thanks seemed to rest very well satisfied, as well with the manner as with the matter, at the least so of their courtesy they protested'.

And taking their leave they departed towards the city.

9

'CONSUMED, FALLEN AND DESPERATE'

AFTER 1588 when Carleill was established at Carrickfergus he showed himself a prudent and diligent governor. Writing a report on his country[1] and its conditions he described the Route as once entirely belonging to the MacQuillans, but they now held but a small part of it. Sorley Boy Macdonnell—now dead—'by Her Majesty's sufferance' had held the land lying between the Boyne and the Bann, and his son James now had it. The MacQuillans, who had anciently been the owners of the Route, were now driven into a part of it only. MacQuillan grudged this division and wished to complain about it in England, but Carleill had restrained him. He begged that he might surrender his land to the Queen and so 'have the same granted and confirmed to him from Her Highness by English service upon fee simple'. He would agree to the payment of a yearly rent and reservation of service to the Queen.

James Sorley, counting himself stronger than his father had been because he had an O'Neill for his mother, wanted his land confirmed to him and his heirs by letters patent from the Queen, yielding the same rent and services as had already been imposed on him.

The Glens, originally belonging to the English Bissets, had been claimed by the Macdonnells of Kintyre in Scotland as their inheritance, and the Queen had granted the country to Angus Macdonnell for a yearly rent of sixty beeves.

On the south side of the Route, in country called the Lower or North Clandeboye, Shane McBryan O'Neill, son of Sir Bryan Phelim O'Neill, claimed lordship, though Neill Ogue, son of an older brother Hugh McPhelim, was in reality chief of the country. But a Commission directed to Sir Henry Bagenal and Captain Henshawe had divided the land between them, one-third to Shane McBryan and the other two parts to Neill McHugh. This was countermanded, through some foolish information put forward by one of Carleill's servants, Marmaduke Nealson, 'somewhat too long to be recited'. Sir John Perrot had tried to raise three hundred beeves of yearly rent from North Clandeboye under Shane McBryan, and he said that Shane had agreed. But Carleill wrote, 'I know very well that it hath hereto been far above Shane's ability to perform any such matter, for he hath had enough to do many times to find meat and drink for his own household.' Carleill continued, 'Some good matter might be drawn out of the country if the people, as well the gentlemen as the meaner sort, were once settled in an orderly estate of English tenure which is greatly desired by them. In the doing whereof I will there may be some freeholders established as depending on Her Majesty only, as having nought to do with the Irish lords or their barbarous customs and extortions.'

In South Clandeboye Turloch Lynneach O'Neill kept fifty soldiers instead of paying a yearly rent, but now he wished to surrender and to take a new estate of fee simple from the Queen, paying yearly rent and other services.

In Killaltaghe Cormac O'Neill was chief, and some of his near kinsmen were likewise desirous of being made freeholders, surrendering their present state to Her Majesty and receiving the same again by English tenure.

And so the report goes on, quietly showing the good order that Carleill was bringing to the country. But the lull was only temporary; just round the corner lay the rebellion of the Earl of Tyrone, the leader that Ulster had been waiting for.

This new stability of tenure, did the Irish really want it? An old way of life must die first before a new outlook is adopted, and there is no evidence that the old way of life *was* dying. The Irish did not need peace in order to foster trade, as the English desired it. For the Irish did not deal in money, but in cattle, and the raiding of cattle was in itself war. The Queen's protection might help a man to score off his neighbours, and here it might be of value, for no man could trust his neighbour. But heaven forbid that a deadly peace should ensue, with the bards silent by the peat fires and the long moonlit nights empty of raiding.

The English and the Anglo-Irish in the garrison towns and in the Pale scratched basely for money and fought together, not with knives, but with their tongues. Their methods of obtaining money were questionable. Deputy Perrot had risen, high and disdainful, above their small contortions, and they had hated him. Now they had won and he was gone.

So the Irish asked for the Queen's protection in 'an orderly estate of English tenure', but before they had received it the old yearning for war was on them again.

Catholicism in Ulster had at last become a live issue. The faith was being spread by priests from overseas, and the English were accused of heresy. Religion was yet another irritant between the two peoples.

In 1578 Fitzmaurice had led a holy Papal war against the English in Munster with Dr. Nicholas Sanders to spread the faith. They had been joined by Baltinglas from Leinster. A Papal force had held Smerwick; when it fell to England, the garrison had been massacred. Then the province of Munster had been laid waste by English soldiers, and more than thirty thousand Irish had been wiped out by starvation, pestilence and the sword; the faith had gained its martyrs.

But though laws against recusants, as in England, had been passed by Sir John Perrot's Parliament in 1585, it had not been thought politic to enforce them at the time. The great lords remained free from controls, and priests continued to live in their houses. In the Council Book of Sir William Fitzwilliam we read for 1587 that the Earl of Tyrone 'shall not wittingly keep friars, monks, nuns and priests in the country unless they conform themselves'.[2] Small chance of this happening, and the Council knew it.

But the leniency was not to continue. By 1594 the Earl of Tyrone was being reported in a letter to Sir Robert Cecil,[3] as having been 'laboured into rebellion by a Spanish Cardinal, so called, and a Romish Bishop', and there is reference to priests 'late come over' being dispersed all over Ireland 'to stir up the heads of the Irishry with their bulls, pardons and excommunications, wounding the consciences of the people'. 'The Lords Deputy', so wrote Cecil's informant, 'had been directed to hold a temporizing course in matters of religion, rather than to suffer them to enjoy their consciences.' And so the Ecclesiastical Commission had long lain dormant, but the Commissioners should now receive letters 'to quicken them to a more earnest zeal'.

This explains why, during the late eighties and early nineties, religion was not mentioned in Carleill's reports about his country.

*

In Carrickfergus the life of the small town was tossed and twisted by the unscrupulous Governor of the castle. Egerton, like most Englishmen in Ireland, was out for what he could get, *had* to be out for this in order to live. He devised a ruse whereby certain inhabitants of the town could avoid paying rates, and himself draw profit thereby.[4] He filled up the ditches enclosing the castle towards the land and raised up heaps of earth, 'dung and filth', on the quay close to its walls. Then he encouraged some inhabitants to build houses there, thus being exempt from the taxation of the town. In 1591 the Corporation complained to the Lord Deputy, and the new householders were ordered to pay taxes as others did.

But there was still conflict, and Sir Henry Bagenal and the Baron Shane were ordered by the Deputy to compose the differences between Egerton and the townsmen.

In 1589 Charles Egerton had himself been Mayor; after this episode he was not honoured again. Always the mayors and the sheriffs were drawn from the English settlers, a little community of merchants bravely building a home for themselves on that desolate coast. With its fine church, its palace and castle, the mills for grinding corn for the soldiers, a frigate or two lying in the harbour, it must have been a symbol of England, of the settled way of life.

Another Carleill came to the Palace of Carrickfergus, one James Carleill of Barham in Kent. He was the younger brother of Jonathan of Barham, and was described in the 1619 Herald's Visitations of Kent as a captain in Ireland.[*5] In 1590 he was appointed from Carrickfergus to collect the rents for the Bishopric of Down and Connor.[6] He had served with his kinsman Christopher on the West Indies Expedition and had proved himself a good soldier. There had been an Alexander Carleill too, but he had died on the expedition. James was to appear strangely linked with Christopher after Christopher's death.

These men had thrown in their lot with Carleill, as had also his nephew Rivers, master of his ship in Ireland.

Carleill had received his pay according to the Privy Council's instructions, when he had first arrived at Carrickfergus. But that state of affairs was not to last long. The usual evasions occurred, the usual docket of Irish suits was sent up, Carleill's name on the list,[7]

* See note 5 in References for Chapter 9, page 192.

yet nothing was done. His pay as Governor of Carrickfergus was supposed to come through Sir Henry Wallop in Dublin, that of the Seneschalship of Clandeboye from the treasury in England.

In the autumn of 1588 Bingham, Carleill, Egerton and their bands had been reduced from sterling pay to Irish pay, but they had complained and become humble suitors to the Privy Council 'because they were unable to run their horsemen and wards with that allowance, cess and other help of the country being taken from them'.[8] Knockfergus was in a remote place and the victualling was difficult, the Privy Council had acknowledged that fact. Indeed Egerton had been forced to sell some of his estate in England and his wife's chain in order to victual his soldiers.[9]

In January 1589 the fault was rectified; the Queen restored all three men to sterling pay.[10] But certain aspects were still in dispute a few months later when the Privy Council was writing to the Lord Deputy that both Carleill and Egerton had not received any imprest of victualling money for some time and the Treasurer should give it to them.[11]

They seemed to have received better treatment than Sir George Carew, for some time before 1590 he was writing to the Lord Chancellor of Ireland with dangerous frankness;[12] he should be restored to his accustomary wages 'having served the Queen with horsemen almost to my undoing'; as the Queen had restored Sir Richard Bingham, Mr. Carleill and others to their accustomed entertainment, he wished to be paid as others were.

Those were the days when men were expected to live by their wits. Can they be blamed for doing so, often at the expense of honesty?

Walsingham did not intend to leave Carleill at Carrickfergus when there was other more important work to do. Early in 1588/9 he moved him to England and used him to review the defences of Ostend. He would be an independent witness, aloof from the politics of the Low Countries. He lived in a lodging in Botolph's Lane, near his boyhood home, and from London he crossed the sea to Ostend to investigate and report.

Ostend was garrisoned by the English, and it had become a great expense. It was 'in decay', a permanent condition of most fortified towns in the Low Countries. Elizabeth was finding her financial obligations in the Netherlands hard to fulfil. The defeated Armada ships were sheltering in the harbours of Santander and San Sebastian, and an expedition under Drake was to sail in the spring in order to destroy them, to set Don Antonio on the throne of Portugal and to attack the Spanish treasure fleet in the Azores.

Norris was sent to the Netherlands to enlist the support of the Dutch; a supply of ammunition and fifteen hundred men were suggested for the Portuguese expedition. The threat of the withdrawal of English forces there was much resented by Lord Willoughby, who had recently replaced Leicester as Governor-General of the Netherlands with instructions to mend the differences between Dutch and Spaniards.

But the hard fact remained, the English treasury was low, the pre-war expenditure of £150,000 a year had risen in 1588 to £420,000.[13] Elizabeth had drawn £245,000 from her private savings; the Portuguese expedition was to be privately financed, with £5,000 from the Queen. But unless this expedition proved a success and produced treasure, there was small hope of money for Lord Willoughby's projects in the Low Countries.

Elizabeth's treaty with the Netherlands obliged her to keep five thousand foot and a thousand horse there, and English garrisons at Flushing and at Brielle. Her annual expenses amounted to £100,000. The Dutch, in return, were to accept the military leadership of the Lieutenant-General, to recognize the wide executive power of the Council of State on which the English had two representatives, and to repay the money they owed the English. Both sides accused each other of evading their obligations.

Willoughby could not agree that economies be made in the defences of Ostend, for the Spaniards were threatening the town. He wished to hold it, and was angry when Carleill arrived from England to make his report for the Privy Council, as if 'no one this side were as sufficient of judgement either for matters of fortification or placing garrisons as Mr. Carleill'.[14]

Carleill met Sir John Conway, the Governor of Ostend, and together they made their investigations. Conway sent a letter to Burghley and it was endorsed by Carleill;[15] the whole side of the old town was broken by the violence of the sea, he wrote, the dike filled with sand and the rampart broken; he had communicated with the Estates, but small help would come from that quarter; he suggested that the town be defended for awhile till the Estates had declared its hand and till Carleill had sent in his full report.

Later in the month an estimate for the repair and defence of Ostend was drawn up by the two men, and indeed it was a sum to put fear into the Queen's heart, being £3,145 sterling.[16]

In May Carleill's full report was received by Burghley;[17] Walsingham was ill, increasingly ill, and for periods of time could not attend to affairs of State. Carleill's report was designed to calm the Queen's objections; by some process the sum of £3,145 had been reduced to £500, and he suggested that the gross sum that the Queen would give to the United Provinces, of which Ostend was a member, should be reduced by that amount. This figure meant that the town could be kept with six companies, should troops be needed elsewhere. If, he continued, it was determined that the town should be given over to the Estates, 'let us look for none other than a dishonourable loss of the town and artillery, and a shameful withdrawing of the garrison which must attend so slack a resolution'. He then wrote disparagingly of the 'indigent, partial and irresolute disposition' of the Estates, of which they had already had too great an experience.

Enclosed with this report was a personal letter to Burghley which is worth quoting. It shows Carleill at the height of his powers: in one and the same year he had flouted the Lord Deputy Fitzwilliam in Ireland, and had revealed his heart to the Lord Treasurer in England in a passionate outburst. He was supremely confident.

He prayed Burghley, 'that in case her Majesty do continue her disposition to abandon the same [i.e. Ostend], that any other man be employed in that work rather than myself, for I protest before God that I had rather spend one of my joints to win such a place than to be spoken of to have been the instrument of leaving it to the enemy altogether, if so by her Majesty's express commandment. And under correction unto your Lordship in private I will say that they who do so earnestly persuade her Majesty therein have seldom paid the price of winning such a place.'

The age-old contempt of the fighting man for the civilian. . . .

Elizabeth was to divest herself gradually of responsibility in the Netherlands. For the Portugal expedition was not a success; no Spanish ships were captured in the harbours, no treasure brought home from the Azores, Don Antonio was no nearer to the throne of Portugal. Drake's reputation fell very low, and he never regained it. His disgrace was the first nail in Carleill's coffin, though Carleill may not have known it at the time. If Drake had prospered, Carleill might have prospered with him.

But now he had the reputation for good fortune on land and on sea. In June 1589, a courier, one John Welles, was writing to Walsingham from Paris.[18] The Protestant King of Navarre was blockading the city which was held by the Catholic League, and Welles suggested that four hundred English horse and five hundred foot could win the country for the King. 'Mr. Carleill were a good man for that purpose', he continued hopefully.

On May 26th, 1591, the Walsinghams had the very expensive honour of entertaining the Queen for three days at Barn Elms, their great house.[19] On the lawns by the sliding Thames all the extravagant follies that delighted the Queen's heart were displayed; there was jousting, there were plays, fantastic fooleries and mummings were performed, the tables were laden with exotic foods, and the company settled down to laugh and to laugh, hour after hour, and no one— we believe—was bored. So the myth of England's Virgin Queen, surrounded by adorers, was maintained.

The Walsinghams gave her costly presents, each gift tearing into their vanishing wealth. They had already made their annual New Year's gift, a homage expected of all prominent courtiers and statesmen. Walsingham, who was by now a very sick man, must have struggled through these difficult days, helplessly watching his fortune drain away. Perhaps Carleill was with him; as a son of the house his place would have been in his stepfather's retinue. Walsingham had always been austere, a Puritan by nature as well as by conviction, and the panoply he had to maintain had never been congenial to him. Now less than ever—for carefully and thoroughly he was preparing himself for death.

He did not live much longer. The following year, on April 6th, he died after a long and painful illness. By now he was so poor that his widow could not give him the funeral that was seemly for a man of his position. He had kept the nation's Secret Service going at his own expense, paying his spies working in England and in other lands. As a student of Machiavelli he realized that it was the necessary corollary to the modern state. But the outlay had ruined him.

His personal involvement in the more unsavoury aspects of the work has brought him into disrepute among Catholics, then and now. Today we live in an age when details of the Secret Service are really secret, and no Minister is tarred in public with that brush. Walsingham was not so fortunate; he had to do the work himself. He lived in a cunning and unscrupulous age and he used all its weapons. There is no doubt that Elizabeth's life was saved through the information provided by his network of spies, many of them traitors who sold their secrets for gain. Perhaps he wielded history more completely than any other statesman of his time in England. He was a single-minded patriot who never faltered, and an untiring worker for the Queen and for the Protestant cause.

But scarcely a smile escaped him to stray into history, and the long, obstinate face beneath the skull-cap could not have commanded great love.

Camden wrote of him that 'he weakened his private estate and being surcharged with debt, he was buried by dark in Paul's Church at London without any funeral solemnity'.[20] That Elizabeth should have let this happen to her faithful servant . . . Bars of iron ran through the hearts of the Tudor monarchs.

As Carleill knelt by his stepfather's grave that April night, in the light of flickering torches, he must have felt the darkness closing in on him too.

In 1602 the Lady Ursula Walsingham was to beg the Queen for the reversion of the Priory of Carisbrook which she had held on lease for the past twelve years; it had originally been the possession of her first husband, and was, she said, the only living left her. Since Walsingham's death she had paid the Queen £1,600 for it, and was now in debt to the state.[21]

If Walsingham's widow received no mercy, what hope was there for his stepson?

Carleill continued to fight for his life. A month after Walsingham's death he wrote to Burghley suggesting that he should be given a commission to search and seize goods belonging to Spaniards in England.[22] This, he pointed out, was granted by the Lord Admiral to any person who captured the same goods on the high seas, the Lord Admiral keeping a tenth of the gain. Carleill then went on to explain how the previous winter he had suggested a like scheme to the Queen, and how he had remained such a long time at the Court at Richmond attending on the Queen's pleasure, while she 'was so long in determining what part I should have', that the goods were conveyed away suddenly to Middelburg and from thence to Antwerp.

He wrote sadly of his condition, 'I have been long time a fruitless suitor, over well nigh the most part of four years time, as also that I have spent my patrimony and all other means in the service of my country, which hath not been less than six thousand pounds, whereof I do owe at this present the best part of £3,000. There is no man can challenge me that I have spent any part of all this expense in any riot, game or in any other excessive or inordinate manner.'

He pointed out that his reward, should his plan be adopted, would not come from the Queen's treasure, nor would any charge fall on her subjects. This was the only opportunity he would have of settling his state and that of his poor wife and children; he had been a professed soldier for eighteen years and was worthy of enjoying as good a fortune as other men who had not so freely adventured the spending of their lives in their country's service as he had done.

There is no record that his proposal received the Queen's blessing.

As early as the spring of 1589 he had begun to compound with William Warren for the Seneschalship of Clandeboye,[23] and long negotiations had ensued. If he sold it he would save the endless expense, this pouring of water into the sea, the repairs done to the crumbling Palace walls, the keeping of spies in Scotland, even the victualling of his own twenty warders. No man without private means could hold such a post, debts piling up while he begged for his pay.

To sell an office was not frowned on by the Lord Deputy if the exchange was a good one. But in this case Fitzwilliam thought that Warren was too friendly with the Earl of Tyrone. Tyrone's rebellion lay very near, and a strong man was needed in Carrickfergus. The Privy Council reviewed the situation in July 1590 when William Warren made unpleasant allegations against Carleill for failing to fulfil the bargain. William Warren, said the Council, was unfit to exercise the office of Seneschal of Clandeboye, and Carleill was exonerated from blame.[24]

So Carleill had to remain in his Palace, borrowing money in order to pay it out again.

In March 1590/1 he was at Court, among a number of other suitors for Irish debts,[25] a distinguished company of men who had served the Queen well. In July he was still there,[26] and seven months later his name appears yet again.[27] How much time he spent in England and how much in Ireland it is hard to say. These begging excursions on the part of the suitors could have done the state of Ireland no good at all.

The Queen's income came from various sources,[28] money from Crown lands, customs, ecclesiastical first-fruits, recusancy fines, proceeds of justice, and the right to purveyance and pre-emption. Parliament raised money in the country by subsidy for special circumstances. These subsidies were becoming more frequent because of the war, loans and benevolences were levied on the wealthy, ship money imposed, customs augmented; the Queen sold Crown lands. But there was still a deficit. The Crown was indeed very poor and there was no prospect of peace.

Clearly the Queen had not enough money to pay her servants regularly. In accepting a public post a man knew he must dig deep into his own pocket; it was up to him to make good in some other way. Public life was a gamble, but sometimes it paid. Monopolies were granted by royal patent for the manufacture or sale of certain commodities, and these were enjoyed by the Queen's servants who deserved well. Ralph Lane, the leader of the Roanoke Colony, devised an original method of becoming rich. He was to pay the Crown an enormous sum for the right to collect Customs' dues in the country; dishonest and inefficient Customs officers had failed to do this effectively in the past; Ralph Lane not only gave the Crown its dues, but made a fat profit for himself into the bargain.

Not everyone was as persistent or as lucky. Sometimes the Queen's mercy shone on a sufferer who fell by the wayside. Captain Nicholas Dawtry, whose career in Ireland had not been unlike that of Carleill and who was to be equally poor, suddenly received a present from her—she had seen the unwieldy form hanging disconsolately about the Court,[29] and her heart had been swiftly touched.

Carleill received no gift, being neither fat nor piteous. He was possessed of none of the qualities that could win the Queen's heart; he was no courtier, he could not speak flattering words, nor feign an adoration that he did not feel.

There may have been some minor excursions into piracy. In December 1589 Luke Plunkett, writing to the Lord Deputy, reported how while in Corunna he had seen a pinnace of Carleill's, which men said was rigged up 'to be used on the coast of England or of Ireland against fishermen'.[30]

Carleill's connection with piracy must have been discussed generally—the Lord Deputy Perrot had spread evil talk—for when his death was reported in Stow's *Annales*, these were the last words written about him, 'He utterly abhorred piracy.'[31]

Carleill seems to have approached the Queen for a reversion of fifty years in a hundred marks of Her Majesty's Duchyland.[32] But nothing came of this.

In July 1592 Mary Carleill tried her hand at begging;[33] there was no longer Walsingham to help them, so she had to write to Lord Burghley. She claimed that £100 was due to her husband and his small company as by warrants signed by the Lord Deputy and Council in Ireland, which were now in Sir Henry Wallop's hands; 'I know my husband has acquainted you with our need which I assure you is rather more than otherwise'; she understood there was now a Privy Seal for Ireland, and she begged Lord Burghley most humbly that some help or a third part of the 'arrearage' might be paid.

Poor woman, it would have been unrealistic to have asked for all that was their due.

She was by now living in the lodging in St. Botolph's Lane in London, for her child may still have been under the care of a very doubtful Walloon surgeon, who had 'uttered certain lewd and seditious speeches'.[34] The Privy Council, understanding that this man had two children under his care, one a child of Captain Carleill's, the other of Sir Thomas Lucy, that steely and bigoted Warwickshire Justice, had agreed that the surgeon be allowed to terminate the cures, if so be it that Carleill and Lucy redeliver him to prison when the children were well again.

What a temptation to the surgeon to leave them uncured.

This negotiation needed Carleill's presence in England, for in April 1592 we find him being authorized by the Privy Council to take post horses for his return to Ireland.[35]

After this, perhaps through the help of Burghley, something was done for him. A sum of money was set aside to pay Irish debts, and Carleill received £50.[36] The Queen made a further gesture, for she gave him the forfeiture of land which might come to her as a result of the murder of a man called Rose who had lived in the county of

Dorset. It was thought that William Webb of Salisbury who held land in Motcomb in Dorset would be found a principal or at least an accessory and thereby lose his goods. Carleill, full of hope, came over from Ireland, on instruction from the Privy Council, to pursue his case.[37]

The story unfolds itself clearly enough. William Webb was the patron of the living at Marnhull, and Thornborough was the incumbent. Webb had 'violently dispossessed him of his parsonage', and in the process Rose had been killed. Who Rose was and whose side he was on does not appear. Probably Webb had ejected Thornborough for his Popish practices, for Webb was a stiff Puritan,[38] and this was the land of the Arundells of Wardour, where Catholicism was still practised openly. Sir Matthew Arundell was outwardly a conformist, putting his friendship with the Queen before his religious conscience, his son Thomas a recusant. In 1597 the father was to put his son, now released from prison for his recusancy, in the protective custody of William Webb, describing him to Sir Robert Cecil as 'a man well affected in religion'. Here Thomas was to pine in the unsympathetic confinement.

Already in 1590 a prisoner who lived at Marnhull and at Shroton, one Thomas Polden, had been procured to go to London by William Hutchinson,[39] another clerk, who seems to have suffered cruelly at the hands of Polden and his friends. But Polden had been sent back to Dorset for a local enquiry to be held, a state of affairs greatly desired by miscreants who could twist justice to their own liking with greater ease in their own county than in London. Six months later Polden was again in London, at the instigation of William Hutchinson, attending daily on the Privy Council till he obtained licence to depart.[40]

In all likelihood this man was connected with the riot which included Rose, William Webb and Thornborough, for Carleill himself was to fail in an attempt to convey a prisoner, a principal in the murder, to London for trial when he arrived in Dorset two years later. He does not mention this prisoner's name, but he may well have been Polden.

Carleill had arrived in that unruly county of Dorset, carrying a letter of commission from the Privy Council to the Justices 'to take down examination of the matter to proceed according to quality of disorder'.[41] His experiences there were unhappy indeed. When he had been frustrated past endurance, he wrote to the Queen herself, the first and only time he appealed in person to the monarch who owed him at least a living.[42]

'I found such unreasonable delays, such open partiality, such packing and practising underhand as little reason could be had amongst them.' The prisoner whom he had contrived to send to London for trial, had been sent back by the Privy Council to be tried in Dorset 'where no help may be, for Webb and his mother being greatly monied and dealing very much in the trade of usury have many or most of the better sort there beholden or indebted unto them'. Carleill wrote on, his mood becoming more desperate, the mood in which now most of his days were spent: 'I am utterly unable to entertain myself to live here, and so much less to follow such chargeable suits. . . . I am therefore driven to return to my former suit, which is a reversion of fifty years in a hundred marks of your Majesty's Duchy land. If the frank employment of my life . . . accompanied with entire expense of my poor patrimony and sundry substantial helps of my good friends already bestowed, may not move your Highness after twelve months' time of being a poor suitor to grant this, then as a man not knowing any other, and as consumed, fallen and desperate must I beseech your leave to withdraw myself from the unsupportable shame which already begins to fall on me . . .' Even then he did not go as far as poor Perrot, who had cried out in his agony, 'If she would use men thus she will have cold service, and one day she will have need of me.'

The last two years of Carleill's life were very terrible. From Ireland he heard bad news;[43] the peace he had established was disappearing; Ulster was now the most disordered province in Ireland and the 'Irishrie' there most inclined to incivility. Sometimes Scots came from the Isles to raid the coast, a thousand of them a night, and carried off cattle and 'took their pleasure of the whole country'. The town of Carrickfergus was unwalled, and no provision made for repair; the victuals of the garrison came by sea either from Dublin or from Cheshire and the tides were strong and terrible, the country bare and hard to fight in. The inhabitants of the town not only feared the Scots, but the Spaniards too, and surely if the King of Spain wished to annoy the Queen of England he would choose this northern realm to invade. There was doubt too about the loyalty of the northern great men. This was written, probably by Sir Henry Bagenal, in the summer of 1592. Henshawe was doing his best at Carrickfergus, but Carleill was in England; the strong soldier was gone.

The northern great lords were indeed plotting rebellion, Hugh Roe O'Donnell, in company with his ancient enemy, Hugh O'Neill, Earl of Tyrone; hatred of England had at last drawn them together. In 1587 it was said of the Earl that 'all men of rank within the province are becoming his men, receive his wages and promise him service according to the usual manner of that country'. What had happened to Carleill's 'orderly estate of English tenure'?

Sir John Perrot had begun to distrust the Earl as early as 1587. He was a dangerous man for England with his courtly ways, his friendship with Philip II of Spain, his belief in a Catholic and Celtic Ireland. 'Religion is now everywhere made a cloak for rebellion', wrote Camden.

During the early nineties Tyrone's war was a diplomatic one, Spain the ally, England the enemy; both were to be played against the other till the time came to strike.

In May 1593 Turloch Lynneach, now old, resigned in his favour, and the Earl became O'Neill, 'in comparison whereof the very title Caesar is contemptible in Ireland', wrote Camden. All Ulster knew by now that rebellion was inevitable.

The trial of Sir John Perrot for high treason at Westminster in April 1592 must have been another sorrow for Carleill.[44] He knew Perrot, his rages, his injustices, his sudden charms and warm friendship; no man had felt his fury more than Carleill had done. But Carleill was a just man, and he knew that Perrot was no traitor. His trial revealed all that was most vile in Elizabethan life; for there was bribery and corruption, the buying of witnesses, and the promotion of the Law Officers involved in the case.[45] The men in Dublin who had conspired against him were his enemies. Carleill knew them all and how little their words could be trusted. Perrot was accused of plotting with the King of Spain, of plotting with Catholic priests in Ireland, of fostering O'Rourke's rebellion. His foul-mouthed abuse of the Queen was enough to have convicted him, without these other fabrications. He confessed his violent speeches; his treachery he denied. In Court he suffered like an aged lion in a circus, and like a lion he roared his defiance.

He feared the violence of his feelings and his own lack of control, pleading in Court that he was 'by nature choleric' and knew not what infection his imprisonment might work on him. And therefore if he 'should hap to fall into any extraordinary speeches in that honourable place he craved pardon, alleging that the same should not proceed from want of duty or obedience'. He did indeed fall into one or two 'extraordinary speeches', crying out that he had been bought and sold. But his fate was already sealed.

He was found guilty of High Treason, and received sentence of death on June 16th. But he was never executed, for while he lay in the Tower awaiting the Queen's decision, he died.

There may have been a tendency towards melancholia in the Carleill family. There is a strange letter written by Ralph Lane to Lord Burghley from Ireland in 1595 where he was Clerk of the Check.[46] If it had been written in 1593 before Christopher Carleill's death the description of the 'Mr. Carleill' in the letter would have perfectly described Christopher. But in fact the Mr. Carleill of 1595 must have been James Carleill, Christopher's kinsman. Ralph Lane had been trying to procure for himself the governorship of one of the Irish provinces, and had asked Mr. Carleill to press his claims at Court in England. But 'Mr. Carleill . . . not finding his acceptance there in Court answerable to his expectations for a late good service by him with his great peril performed in a practice with the Scots appointed to him by the Lord Deputy . . .' had given over his own suit and that of Ralph Lane, and had quite suddenly gone with Sir Francis Drake to sea 'who favouriteth him greatly for the experience in his last Indian voyage for Cartagena, that he had of his worth'. Lane had given a letter to Carleill for the Queen and told him to deliver it to Lord Burghley or Sir Robert Cecil to pass on at their discretion. But 'Mr. Carleill' had not done this. And Ralph Lane could find no adequate reason for this irresponsibility, except that 'I do find that Carleill in a natural melancholy humour abounding in him, albeit otherwise truly approved a right honest man and a very sufficient resolute soldier and of singular experience of all the factions of these northern parts and particularly amongst the Scots'.

How like Christopher was this James. The sudden throwing over of the diplomacy at which he was no good and his escape into action, to sea with Drake. The impulsiveness . . . the melancholy . . . It was as if Christopher himself had risen from the grave.

During the summer of 1593, despite his moods of desperation, Carleill was still capable of practical dealings with the College of

Heralds, trying to establish for himself a coat of arms and a crest. There was a sum of money to be paid, possibly about £10. And if he did not possess £10? There was his brother-in-law, Christopher Hoddesdon, an obliging person who was always ready to help him; at Carleill's death he owed Hoddesdon £40.[47]

To us this seems rather improvident. But it was an age when men were busy establishing ancestors for themselves—some real, some false—in order to buy with their new wealth the right to arms that their ancestors had borne. Very great store was placed on a man's family; and for Christopher Carleill to link his name with that of Lord William de Carleill of the time of Edward I would do him no harm at all in his search for advancement. He might be forced to loiter round the Court, consigned with a gesture to the company of Nicholas Dawtry and men of his kind, but he would not be entirely insignificant there. Perhaps the 'unsupportable shame' of which he had spoken to Elizabeth urged him to seek this outward show, rationalizing it into a benefit for himself and his family.

He had to prove his descent from Lord William de Carleill in the county of Cumberland in the reign of Edward I, and this must have needed some research. His father's brother, William Carleill, was living in Carlisle at the time of Alexander's death in 1561.[48] Alexander, Christopher's father, had been granted a coat of arms shortly before he died,[49] but it bore absolutely no resemblance to the arms borne by Lord William. Presumably Christopher Carleill must have carried his father's arms in battle for the last twenty-one years, and one can only suppose that he now preferred to link his name with his more distinguished ancestor, Lord William. Two heralds busied themselves with Carleill's request, Norroy King of Arms and Walter Dethick, Garter King of Arms. In the opinion of Christopher Carleill, Lord William's crest did not seem to belong to his arms, and Norroy King of Arms therefore granted a new crest to Christopher Carleill and confirmed the arms. This grant is dated October 10th, 1593,[50] barely a month before Carleill's death. Because of his distinguished career the herald recorded an appropriate crest, 'an arm and right hand rising with gold armour and red decoration, holding a sign, a staff or military rod of a General or Captain of the Field'.

It is doubtful if Carleill ever bore these arms. By 1619 they had been transferred to the Carleills of Barham.*[51]

* See page 166.

On October 29th, 1593 Carleill administered his father's will.[52]
Why this was not done before it is impossible to say. Why his
mother Anne, Alexander's widow, had not administered it is equally
strange. Perhaps there was some legal mistake made which was not
rectified till 1593. Christopher had referred to his 'poor patrimony'
when writing to his stepfather, so he must not only have been
enjoying it, but spending it. Equally curious is the fact that on April
27th, 1594, five months after Carleill's death, the administration of
the goods, 'not administered both by Anne, relict and executrix, and
by Christopher Carleill, administrator of the deceased, was committed to Mary Carleill, relict of the said Christopher, to the use of
the children of the same Christopher'.[53]

She had already in December 1593, the month after Christopher's
death, renounced the administration of his goods, rights and credits,
for some reason that is not stated.[54] Perhaps her husband's debts
were greater than the sum of money involved.

All that summer the Plague raged in London; the Court moved
into the country and St. Giles's Fair was cancelled. The carts were
out at night, rumbling on the cobble-stones, collecting the dead for
burial; herbs were burned in the houses to ward off the infection,
rosemary, lavender, rue and marjoram, sweet and sickly, mingling
with the smell of death; men and women knelt long in prayer. This
was a mad world, but somehow it suited Carleill, for he was a little
mad too. Now he no longer moved, isolated in his grief, but could
weep with other people. He himself was to die in November, but
not of the Plague. No, he was to die, Stow's *Annales* record, 'as is
supposed for grief of his friend's death'.[55]

This would argue some personal affection of which we know
nothing at all, so that at the end of a life of which we know a great
deal, we must remain perplexed. And why was the friend's name not
mentioned? Was it because the association was too well known for
definition? Was it because the friend was in disgrace? Why did this
man, Christopher Carleill, once so cheerful and affable, die of grief?
There are no answers to these questions, only conjectures.

Curious and original reasons for death were often given at the
time, afflictions of the spirit rather than of the body; one man was
said to 'have died of vexation'; one might define his death more
prosaically as being the result of a stroke. Carleill, distracted by his
poverty, with a mind weakened by worry, may have felt his friend's

death to be a crescendo of sorrow he could not endure, his reason toppling into a melancholia so profound that life itself was refused. Pondering on these forgotten griefs, one sees nothing clearly; only there is a chill that creeps in, like the approach of snow.

Camden was more practical in his description of Carleill's death. Here is his statement, bringing us to earth.[56] He gives a list of important men who died in 1593; there was the Earl of Derby, Henry Ratcliffe, Earl of Sussex, Arthur Lord Grey of Wilton, Henry Lord Cromwell and Henry Lord Wentworth, 'Neither is Christopher Carleill to be passed over in silence', he continued, 'whose martial prowess was famous by sea and by land . . . which with those above named departed into a better life.'

Abbreviations used in the Sources

A.P.C.   *Acts of the Privy Council*
B.M.   British Museum
Cal.   *Calendar*
H.C.A.   High Court of Admiralty
H.M.C. *Historical Manuscripts Commission*
MSS.   Manuscripts
P.C.C.   Prerogative Court of Canterbury, Register of Wills
P.R.O.   Public Record Office
Soc.   *Society publications*
S.P.   State Papers
   All references in the text whose whereabouts are not indicated are in the Public Record Office.

Printed Sources Extensively used throughout the Book. Not Referred to in Full Again, after the First Reference

Camden, William.   *The History of the most renowned and victorious Princess Elizabeth, composed by way of Annales,* trans. R. N[orton] 1630.

Carlisle, Nicholas.   *Collections for the history of the ancient family of Carlisle* (1822).

Holland, Henry.   *Herologia Anglica* (1620).

Stow, John.   *Annales, or a General Chronicle of England,* continued by Howe, E. (1613).

BRIEF BIBLIOGRAPHIES, REFERENCES AND NOTES

Chapter 1: THE BOY

Bibliography
For Carleill family, Carlisle, Nicholas, *Collections for the history of the ancient family of Carlisle* (1822). For Sir Francis Walsingham, Read, Conyers, *Mr. Secretary Walsingham and the policy of Queen Elizabeth* (1925). Stählin, *Die Walsinghams bis zur Mitte des 16. Jahrhunderts* (1905). For Russia, Willan, T. S., *The early history of the Russia Company, 1553–1603* (1956); also *Muscovy Merchants of 1555* (1953). *Early Voyages and travels to Russia and Persia*, edit. Morgan and Coote in *Hakluyt Soc.* vol. 72 (1886). For City Companies, Milbourne, Thomas, *The Vintners' Company* (1888). Hannay, David, *The Great Chartered Companies of the City of London* (1926). Hazlitt, William Carewe, *The Livery Companies of the City of London* (1892). Beaven, Rev. Alfred, *The Aldermen of the City of London*, vol. II (1913). For London, Besant, Sir Walter, *London in the time of the Tudors* (1904). Stow, John, *Survey of the Cities of London and Westminster*, continued by John Strype (1720). For the funerals, *The Diary of Henry Machyn*, in *Camden Soc.*, vol. 42 (1848).

1 *Diary of Machyn*, 166.
2 Willan, *Muscovy Merchants*, vol. I, 78.
3 Beaven, vol. II, lv.
4 Willan, *Muscovy Merchants*, vol. II, 97–8.
5 *Ibid.*, 119.
6 *Ibid.*, 85.
7 Carlisle, 14.
8 Willan, *Muscovy Merchants*, 15.
9 *Vintners' Company*, 32.
10 P.C.C. 31 Loftes.
11 Carlisle, 14.
12 P.C.C. 31 Loftes.
13 *Register of St. Michael in the Royal, alias Whittington College*, Guildhall Library.
14 Read, Conyers, vol. I, Chap. I.
15 P.C.C. 32 Stevensen.
16 Stählin, vol. I, 124.
17 Willan, *The early history of the Russia Company*, 34.
18 *Oglander Memoirs*, ed. W. H. Long, (1888), 155.

19 Venn, *Alumni Cantabrigienses* (1940), vol. I, 293. Cooper, J. C. H. and T., *Athenae Cantabrigienses* (1861), vol. I, 161. Both books give biographical details of Christopher Carleill, but no scholastic details of his university career. A search in the University archives has not produced his name anywhere. He does not appear to have matriculated or taken a degree. This, however, is not conclusive evidence that he was not at Cambridge. Venn states that he was admitted to Lincoln's Inn, see *Admission Register*, 80. He could only have been there a few months before joining the English volunteers in the Netherlands.

20 Read, Conyers, vol. I, 18–20.

Chapter 2: FIGHTING FOR THE PRINCE OF ORANGE

Bibliography
For England and the Netherlands, Read, Conyers, *Mr. Secretary Walsingham* (1925), vol. I, chapter on Low Countries. Motley, John Lothrop, *The Rise of the Dutch Republic* (1899). Geyl, P., *The Revolt of the Netherlands, 1555–1609* (1932). de Meteren, Emanuel, *Histoire des Pays Bas* (1618). Wedgwood, C. V., *William the Silent* (1944). Gascoigne, George, *The Spoil of Antwerp* (1576) in Arber, *An English Garner*, vol. VI, *Tudor Tracts* (1903). For contemporary accounts of the English volunteers in the Netherlands see (i) *The Action of the Low Countries, written by Sir Roger Williams, knight*, printed 1618 in the Somer's Collection of Tracts, *A Collection of Scarce and Valuable Tracts*, arranged by Walter Scott (1809) referred to here as *Action of the Low Countries*; (ii) *The complete poems of George Gascoigne*, arranged by W. C. Hazlitt (1869). Prouty, G. T., *George Gascoigne* (1942).

1 Read, Conyers, vol. I, 55.
2 Wedgwood, 122.
3 Gascoigne, *Voyage into Holland* (1572) in Hazlitt, vol. I, 384–94.
4 Camden, William, *Annales*, 231.
5 *Action of the Low Countries.*
6 Carlisle, *Grant of Arms to Christopher Carleill*, 27–8.
7 Gascoigne, *Dulce Bellum Inexpertis*, in Hazlitt, vol. I, 149–96.
8 S.P. 63/116, f. 11.
9 S.P. 63/114, f. 68.
10 *Herologia Anglica*, 94–6.
11 Camden, 48.

Chapter 3: SAILOR AT LA ROCHELLE: SOLDIER IN THE LOW COUNTRIES

Bibliography
For England and France, Read, Conyers, *Mr. Secretary Walsingham*, vol. I, Chap. V. For England and the Netherlands, as in my last chapter, Bibliography. For fighting in Friesland, de Meteren, Emanuel, *L'Histoire des Pays Bas* (1618). For siege of Brouage, Vincent, J., *Un grand port français oublié*, in *La Revue Maritime*, vol. CCII. For English Army, Cruikshank, C. G., *Elizabeth's Army*, 2nd edit. (1966). Fortescue, Hon. John, *History of the British Army* (1899), vol. I.

1 Carlisle, Nicholas, *Collections, Grant of Arms to Christopher Carleill*, 27–8.
2 Vincent, 26–9.
3 *Cal. S.P. Foreign 1577–78*, no. 20.
4 *Ibid.*, no. 41.
5 Salisbury MSS. 9/71.
6 *Cal. S.P. Foreign 1577–78*, no. 153.
7 *Ibid.*, no. 135.
8 Gascoigne, George, *The Spoil of Antwerp*, in Arber, *op. cit.*, in Bibliography, my Chap. 2.
9 *Cal. S.P. Foreign 1577–78*, no. 871.
10 *Ibid.*, no. 342.
11 *Ibid.*, page 426.
12 *Ibid.*, no. 759.
13 *Ibid.*, no. 732.
14 *Ibid.*, no. 913.
15 Digges, Leonard (1579), and Thomas (1590), *An arithmetical warlike treatise named Stratioticus.*
16 Cruikshank, 50–1.
17 Fortescue, 143–4.
18 *Cal. S.P. Foreign 1578–79*, no. 472.
19 *Cal. S.P. Foreign 1581–82*, no. 388.
20 *Cal. S.P. Foreign 1577–78*, page 427.
21 *Cal. S.P. Foreign 1579–80*, no. 470.
22 Blandy, William, *The Castle* (1581).
23 *Herologia Anglica*, 92. Round the engraving are the words *Carleill Armiger Christopherus. Carlellum Gallus, Carlellum Sarmata laudat virtutesque huius Belgica terra probat.* An engraving in Windsor Castle has the word '*Steenwick*' [*sic*] written behind the figure.
24 Waters, David, in *Americanum Nauticum*, Number Three, 28.
25 *The Four Books of Flavius Vegitius Renatus*, trans. Sadler (1572).
26 S.P. 83/12, f. 1.
27 Hymans, L., *Bruxelles à travers les âges*, vol. II.
28 *Cal. S.P. Foreign 1579–80*, no. 332.
29 de Meteren, *op. cit.* in Bibliography, my Chap. 2.
30 *Cal. S.P. Foreign 1579–80*, no. 496.
31 *Ibid.*, no. 529.
32 *Ibid.*, no. 532.
33 *Cal. S.P. Foreign 1581–82*, no. 67.
34 de Meteren, 198.
35 *Cal. S.P. Foreign 1581–82*, no. 42.
36 *Cal. S.P. Foreign 1579–80*, no. 511.
37 *Cal. S.P. Foreign 1581–82*, no. 70.

Chapter 4: MERCHANT ADVENTURE

Bibliography
For Fenton's voyage, *The Troublesome Voyage of Captain Edward Fenton 1582–1583*, ed. Taylor, E. G. R., *Hakluyt Soc.*, 2nd ser., vol. CXIII (1957), referred

to here as *Troublesome Voyage*. It contains the *Private Diary of Richard Madox*, pages 150–98. The B.M. references in above book are repeated here. Quinn, D. B., *Voyages and Colonising Enterprises of Sir Humphrey Gilbert*, Hakluyt Soc., 2nd ser., vol. LXXXIV (1940), referred to here as *Voyages of Gilbert. The Original writings and correspondence of the two Richard Hakluyts*, ed. Taylor, E. G. R., *Hakluyt Soc.*, 2nd ser., vol 76 (1935), referred to here as *Writings of the two Hakluyts*; Hakluyt, Richard, *Principal Navigations, traffiques, voyages and discoveries of the English nation*, MacLehose edition (1903), vol. III, referred to here as *Principal navigations*. For Russia, Fletcher, Giles, *Of the Russe Commonwealth*, pages 1–153 in Bond, A., *Russia at the close of the Sixteenth Century*, *Hakluyt Soc.*, vol. 20 (1856), also *Sir Jerome Horsey, his travels*, pages 155–265 in above volume. Willan, J. S., *The early history of the Russia Company* (1956). For the *Tiger*, Williamson, J. A., *Sir John Hawkins, the time and the man* (1927). Oppenheim, Michael, *History of the Administration of the Royal Navy and Merchant shipping in relation to the Navy* (1896). Corbett, Sir Julian, *Drake and the Tudor Navy* (1899). Waters, D. W., *Elizabeth's Navy and the Armada Campaign*, in *Mariner's Mirror*, vol. 35 (1949). Clowes, W. David, *The Royal Navy* (1897).

1 *H.M.C. Cal. Salisbury MSS.* vol. II, no. 903.
2 *S.P. 83/13*, f. 83.
3 *Cal. S.P. Foreign 1582*, no. 190.
4 *Cal. S.P. Foreign 1581–82*, no. 680.
5 *Ibid.*, no. 717.
6 H.C.A. 38/9, 2 April 1579.
7 H.C.A. 14/21, no. 203.
8 H.C.A. 14/21, no. 92.
9 Willan, *op. cit.*, above, 286.
10 *Sir Jerome Horsey, his travels*, in *Hakluyt Soc.*, vol. 20, 194.
11 *Cal. S.P. Spanish 1580–86*, p. 101.
12 *Troublesome Voyage*, 10.
13. *Cal. S.P. Spanish 1580–86*, p. 306.
14 B.M. Cotton MSS., Otho E viii, f. 127.
15 *Ibid.*, f. 129.
16 *Ibid.*, f. 151.
17 *Cal. S.P. Spanish 1580–86*, p. 306.
18. *Troublesome Voyage*, 51, note.
19 *Ibid.*, 50.
20 B.M. Cotton MSS., Otho E viii, f. 150.
21 *Writings of the two Hakluyts*, 147.
22 B.M. Cotton MSS., App. XLVII and Cotton MSS., Titus B VIII, ff. 179–221.
23 B.M. Cotton MSS., Otho E viii, f. 130.
24 *Ibid.*, f. 144. The suggestion that Carleill was jealous of Hawkins and so backed out of the voyage has been accepted by Taylor, E. G. R., in *Troublesome Voyage*, xxxii, also by Quinn, in his *Voyages of Sir Humphrey Gilbert*. But Fenton was the only known author of this theory, and so this shifting of the blame for losing Carleill on to Hawkins and away from himself must be looked at cautiously.

25 *Troublesome Voyage*, 181–2, 84.
26 *Ibid.*, 38.
27 S.P. 83/12, f. 29.
28. *Cal. S.P. Spanish 1580–86*, p. 329.
29 *Ibid.*, p. 463.
30 *Ibid.*, p. 381.
31 *Ibid.*, p. 385.
32 *Ibid.*, pp. 386–7.
33 *Cal. S.P. Foreign 1572–74*, p. 386. Willan, J. S., in *op. cit.*, 158, suggests that this should be calendered July 1582.
34 *Principal Navigations*, vol. III, 308.
35 Clowes, vol. I, 421.
36 *Ibid.*, 423.
37 Corbett, vol. II, 13–14.
38 Clowes, vol. I, 580.
39 *Williamson*, 343.
40 Fletcher, Giles, in *Hakluyt Soc.*, vol. 20.
41 *Herologia Anglica*, 95.
42 *Principal navigations*, vol. III, 102–3.
43 *Hakluyt Soc.*, vol. 20, XIX, XX.
44 *Principal navigations*, vol. III, 463.
45 *Reliquary*, vol. XVII (1875–6), 14.
46 *Travels of Sir Jerome Horsey*, 195.
47 *Willan, J. S.*, 180.
48 *Hakluyt Soc.*, vol. 20, 1.
49 *Voyages of Gilbert*, vol. I, 59.
50 *Ibid.*, vol. II, 278–9.
51 *Ibid.*, vol. I, 60–1.
52 *Ibid.*, 83.
53 *Ibid.*, vol. II, 347.
54 *Writings of the two Hakluyts*, 199.
55 *Ibid.*, 196.
56 *Voyages of Gilbert*, vol. II, 350.
57 Hakluyt, Richard, *Principal Navigations*, vol. VIII, 134–7. There are two MS. versions, S.P. 12/155, f. 87 and S.P. 12/155, f. 88.
58 *Voyages of Gilbert*, vol. II, 365–9.
59 *Ibid.*, vol. II, 373.
60 *Writings of the two Hakluyts*, 206.
61 *Cal. S.P. Foreign 1583–84*, no. 552.
62 *Ibid.*, no. 598.
63 *Ibid.*, no. 779.

Chapter 5: SOLDIER AND SAILOR IN ULSTER

Bibliography
For Ireland, Bagwell, Richard, *Ireland under the Tudors* (1890), vol. III. Colles, Ramsey, *The history of Ulster* (1919). Quinn, David Beers, *The Elizabethans and the Irish* (1966). *The Chronicle of Ireland by Sir James Perrot*, ed. Henry Wood

(1933). *Annals of the Kingdom of Ireland by the Four Masters*, ed. John O'Donovon
(1851). Ware, Sir James, *Antiquities and History of Ireland* (1705). *The Itinerary
of Fynes Morison* (1617). Dawtry, John, *The Falstaff Saga* (1927). For Scots in
Ulster, McCoy, Hayes, *The Macdonnels prior to Sorley Boy*, in Ulster Journal of
Archaeology, vol. 7. *Sixteenth Century Schemes for the Plantation of Ulster*, in
Scottish Hist. Review, vol. XXII, 22. For Elizabeth's Army, Cruikshank, *op.
cit.* in Bibliography my Chap. 3. Fortescue, *op. cit.* in *ibid.*

  1 H.C.A. 1/42.
  2 *Ibid.*
  3 S.P. 63/112, f. 4.
  4 *Ibid.*
  5 S.P. 63/113, f. 4.
  6 S.P. 63/111, f. 88.
  7 *History of that most eminent Statesman Sir John Perrot, Knight of the Bath and
    Lord Lieutenant of Ireland, by Sir James Perrot*, ed. Richard Rawlinson (1728).
  8 S.P. 63/111, f. 76.
  9 S.P. 63/111, f. 85.
10 B.M. Lansdowne MSS., 111, f. 46.
11 *Annales of the Four Masters.*
12 Bodleian, Perrot MSS., I.
13 S.P. 63/111, f. 85.
14 Fitzwilliam MSS. in Northants Record Office.
15 *Ibid.*, a particular description of Ulster.
16 S.P. 63/112, f. 14.
17 S.P. 63/112, f. 49.
18 S.P. 63/112, f. 77.
19 S.P. 63/112, f. 90 (i), (ii), (iii).
20 S.P. 63/111, f. 94.
21 Bodleian, Perrot MSS., I.
22 S.P. 63/113, f. 4.
23 Bodleian, Perrot MSS., I.
24 S.P. 63/114, f. 11.
25 S.P. 63/114, f. 29 (i).
26 *Ulster Journal of Archaeology*, vol. 8, 14
27 S.P. 63/114, f. 29 (ii).
28 S.P. 63/114, f. 68.
29 S.P. 63/114, f. 69.
30 S.P. 63/116, f. 11.
31 S.P. 63/112, Nov. 6th 1584. Perhaps despatched Jan. 1584/5.
32 S.P. 63/116, f. 14.
33 S.P. 63/118, f. 6.
34 S.P. 63/112, f. 76.
35 Dawtry, 81, quoting B.M. Cotton MSS., Titus B. XII, f. 283.
36 Bodleian, Perrot MSS., I.
37 *Ibid.*
38 Cruikshank, 40.
39 S.P. 63/117, f. 37.
40 P.C.C. 37 Butts.

Chapter 6: THE WEST INDIES VOYAGE 1585–6

Bibliography
For the Vigo incident, Despatch Carleill to Walsingham, S.P. 12/183, f. 10, printed in *Papers relating to the Spanish War, 1585–87*, ed. Corbett, J. S., *Navy Record Soc.* (1898), vol. XI, 39. For the West Indies Voyage, *The Primrose Log*, in *ibid.* Bigges, Walter, *A summary and true discourse of Sir Francis Drake's West Indies Voyage*, in Hakluyt, Richard, *Principal Navigations, Voyages, Traffiques and discoveries of the English nation*, Hakluyt Soc. (1903–5), vol. X. Greep, Thomas, *The true and perfect news of the worthy and valiant exploits performed and done by Sir Francis Drake, 1587*, in *Americanum Nauticum, Number Three*, Introduction, David Waters (1955). For Spanish accounts of the voyage, Wright, Irene, *Further English voyages to Spanish America 1585–1594*, in *Hakluyt Soc., 2nd ser.*, vol. 99 (1951).
  1 *Americanum Nauticum.*
  2 Wright, xxviii–xxix.
  3 Note on *Tiger.* See my Chap. 4, pages 72–3, This ship may have been a London privateer; one existed in 1591, see Andrews, *Elizabethan Privateering 1585–1608.* The Queen's *Tiger* was being 'remade' in 1585; she appears in a list of ships going to the Isle of Wight in December 1585, see S.P. 12/185, f. 53; see also Corbett, *Drake and the Tudor Navy* (1898), vol. II, 13. She therefore could not have sailed in September in Drake's West Indies expedition; there were only two H.M. ships recorded on this voyage, the *Elizabeth Bonaventure* and the *Aid*, see E. 351/2222. Another *Tiger* of 140 tons had sailed with Sir Walter Raleigh's convoy to Roanoke in April 1585. Therefore there would seem to have been three *Tigers* afloat in 1585.
  4 Waters, in *Americanum Nauticum.*
  5 Corbett, 27–32.
  6 Waters, in *Americanum Nauticum*, 26.
  7 *The Life of the renowned Sir Philip Sydney*, by Sir Fulke Greville, knight (1651).
  8 *Navy Record Soc.*, vol. XI, 139.
  9 *Cal. S.P. Foreign 1585–86*, p. 79, Oct. 11/21.
 10 *Ibid.*, p. 64, Oct. 4/14.
 11 *Cal. S.P. Foreign, 1585–86*, 279.
 12 Digges, *Stratioticus, op. cit.* in my Chap. 3, reference 15, p. 185.
 13 *Wright*, xxvi.
 14 *Ibid.*, 22.
 15 *Ibid.*, xxxv.
 16 *Americanum Nauticum*, 64. Engraved plan of the attack on San Domingo designed by Baptista Boazio, probably engraved by Jodocius Hondius.
 17 *Wright*, xxxvi.
 18 *Ibid.*, 26.
 19 *Ibid.*, xxv.
 20 *Ibid.*, 28.
 21 *Ibid.*, 223–5.
 22 *Ibid.*, xli.
 23 *Ibid.*, 47.

24 *Ibid.*, 131.
25 *Ibid.*, 133.
26 *Ibid.*, 49.
27 *Ibid.*, 111.
28 *Ibid.*, 42.
29 *A Summary and true discourse*, 121.
30 *Wright*, 44.
31 *Ibid.*, 52.
32 *Ibid.*, 199.
33 *Ibid.*, lxiii.
34 *Ibid.*, 26.
35 Greep, in *Americanum Nauticum.*
36 *Navy Record Soc.*, vol. XI, 86, 92.
37 *A.P.C.*, May 8th, 1587.
38 *Navy Record Soc.*, vol. XI, 84.
39 *Cal. S.P. Foreign 1585–86*, 279.

Chapter 7: IRELAND AND THE ARMADA

Bibliography
For Scotland, Read, Conyers, *Lord Burghley and Queen Elizabeth* (1966), Dawtry, John, *op. cit.*, in Bibliography my Chap. 5. For Ireland, Quinn, *op. cit.* in same Bibliography. For Carleill and the Armada prisoners, *The Spanish Armada*, ed. Naish, G. B., in *Naval Miscellany*, IV, *Naval Record Soc.* (1952). For Armada wrecks in Ulster, Mattingly, Garrett, *The Defeat of the Spanish Armada* (1959), Hardy, Evelyn, *Survivors of the Armada* (1966), McKee, Alexander, *From Merciless Invaders* (1963).

1 *A.P.C.* April 31st, 1587.
2 *Cal. Carew MSS.*, *1575–1588*, 463.
3 *A.P.C.*, April 31st, 1587. *Cal. Patent and Close Rolls, Ireland*, vol. II, 159–160.
4 P.R.O. E 351/234.
5 S.P. 84/36, f. 45.
6 S.P. 63/135, f. 79.
7 S.P. 63/141, f. 20.
8 S.P. 63/137, f. 13.
9 Read, Conyers, *op. cit.* above (1966), 423.
10 B.M. Cotton MSS., Caligula, printed in *Cal. S.P. Scottish*, ed. Boyd, vol. IX, 531.
11 Dawtry, John, *The Falstaff Saga* (1927), 76, quoting B.M. Cottonian MSS., Titus B XII, f. 282. B.M. Lansdowne MSS., 111, f. 46.
12 *H.M.C. Cal. Salisbury MSS.*, vol. II, 560.
13 Ware, Sir James, *Antiquities and History of Ireland* (1705), 41.
14 *Ibid.*, 42.
15 S.P. 63/135, f. 96.
16 S.P. 63/136, f. 1.
17 *Ulster Journal of Archaeology*, vol. 7.
18 *Ibid.*

19 McSkimin, Samuel, *History and Antiquities of Carrickfergus* (1909).
20 B.M. Lansdowne MSS., III, f. 46.
21 Quinn.
22 S.P. 63/136, f. 39.
23 S.P. 63/136, f. 58.
24 *Cal. S.P. Spanish 1587–1603*, p. 448.
25 S.P. 63/136, f. 48. Mattingley in *op. cit.*, 311, states that almost from the Armada year the English spread the story that the Spaniards who came ashore were spontaneously murdered by the Irish for their clothes, arms and jewellery. He goes on to say that this happened only in a few cases, and gives no proof of his statement. Hardy, Evelyn, in *op. cit.*, 46, repeats this theme. But we have the account of de Cuellar, a Spanish survivor, who tells us of the brutality of the Irish peasant in killing and wounding drowning men while robbing them, as opposed to the Irish chieftains who treated them kindly on the whole. His account coincides with the reports of the English eyewitnesses in *Calendar of State Papers Ireland 1587–88*. The English would find it unnecessary to shift any blame on to the Irish (as Mattingley asserts that they did) since they would not regard their own conduct as blameworthy in killing a large number of Spanish survivors of a fleet that had just attempted an invasion of England.
26 *Cal. S.P. Spanish 1587–1603*, pp. 506–10.
27 S.P. 63/136, f. 58.
28 S.P. 63/137, f. 1 (1).
29 *Ibid.*, f. 10 (iv).
30 S.P. 63/137, f. 32.
31 Entry Book, Ireland, Folios, vol. XII, p. 179.
32 S.P. 63/136, f. 34.
33 *Cal. Carew MSS., 1575–1588*, p. 471.
34 S.P. 63/137, f. 10 (iv).
35 S.P. 63/136, f. 36.
36 S.P. 63/136, f. 40.
37 *A.P.C.* Sept. 18th, 1588.
38 *Cal. Carew MSS., 1575–1588*, 491.
39 S.P. 63/136, f. 58.
40 *Cal. Carew MSS., 1575–1588*, 471.
41 Entry Book Ireland, Folios, vol. XII, p. 175.
42 *Ibid.*
43 *Ibid.*, p. 176.
44 S.P. 63/136, f. 42.
45 S.P. 63/137, f. 52.
46 S.P. 63/139, f. 25.
47 Entry Book Ireland, Folios, vol. XII, p. 207.
48 *Cal. S.P. Spanish 1587–1603*, 510. S.P. 63/137, f. 39.
49 B.M. Cotton MSS., Caligula D, f. 226. Printed in *Cal. S.P. Scottish*, ed. Boyd, vol. IX, 531.
50 *Cal. S.P. Spanish 1587–1603*, 283.
51 *The Spanish Armada*, in *Naval Miscellany*, IV (1952), *Navy Record Society*, 80–1.

52 *Extracts from the Records of the Burgh of Edinburgh, 1573–87*, 80–81, *Burgh Record Society*.

53 S.P. 63/153, f. 53.

54 *Cal. Carew MSS., 1589–1600*, p. 12.

55 *Ibid.*, p. 10.

Chapter 8: A SIXTEENTH-CENTURY SYMPOSIUM

Bibliography

Bryskett, Ludovick, *A discourse of Civil life, containing the Ethic part of Moral Philosophy for the instructing of a gentleman on the course of a virtuous life adapted from the Dialogues of B. Giraldi* (1606). Mitford, Rev. John, *The Life of Edmund Spenser* (1852). Jones, Deborah, *Ludowick Bryskett and his family*, in *Thomas Lodge and other Elizabethans*, ed. Sisson, C. J. (1933).

1 Dawtry, John, *The Falstaff Saga* (1927).

Chapter 9: 'CONSUMED, FALLEN AND DESPERATE'

Bibliography

For Ireland, as in Bibliographies my Chapters 5 and 7, also for Carrickfergus, McSkimin, Samuel, *The history and antiquities of the country of the town of Carrickfergus* (1811). For Ostend, Read, Conyers, *Lord Burghley and Queen Elizabeth* (1960). For Carleill's Grant of Arms, Carlisle, Nicholas, *Collections*, *op. cit.* in Bibliography my Chapter 1.

1 S.P. 63/167, f. 66. This is undated, though calendered for 1592. In my view it must have been written before 1591, as there is no mention of trouble from the Earl of Tyrone.

2 B.M. Addit. MSS., 4792, f. 28.

3 H.M.C. *Cal. Salisbury MSS.*, vol. IV.

4 McSkimin, *Appendix IV*, 382.

5 *Visitations of Kent, 1619, Harleian Soc.*, vol. 42. It is tempting to see James and Jonathan as the nephews of our Christopher Carleill, being sons of his elder brother who had died shortly before their father Alexander, in 1561, see Carlisle, *Collections*. But the dates do not fit in, for Christopher, the father of Jonathan and James of Barham, was still alive in 1568, *see* P.R.O. C 66/052, m 35. Christopher of Barham had married the widow of Sir Walter Mantell of Horton Priory who had been executed after Wyatt's Rebellion in 1553. She had brought him Shelving Manor in Barham, near Canterbury. This Christopher was probably of the same generation as our Christopher's father, Alexander.

6 Public Record Office, Northern Ireland, T. 707, p. 20.

7 S.P. 63/149, f. 37.

8 *A.P.C.* Jan. 17th, 1589. S.P. 63/149, f. 37.

9 S.P. 63/149, f. 57.

10 *A.P.C.* Jan. 17th, 1589/90.

11 *A.P.C.* April 10th, 1590.

12 *Cal. Carew MSS., 1589–1600*, 40.

13 Read, Conyers, *op. cit.*, above, 439.

14 S.P. 84/30, f. 102.
15 S.P. 84/30, f. 110.
16 S.P. 84/34, f. 21.
17 S.P. 84/32, f. 207.
18 *Cal. S.P. Foreign, Jan.–July 1589*, 342.
19 Nichols, John, *The Progresses of Queen Elizabeth* (1821), vol. IV, pt. I, 47.
20 Camden, 21.
21 *Oglander Memoirs*, ed. Long, W. H. (1888).
22 B.M. Lansdowne MSS., vol. 64, f. 54.
23 S.P. 63/155, f. 10. S.P. 63/153, f. 53. S.P. 63/155, f. 11.
24 *A.P.C.* Dec. 28th, 1590.
25 S.P. 63/157, f. 48.
26 S.P. 63/149, f. 19.
27 S.P. 63/163, f. 42.
28 Black, J. B., *The reign of Queen Elizabeth* (1959), 228–9.
29 Dawtry, *op. cit.* in Bibliography, my Chap. 5, 66.
30 S.P. 63/149, f. 30.
31 Stow, 805.
32 *Cal. Salisbury MSS.*, Part IV, 271.
33 S.P. 63/166, f. 6.
34 *A.P.C.* Dec. 24th, 1591.
35 *A.P.C.* April 30th, 1592.
36 S.P. 63/166, f. 25.
37 *A.P.C.* Jan. 1592/3.
38 Lloyd, Rachel, *Dorset Elizabethans* (1967), 85.
39 *A.P.C.* Sept. 12th, 1590.
40 *A.P.C.* Mar. 17th, 1590/2.
41 *A.P.C.* Jan. 21st, 1592.
42 *Cal. Salisbury MSS.*, Part IV, 277.
43 S.P. 63/170, f. 21.
44 *Cobbett's Complete Collection of State Trials* (1809), vol. I, 1315.
45 B.M. Lansdowne MSS., 72/8.
46 S.P. 63/121, f. 54.
47 P.C.C. 18 Wood.
48 P.C.C. 31 Loftes.
49 B.M. Harleian MSS., 1096, f. 4, f. 102. Addit. MSS. 16, 940, f. 34. College of Heralds, C 16, f. 225b.
50 College of Heralds, *Miscellaneous Grants I*, f. 27b. *Vincent*, 169, f. 50. R. 21, f. 293. *Vincent Old Grants I*, 239. The Latin version of the Grant is printed in Carlisle, Nicholas, *Collections*, 26–8.
51 B.M. Harl. 1507, Plut. LXII C, 6138. Printed in *Visitations of Kent* (as in Note 5).
52 P.C.C. Loftes (in margin).
53 *Ibid.*
54 Guildhall 9050/2, f. 137.
55 Stow, 805.
56 *Camden*, 424.

INDEX

All references to a woman several times married are listed under one family and italics used for that family name in other references.

2